SAVAGE ENT

"A very decent, impeccably
happened to fans down the age
maker out there who could seize on *Savage*
basis of a script for a four-part series on the history
football fans" – *When Saturday Comes*

"A splendid new book by [an] always exemplary researcher"
– *Sports Journalists' Association*

"An excellent read, rich in anecdotes and explanation... An accessible and enjoyable chronicle of supporting football through the ages" – *Game of the People*

"An important addition to efforts that seek to put a history of football fans on a par with the well-written histories of players, owners and administrators to form a complete picture of a sport that is so dominant in our culture"
– Martin Cloake, author *A People's History of Tottenham Hotspur*

"Guides the reader through the ages of the game we love and our experience and consumption of it down the ages with the sensitivity that topics such as Hillsborough, Bradford and Heysel deserve while also reminding us that, despite the pitfalls, being a football fan is a fun and life-affirming state of being" – *The Football Pink*

Also by Paul Brown:

THE VICTORIAN FOOTBALL MISCELLANY

"One of the greatest books ever written about football since Charlie Buchan put down his pen!" – Danny Baker, BBC 5 Live

"A veritable cornucopia of eclectic Victorian footballing splendour!" – FootballBookReviews.com

"Hugely entertaining." – *When Saturday Comes*

ALL WITH SMILING FACES:
HOW NEWCASTLE BECAME UNITED, 1881-1910

"A perfect Christmas gift... I loved it! NUFC + history = ☺." – Ant McPartlin, Twitter @antanddec

"A fantastic new book, which charts the club's early years and meteoric rise in the Victorian and Edwardian eras." – *Newcastle Chronicle*

UNOFFICIAL FOOTBALL WORLD CHAMPIONS

"A fascinating history of football. Five stars." – *FourFourTwo*

BALLS: TALES FROM FOOTBALL'S NETHER REGIONS

"Football has been given compendiums of curiosities before, but surely none so comprehensive as this." – *FourFourTwo*

Non-football:

THE ROCKETBELT CAPER:
A TRUE TALE OF INVENTION, OBSESSION AND MURDER

"A delight to read. Genuinely stranger than fiction. Recommended." – *Popular Science UK*

"Reads like good movie material." – *BBC Focus*

SAVAGE ENTHUSIASM

A History of Football Fans

Paul Brown

Goal Post

Published in 2017 by Goal Post
www.goalpostbooks.co.uk

An imprint of Superelastic
County Durham, UK
www.superelastic.co.uk

ISBN-13: 9780995541221

www.stuffbypaulbrown.com
www.twitter.com/paulbrownuk

A CIP data record for this book is
available from the British Library

Cover by Tim Fox-Godden
www.timgoddenillustrations.bigcartel.com

If you enjoy reading this book please consider leaving a
review on your favourite book store or reader website

www.twitter.com/goalpostbooks
www.facebook.com/goalpostbooks

"People come home from these games: 'We won, we won!' No, they won. You watched."
– Jerry Seinfeld

Contents

Introduction

Being a football fan is both a privilege and a burden. When you're winning, it's the best thing on Earth, and when you're not, it's the end of the world. And the thing about being a football fan is, whichever way fortune swings, you're stuck with the game and your team for life. We fans have come to accept the great hold football has on us. But how did this happen? How did we become so entirely wrapped up in the game? How did we become football fans?

Many of us can trace the lineage of our support through our parents, our grandparents and so on. But association football has only been around for 150 years or so. At some point, several generations ago, our ancestors discovered and embraced the emerging game, developed affinities for individual clubs, cheered and sang, and helped initiate the fan culture that we're part of today. But the roots of football fandom were established long before the association game was invented.

People have been fanatical about football ever since feet and balls were first introduced to each other, from ancient games in China, Greece and Rome, through Britain's violent medieval football battles, to the (slightly) more refined public school games and, eventually, the codified game of association football. In vase paintings, ancient poems and old chronicles, there is evidence of football fanaticism that predates the formation of the Football Association and the creation of the Laws of the Game in 1863. Even in its earliest forms, football was able to inspire savage enthusiasm.

Football fever really took hold among the general public around the 1880s, fuelled by social changes that allowed working people the time and means to pursue new pastimes. Although their fanaticism was rapidly being established, these enthusiasts weren't labelled as "football fans" until the early 20th century. Before that they were "spectators" and then "supporters" (terms that are still used pretty interchangeably today). The term "fan", as a contraction of "fanatic", was first used to describe keen baseball spectators in the sports columns of US newspapers in the 1890s. A 1900 edition of language journal *Dialect Notes* includes the entry: "Fan, *n.* A baseball enthusiast; common among reporters."

In 1913, the London *Sketch* newspaper published a column with the headline "Football 'Fans'" that compared the feverish behaviour of British football spectators to that of American baseball enthusiasts, "who are called 'fans', as short for fanatics". And in 1914, the *Daily Express* used the term (again cautiously protected by inverted commas) in a reference to "First League football 'fans' in London". It has since become common for people to be categorised as fans of anything and everything, but football fans, perhaps more than any other set of enthusiasts, occupy a significant and highly-visible place in society. Football fandom has become an integral and inescapable part of modern culture.

The traditional football fan, in an image captured somewhere between the game's post-war boom and its satellite TV-fuelled commercial explosion, is a familiar – if clichéd – character. He'll most likely be male, wearing a replica team shirt, or perhaps a woollen hat and scarf in his team's colours. He may have a rosette pinned to his chest, and a wooden rattle in his hand. He'll arrive at his local football ground and hand over a paper ticket stub before pushing through a mechanical turnstile. He'll procure a steaming cup of Bovril, and perhaps a match pie, then make his way to the standing terrace. There, he'll sing and sway, and ride an emotional rollercoaster that rises and falls with the ebb and flow of the match. And afterwards he'll head home, his mood altered for better or worse by the result of the game. A win makes the next week of work easier to contemplate. A defeat makes it a slog, but there is always the next match to look forward to. There is always the next match.

This routine might baffle outsiders, who fail to understand the vital importance of football. Ever since trainloads of provincial folk began to arrive in London for the first FA Cup finals, football fans have been viewed with bemusement and derision by sections of society. Initially there was a broad class divide. Football was the working-class game, and those of a higher standing who did not feel its popular appeal were wary of invasion by flat-capped northern factory workers. Noisy groups of football fans were at best boisterous, and at worst hooligans. To be fair, during the long history of football fans, a minority have earned a bad reputation with behaviour that would not be becoming of (by hackneyed contrast) opera fans. In certain periods, most notably in the 1970s and 1980s, high-profile incidents of disorder and violence led to the general vilification of football fans. The contempt with which fans came to be regarded would have tragic consequences, leading to a series of wholly-preventable disasters.

Things did change, and the reputation and treatment of football fans improved over the 1990s and 2000s, during what some might call the gentrification of the game. But, while few would mourn the gradual disappearance of the hooligan, the traditional football fan is also disappearing. As cash has been pumped into the game, the traditional working-class fan has been increasingly priced out. Today, top-flight football belongs primarily to the middle classes. And, with ex-prime ministers and heirs to the throne claiming dubious affiliations to Aston Villa, football's popular appeal has also reached the upper classes. Politicians and royals recognise that an affiliation with football can foster an affiliation with the people. It has become fashionable to be a football fan.

It has also become possible to be a football fan without ever attending football matches. This has been enabled by expanding media coverage of football, which has made it easy to follow the game and watch matches from our homes, in the pub, or on the go, virtually anywhere in the world. The media has long been an enabler of the football fan. The rise in popularity of football and the growth in circulation of newspapers were indelibly linked from the late-1800s. Newspapers nurtured and promoted football, increasing the game's popularity, and football fans bought newspapers to read their coverage, expanding newspaper readerships. Then came radio and TV, and it became increasingly possible to follow football from afar. Further technological advances, notably the internet and social media, have expanded football coverage and extended the game's reach. What it means to be a football fan has evolved and shifted to such an extent that a 19th century fan might struggle to recognise a 21st century fan as a fellow round-ball enthusiast.

In the modern era, the vast majority of football fans never go to matches. Take Manchester United's claim, based on a market research survey, to have 659 million supporters. Old Trafford's capacity is 75,731. So, according to a back-of-an-envelope calculation, only 0.01% of the club's fans can fit into their ground. While the average attendance for Premier League matches in 2015-16 was just under 36,500, the average UK TV audience for those matches was 800,000. And that was just the UK audience. The Premier League says its worldwide TV audience is three billion. And then there's social media. Real Madrid have more than 100 million fans on Facebook. The capacity at the Bernabéu is 81,044. Those fans who do go to matches are part of a vastly-outnumbered minority.

But fans do still pass through the turnstiles. And, at football's lower levels, they remain the lifeblood of the game. The modern fan is still more likely to be male than female, although research shows that a third of football fans are now women. They may still wear a replica shirt, but the woollen hat and scarf have fallen out of fashion. (The rosette and rattle are now football museum pieces.) The turnstile they pass through may be electronic, with a plastic smartcard placed into a scanner rather than a paper ticket handed to an operator. Most likely they will sit rather than stand, in plastic flip-up seats that clatter when a passage of play brings fans to their feet. There is still singing, and the ebb and flow of emotion. And the result still matters, and affects the mood, until overtaken by anticipation for the next match. There is always the next match. Some things never change.

This history of football fans is a social history, a political history, a history of the media, and a history of the game itself. Primarily, though, it's a history of people going out to watch their teams, win or lose, then going back again and again. It's a celebration of watching football, dedicated to anyone who has ever had their heart gladdened or saddened by the game. It's about being a football fan. It's about being us.

1

Alive with expectation

They gathered at the market place from noon, crowding at windows and clambering on rooftops, eager for a safe vantage point. It was Shrove Tuesday, a general holiday, and men, women and children of all ranks and ages streamed into the square from surrounding streets. Shops were closed, and workers and apprentices were released from their duties. Public houses prepared for brisk trade, and vendors stacked stalls with refreshments. It was the day of the great football game, and the entire town of Derby was turning out to watch.

The year was 1827, but it could have been almost any year from several centuries past, so long-standing was the tradition of Derby's Shrovetide football game. Shrovetide was a major festival (along with Eastertide and Christmastide), and Shrove Tuesday, the last day before the beginning of the religious season of Lent, was a rare holiday. From at least the late-medieval period, Shrovetide was associated with the eating of pancakes, cock-fighting and football. It was an indulgent celebration during which, according to an old gazette, "men ate and drank, and abandoned themselves to every kind of sporting foolery, as if resolved to have their pleasure before they went to die".

Football was a particularly popular pleasure in this late-Georgian era. There were relatively few pastimes available to the masses. In the days surrounding the match, the *Derby Mercury* reported on a horse race, a choral concert, and a dance for farmers' wives, but said none of those entertainments could be compared with football. "No public amusement is calculated to call forth such a high degree of popular excitement," said the paper. "The aged and the young are drawn from their homes to witness the strife which the robust and vigorous population of the town and immediate neighbourhood engage with all the energy of eager but amicable competition."

The annual football game was a rare treat, and the people of Derby looked forward to it like little else. It was one of the most significant events on the calendar, and anticipation built steadily over the year. It was a celebration, and also a release from hard lives and from boredom. And it was a chance to come together, with family and friends as a community, away from the constraints of work and the struggles of life. After Christmas, through January and into February, talk was of football, football and more football. By Shrove Tuesday, with a respite from graft and toil, Derby was ready to enjoy itself. "At two o'clock begins the sport," said an early account, "and as the hour approaches, the whole town seems alive with expectation."

As kick-off neared, the players began to arrive, in groups of a dozen or more, coats and waistcoats removed, arms bare, and trousers "tightly strapped around the loins", so as not to restrict their movements – or allow their opponents a grab-hold. They assembled at opposite ends of the market place, two teams gradually swelling in numbers, from tens, to scores, to hundreds. There were five parishes in Derby, and the players and spectators were drawn from all of them. The teams were named to represent the two largest parishes. This great game would pit All Saints against St Peter's.

The market place represented the starting point, but the game was played over a much larger area, between two goals set several miles apart. The All Saints "goal" was the wheel of a water mill about a mile to the north-east of Derby, on the road to Manchester. The St Peter's goal was the gate of a plant nursery out to the south-west, on the road to London. The rules of the ancient game were fairly negligible. The aim was to kick, carry or force the ball towards one of the distant goals, and strike it three times against the wheel or the gate. The first team to score a goal would win the game. Few restrictions were placed on how this was to be accomplished. The use of hands, brute force and minor physical violence was not discouraged. This was football, but not as we know it.

Some spectators grew impatient. Boys amused themselves by throwing wet rags and muddy wisps of straw into the crowd, to the great annoyance of their targets. Then the ball arrived, and impatience gave way to "all-engrossing eagerness". The ball – a large leather caser filled with cork shavings – was carried in the arms of a victorious hero from the previous year's game. The awaiting horde of players parted to let him through. He proceeded to the middle of the market place, and a hush of anticipation fell upon the crowd. At two o'clock, the ball was thrown up into the air, and the great game began.

Those gathered around the market place were witnesses to a remarkable scene. A huge mass of hundreds of bodies heaved and churned, the prized ball hidden somewhere within its seething centre. Spectators yelled encouragement, and threw oranges to their favourite players for refreshment. Ladies waved handkerchiefs and searched for glimpses of their husbands and sons. The tumultuous battle went on and on, with neither side giving up ground. As exhausted and bloodied men pulled themselves from the steaming fray for brief respite, spectators revived them with cups of ale. Then the men were returned to the action.

The struggle was contained within the market place for an hour or more, before St Peter's somehow managed to force the ball out through narrow streets and confined yards, pushing slowly towards the River Derwent. Once there, the ball was thrown over a fence into the river, and the players hurtled down after it into the water. Here, the battle became more frenzied and dangerous – and even more enthralling – as St Peter's attempted to bear the ball downstream towards their goal, and All Saint's tried to block their progress by any means possible.

The spectators, who had followed the action en masse from the market place to the river, filled the air with a hubbub of impartiality. These early football supporters inevitably favoured their friends and neighbours from their own parishes. "The opposite banks were lined with spectators eagerly urging on their respective partisans to fresh exertions," reported the *Mercury*. "The mothers, wives and sisters of the combatants were at hand to stimulate them to every effort of strength, and were even heard instructing their infants to call out '*All Saints* or *St Peter's forever*'."

Eventually, after a struggle that covered miles and lasted hours, St Peter's reached their goal, and one of their number touched the ball three times against the nursery gate. St Peter's had won the game. The goalscorer was hoisted onto the shoulders of his teammates and paraded through the streets of the St Peter's parish to receive "the plaudits of an admiring multitude". For All Saints and their supporters, there was nothing to be done but nurse wounded limbs and pride. There would always be next year.

The spectators who witnessed the fun at Derby can be categorised as football fans, even if the football they were watching was very different to the game we know today. The Shrovetide match was an example of mob football, a hectic, rule-shy folk game, which brought havoc to the streets of towns and villages across Britain for hundreds of years, from medieval times through to the Victorian era. It was chaotic and violent, and there were numerous reports of broken legs, fatalities, and matches turning into full-scale riots. The game, often involving hundreds of players and lasting for many hours, must have been a compelling spectacle, with contemporary reports evoking something like a round-ball version of the Pamplona Bull Run. No wonder it so enthralled its spectators.

The mob game was an early form of football, but it was by no means the earliest. People have most likely kicked balls about for as long as balls (and feet) have been around. There is something inherently pleasing about kicking a ball. Those of us who recognise this simple pleasure can gain immense satisfaction from trapping an errant football and booting it back to its park-playing owners. We don't even require a proper football. A not-insignificant amount of joy can be obtained from kicking a pebble against a wall, or from rattling a crushed drinks can between a pair of lampposts.

The compulsion to kick a ball feels so primal that it's easy to imagine it could have been around since man's earliest days, with stone-age man kicking around, well, a stone, simply because it felt good to do so, to cause and affect a rolling motion with the swing of a leg. A rolling stone gathers no moss, but it does generate a pleasing sensation when kicked straight and true between a set of imaginary goal posts.

Whether or not stone age man played with a ball, he did, according to the opinions of some scholars, play other sports. Cave paintings found in Lascaux, France, dating from at least 15,000BC (the Upper Palaeolithic period) may depict figures participating in sprint races and wrestling bouts. Certainly, cave paintings from around the world habitually depict figures participating in hunting, which could perhaps be considered the original sport. Hunting required athleticism and skill, and provided excitement and reward. The reward, for early man, was food – and survival. The primal need to hunt was an important factor in human evolution, and may drive our enthusiasm for sport today.

In his book *The Soccer Tribe*, zoologist and "Human Ape" behaviourist Desmond Morris used evolutionary theory and man's need to hunt to help explain our deep connection with football. "Almost the whole of man's evolutionary history belongs to that hunting period," wrote Morris. "It moulded us and made us, genetically, what we are today." Man was - and still is - a hunter, and while the need to hunt may have dissipated, the urge to hunt remains. According to Morris, that urge is satisfied by the playing of sports - including football. And if the urge to play football is in our genes, then so too is the urge to watch it.

Evidence suggests man has watched football for as long as he has played it. Indeed, the earliest known depiction of someone playing football also depicts someone watching it. The Acropolis Museum in Athens holds an *Attic lekythos* (an Athenian vase used for storing oil) dating from the fourth century BC and bearing a clear image of a man juggling a football while a small boy looks on. This Ancient Greek boy is the earliest known football fan.

Ancient Greece also provides the earliest known form of organised football. From around 350BC the Greeks played a game called *episkyros* ("on the lime"), also known as *sphairomachia* ("battle-ball"). It seems to have been every bit as violent as the latter name suggests, and some distance removed from what we might recognise as our beautiful game. There is some debate over whether or not episkyros involved the kicking of a ball, and it certainly allowed the use of hands. Contemporary descriptions suggest a fiercely-odd cross between rugby and volleyball that involved throwing the ball into the air and forcing the opponent team over a central dividing line, which was marked out on the ground in white lime (hence the name "on the lime").

From around 250BC, a game called *tsu' chu* or *cuju* ("kick-ball") was played in Han Dynasty China. There were various forms of tsu' chu, but they generally involved the now familiar aim of kicking a ball into a goal. Although primarily a form of recreation (or military training) for its participants, it does seem that tsu' chu was attractive to spectators, as it's recorded as being played for the pleasure of watching dignitaries.

And then, from around 100BC, the Romans played *harpastum*, or the "small ball game". The rules of harpastum are mostly lost to history, but we do know it involved passing and dodging within boundaries. We also know that harpastum attracted spectators. The historian Athenaeus described a game of harpastum that was watched by a crowd around AD200: "He seized the ball and passed it to a team-mate while dodging another and laughing. He pushed it out of the way of another. Another fellow player he raised to his feet. All the while the crowd resounded with shouts of 'Out of bounds!', 'Too far!', 'Right beside him!', 'Over his head!', 'On the ground!', 'Up in the air!', 'Too short!', 'Pass it back in the scrum!'"

This surprisingly familiar-sounding description of shouts from onlookers is one of the earliest written references to a football crowd, and to football as a spectator sport. The very earliest reference may be from the anonymous poet who wrote in in the first century AD in praise of the harpastum skills of a man named Piso, thought to be the Roman senator Gaius Calpurnius Piso. "It is your pleasure to return the flying ball or recover it when falling to the ground, and by a surprising movement get it within bounds again in its flight," cooed the poet. "To watch such play the populace remains stock still, and the whole crowd suddenly abandons its own games."

Harpastum may be an archaic form of football, but these two writings highlight something that has remained constant right through to the modern form, and that is football's ability to draw a crowd. Harpastum stopped people in their tracks, generated excitement within them, and compelled them to yell words of encouragement – and criticism. These Romans were among the first recorded football fans. (And Gaius Calpurnius Piso may have been football's first fan-favourite.) So, some 2,000 years ago, football was established as a game that was not just fun to play but also fun to watch.

The question of *why* football is fun to watch has many possible answers, but key to several of them is the concept of the vicarious thrill. By watching football, we can vicariously experience what it's like to play football – generally at a more proficient level than we could manage ourselves. Most of us can kick a ball, but few of us can do so with real skill. The harpastum crowd could kick a ball, but not with the skill of Piso. If we cannot play, then to watch is the next best thing.

There is science behind this, too, although it centres around the widely-disputed mirror neuron theory. The idea is that, when an individual observes an action being performed by others, neurons in the individual's brain create a "mirror" response, allowing the individual to experience, to some extent, what it would be like to perform the action themselves. So, if an individual watches another person eating a cake, mirror neurons allow them to experience, to some extent, what it would be like to eat the cake themselves. Detractors argue that, while mirror responses have been recorded in monkeys, mirror neuron theory has not yet been proven to apply to humans.

Nevertheless, science writer Sandra Blakeslee, in the *New York Times*, explained how mirror neurons could hook spectators watching football: "They respond when someone kicks a ball, sees a ball being kicked, hears a ball being kicked and says or hears the word 'kick'". Blakeslee went on to say that tests show mirror neurons respond even in individuals who have never played a particular sport. The response may not always be positive, which would explain why not everyone enjoys watching sport. But such a primal, genetic attachment to sport might help to explain how so many of us became sports spectators and, specifically, football fans.

The Ancient Greeks and the Romans both enjoyed spectator sports. The stadium at Olympia, where the Ancient Olympic Games took place from around 350BC, held around 45,000 spectators, who crowded onto a sloped embankment around a rectangular track. The original Olympic event was *stadion*, a sprint race over approximately 200 metres. Subsequent Olympic Games added longer-distance running events, boxing, wrestling, chariot racing, and a pentathlon consisting of stadion, wrestling, long jump, discus and javelin. There was no room for episkyros (and football would have to wait more than 2,000 years, until 1900, to be included in the modern games).

The Olympics were a celebration of sporting prowess, and also a celebration of the human body. To promote the latter, the athletes (all of them male) competed in the nude, lathered in olive oil. Clearly this may have added to the aesthetic appeal of the event for many spectators, but it also had an effect on the make-up of the crowd. Due to the abundant male nudity, married women were not allowed to be present – on penalty of death – and so the vast majority of spectators were men.

The majority of spectators were well-off, too, if only due to the high costs associated with travelling to and staying in Olympia for the event. Records show spectators travelled long distances to attend what was a major festival and social event. It's fair to say that they came not just for the sport but for the occasion, which drew politicians, military leaders, merchants and artists, and became an important forum for discussion and trading. The event was a political and commercial pageant with significance that went way beyond athletics.

In Ancient Rome, spectator sport was perhaps a more proletarian affair – a mass entertainment for the benefit of the populace, to keep them satiated and subservient in the presence of their superiors. The Circus Maximus, first built around 530BC, seated up to 250,000 spectators – around a quarter of the population of the city at that time. The venue hosted athletics, chariot racing, and *damnatio ad bestias* ("condemnation to beasts"), which involved throwing criminals and Christians to bears and lions. The nearby Colosseum, built around AD70, held 50,000 spectators, and staged gladiatorial contests, simulated sea battles (for which the arena was flooded) and *venatio*, or staged animal hunts.

Desmond Morris placed great significance on these staged animal hunts in the development of football as a spectator sport. If the hunt was the original sport, it was no longer widely played. The development of farming and trading meant hunting was no longer essential to survival. The citizens of Rome had no real reason or opportunity to hunt, but they still craved its challenge and excitement – the thrill of the chase. To satisfy this craving, Rome brought the hunt to the people, shipping in from all over its empire such huge numbers of animals that some species were driven towards extinction. Some 9,000 beasts were killed in staged hunts during the inauguration of the Colosseum alone. And the Colosseum was just one of around 70 Roman arenas that hosted staged hunts over a period of 500 or so years.

"If the city dweller could not rush out to the countryside to hunt, then the animals would be brought into the centre of the city and challenged there in an enclosed space, watched by thousands of frustrated hunters," wrote Morris. The ancient Colosseum resembles a modern football stadium, in size and capacity, and it's certainly possible to see elements of the roots of football fandom in Rome's popular blood sports. Roman spectators gained vicarious thrills from watching staged hunts, just as football fans gain vicarious thrills from watching matches. Football fans remain "frustrated hunters".

It seems likely that the Romans brought the game of harpastum to Britain when they visited for an extended stay from around AD50. Various forms of football were played in the centuries that followed. The Anglo Saxon text *Historia Brittonum*, thought to have been written in AD828, contains a reference to "a party of boys playing at ball". Then the first reference to football spectators in Britain comes from the cleric William Fitzstephen in his description of London, written around 1180. Fitzstephen was writing about the festival of Carnival, now known as Shrovetide.

"After dinner, all the youths go into the fields to play at the ball," wrote Fitzstephen. "The scholars of every school have their ball in their hands. The ancient and wealthy men of the city come forth on horseback to see the sport of the young men, and to take part of the pleasure in beholding their agility." The ancient and wealthy (perhaps too ancient and/or wealthy to play the game) gain their vicarious thrills from watching the more able youths "play at the ball".

There are many fascinating accounts of Shrovetide football games, such as that played at Derby. At Scone, in Perthshire, an annual Shrovetide mob football game was played between the unmarried and married men of the town, who played from two o'clock until sunset. At Inveresk, in East Lothian, an annual match was played between married and unmarried women, and records state the married women always won. In Alnwick, Northumberland, at two o'clock every Shrove Tuesday, "a football was thrown over the castle walls to the populace". An account of the Alnwick game refers to "a large concourse of spectators" who "seemed to watch the eager struggles of the game with as much interest and excitement as those whom were actively engaged in the sport".

Although many onlookers were instinctively drawn to the great spectacle of Shrovetide football, their attendance was not always voluntary. "At some places every man in the parish, gentry not excepted, was obliged to turn out and support the side to which he belonged," recalled the *Monthly Chronicle*. "Any person who neglected to do so was fined." It's easy to see why some residents might be reluctant to support the often violent and disruptive tradition. In advance of games, townsfolk would barricade their doors and board up their windows. Players would carry their football from door to door, begging for money to be used for refreshments. "It was dangerous to refuse," said the *Chronicle*, "because the recusants' windows were very likely to be broken as soon as it was dark."

The violent and disruptive nature of the mob football game led to repeated attempts by the authorities to ban it. Tudor-period author and veritable spoilsport Philip Stubbes, in his 1583 diatribe *Anatomy of Abuses*, said of mob football: "It may rather be called a friendly kind of fight, than a play or recreation; a bloody and murdering practice, than a fellowly sport or pastime." But, according to Stubbes, the game was "rooted in the affections of the people", and successful players would be popular and well-known in their towns and villages.

Attempts to properly suppress football began in 1314 with a decree from Edward II, which banned the game from being played in London due to "great noise in the city caused by hustling over large balls from which many evils may arise". Edward III, Richard II, Henry IV and Edward IV all attempted bans, as did Henry VIII, despite the fact that the latter is known to have once ordered a pair of football boots, so most probably played the game himself.

In the early part of the 19th century, there were scores of arrests and trials involving football-related disturbances and breaches of the peace, and then the Highway Act of 1835 actually outlawed the playing of football on public highways, "with a maximum penalty of 40 shillings". (Playing football on a highway "to the annoyance of a user" is still prohibited today.)

Even the famous Derby game was eventually banned, in 1846, after the mayor was forced to call in the military and literally read the Riot Act (an Act of Parliament outlawing "tumults and riotous assemblies") to suppress a particularly rowdy game. In the following year, 1847, soldiers and special constables blocked thoroughfares to stop crowds from gathering, and successfully prevented the game from taking place. Mob football was being pushed towards extinction, and football fans would have to find a less violent and disruptive form of the game to support.

2

Surrounded by partisans

It was Boxing Day 1860, and the bright sun reflected prettily on the blanket of snow that lay across Hallam Cricket Club's Sandygate Road ground. It was beautiful, but cold, and certainly not a day for cricket. It was, instead, a day for football. Despite the weather, a large number of spectators were in attendance, arriving on foot and by horse-drawn hansom cab, then crowding into the pavilion or pushing up against the roped-off field. Collars were turned up, hands were pushed into pockets, and clouds of warm breath floated into the air. The spectators were gathered in the snow to watch what would come to be regarded as a uniquely historic football match. It was the first match between two of football's oldest clubs, and the spectators were among football's earliest supporters.

The visiting club was Sheffield FC, formed in 1857 and recognised in the modern era as the world's oldest surviving football club. Ordinarily, Sheffield FC (not directly related to either Sheffield United or Sheffield Wednesday) arranged matches internally between its members, splitting them into teams using criteria such as "tall v short" and "married v single". In the previous week, they had played a match against infantrymen from the 58th Regiment of the British Army. Today, for the first time, Sheffield would play a match against another football club – Hallam FC.

Only recently formed as an adjunct of Hallam Cricket Club, home side Hallam FC didn't yet have enough players to make up a team and were bolstered by players from the nearby Stumperlowe Cricket Club. So Hallam FC began its life billed in local papers as "Hallam and Stumperlowe". Nevertheless, Hallam FC can claim to be the world's second-oldest surviving football club, and Sandygate Road can claim to be the oldest surviving football ground. And, while there had been earlier matches between earlier now-extinct clubs, this 1860 Sheffield v Hallam meeting was the earliest football match played between clubs that still exist in the modern era.

The spectators, of whom there were several hundred, were dressed for the occasion and the weather, with the Boxing Day holiday allowing an opportunity to wear their finest clothing – frock jackets, waistcoats and colourful neckerchiefs, under heavy winter overcoats. Moustaches and mutton-chop sideburns were very much in fashion, and there were plenty of shiny top hats to be seen in among the more workaday soft flat caps. There was no segregation and little distinction between the spectators from Sheffield and those from Hallam. These club members and friends and neighbours did not display the colours of their respective teams (scarlet and white for Sheffield, and navy blue for Hallam), nor did they display any real kind of favouritism. They were gathered together to watch an entertaining match, regardless of the result. For this first game, there was a genial, communal atmosphere. It wouldn't last.

The snow-white field under a bright blue sky provided a glorious setting for the game. "The uniforms of the men contrasting with each other and the pure snow had the most picturesque appearance," said the *Sheffield Telegraph*. This was an early indication that football could be enjoyed throughout the depths of the British winter. Distinct in that regard from cricket, football would become known as "the winter game". Certainly, the wintry conditions did not seem to hamper the action, and spectators saw a match that was contested with "great pluck and courage".

According to the *Telegraph*, "The spirit exhibited by those who were present prevented the game from becoming uninteresting to the observers, who were extremely liberal with their plaudits on the successful 'charge' or quiet 'dodge', and equally unsparing in their sarcasm and country 'chaff' on the unfortunate victims of the slippery ground." Dictionary definitions of "chaff" include "banter", which has therefore been associated with football since the earliest club-versus-club match.

On the field, the *Telegraph*'s reporter refused to single out any individual player, as all had done well, but did "give the palm" to the Sheffield team for being "the most scientific and also more alive to the advantage of upsetting their opponents". When darkness brought the game to a close (the 90-minute game of two halves had yet to be invented), Sheffield had won by two goals to nil. The Sheffield players and supporters "went home fully satisfied with their victory".

As if it were not historically significant enough, the 1860 meeting between Sheffield and Hallam can also be regarded as football's first derby match – the first match played between local rival clubs. The origin of the term "derby match" may be connected to the Derby Shrovetide football game, but is more likely to be derived from horse racing's Epsom Derby, the blue ribbon event that has lent its name to other prestigious racing and non-racing sporting events around the world. Sheffield v Hallam would become known as the "rules derby". That's because it was played under Sheffield Rules, an influential code that pre-dated the Football Association's Laws of the Game.

Although the Sheffield and Hallam clubs were only just getting to know each other, their supporters were predestined to be rivals. Sheffield were based in the town centre, while Hallam were based two or three miles out to the west. Those two or three miles made a big difference. Local rivalry existed long before football rivalry, and in the 1860s centred primarily around industry. Competition between rival firms and workers, combined with associated economic and social differences, created inequality, envy and one-upmanship. While their respective teams had only just begun to play each other, there was a pre-existing rivalry between the people of Sheffield and Hallam. Football would provide an outlet through which to channel that rivalry.

There were also differences in social class between the two clubs and their supporters. Although based in a mainly working-class industrial town, Sheffield FC was very much a middle-class club. Membership was restricted to "gentlemen" only, with the *Telegraph* referring to Sheffield FC's doctors, solicitors and architects as "the elite of the town". "Its members are exclusively of the middle class," the paper commented, "and its patrons and supporters include most of the leading men in the neighbourhood."

By contrast, Hallam FC was formed with the intention of creating a more inclusive club, representing a broader section of the town's residents. Hallam was founded by ex-Sheffield "gentlemen", and its inclusivity may not have been broad enough to include the town's steelworkers, miners and other blue-collar men. Nevertheless, here were the beginnings of football played along class divides, where supporters would be drawn towards clubs that best represented their social groups. Class has always been a divisive issue in British society, and it would play a key role throughout the history of the football fan.

Sheffield and Hallam met again in December 1861, at Sheffield's Hyde Park, to play a benefit match in aid of the Sheffield Public Hospital and Dispensary. Once again, there was no mention in newspaper reports of rivalry or partisanship, and there was no indication that the two sets of fans had come together for anything other than to enjoy a communal game of football, and to support a good cause. Reports did contain an early record of a football attendance figure. "The spectators numbered between 600 and 700," said one newspaper, "and from their loud and frequent cheering, evidently enjoyed the sport." The sum of £15 was raised for the hospital.

Twelve months later, on 29 December 1862, "a very fair number of spectators" attended another derby at Sheffield FC's Bramall Lane. This time, though, there was clear evidence of the emerging football rivalry. Hallam had the best of the attacking play, and were determinedly resolute in defence, being loudly cheered by their supporters. "They appeared to have many partisans present," reported the *Sheffield Independent*, "and when they succeeded in 'downing' a man, their ardent friends were more noisily jubilant."

These partisans wanted to watch an entertaining match, but they also wanted to see their own team win. They were no longer neutral observers, and, within the space of a couple of years, had shifted from being spectators to being supporters. And they demonstrated their support vocally and physically. At one point, a bout of fisticuffs between opposition players caused supporters to spill onto the pitch. "[The players] were surrounded by partisans, and for a few minutes there was every appearance of a general fight amongst players and spectators," the *Independent* reported. "The advice of older and cooler heads at length prevailed, the field was cleared, and play again resumed."

The match ended as a draw, "there being neither a goal nor a rouge scored by either party". The reference to a "rouge" reminds that matches played under Sheffield Rules, while substantially more advanced than mob games, would still have looked rather strange to modern football fans. A rouge was a type of touchdown, with the Sheffield Rules allowing players to handle the ball, but not hold on to it.

Pushing and charging were also allowed, but hacking and tripping were outlawed. As unusual as some of these laws might seem, the Sheffield Rules were highly influential, and helped to shape the modern game.

The codification of football had begun in the public schools, where various incarnations of the game were prevalent by the mid-1800s. The once-popular mob game had all but died out following a clampdown on the often-disruptive tradition. Football had effectively been banned in public places, but it continued to be played in public schools. However, not all public schools had playing fields, and the game was necessarily adapted to fit available playing areas, such as the Charterhouse cloisters, where a mob game was impossible, but a kicking and dribbling game thrived. Each school developed its own idiosyncratic set of rules – which made playing matches between different schools somewhat problematic.

Public school games were instead played internally between the school houses, which could draw upon their boarders for support. House system divisions guaranteed rivalry and partisanship, with spectators inevitably supporting the house to which they belonged. Newspaper reports indicate that public school games were well-attended, whether the boys thronged the touchlines through choice or by the will of a schoolmaster or prefect. (At Winchester school, the spectators were part of the game, surrounding the playing pitch as "kickers-in" – effectively a horde of straw boater-wearing ball-boys.)

In 1852, *Bell's Life in London* reported that a match at Harrow between the Middlemist and Simpkinson houses was "attended by a considerable muster of spectators". In 1853, *Bell's* described "a match for cock of college" at Eton between Mrs Drury's and Mr Balston's houses. "After much good play on both sides, Mrs Drury's were hailed 'cocks' by a hearty cheer from the spectators, by obtaining three goals to two goals and one rouge," reported the paper. A "match for cock", by the way, was effectively a public school championship match.

The hearty cheers of these early football spectators did sometimes turn to jeers. Describing an 1854 match at Eton between Mrs Drury's and Reverend Coleridge's houses, *Bell's* reported that "a most exciting match" had been won by Mrs Drury's, "to the great satisfaction of the majority of the spectators". However, the paper added: "We were sorry to hear the offensive shouts of one 'Mackintoshed stranger', which, however, were almost entirely drowned out by the universal supporters of the Druryites."

By now, football was no longer such an unusual spectacle, and observers came to anticipate good games and appreciate good play. Ahead of one match at Eton in 1858, between Collegers and Oppidans, *Bell's* reported that "the excitement of the spectators was intense". In 1861, when Wimbledon School played Kensington Grammar, "the favourable state of the weather, and the character for prowess and skill obtained by both schools in this their favourite game, did not fail to draw together a large number of spectators".

Away from the public schools, clubs were being formed. One of the earliest clubs dedicated to football was London's Gymnastic Society, formed in the late 1700s by men from Cumberland and Westmorland. The club played matches for cash wagers on Kennington Common in Lambeth, until a "want of room" forced them to stop. The short-lived run of matches nevertheless attracted many interested spectators. One of them was the editor of the *Lancaster Gazette*, who recalled one such match that occurred during the last years of the 18th century.

"I well remember being a spectator at a *foot-ball* match in the neighbourhood of London," he wrote, "between ten young men from Cumberland and ten from Westmorland. The sum played for was, I think, 20 guineas. The novelty of the diversion, as it may be thought, attracted a great number of spectators. The game was played with great spirit by both parties, who discovered an agility that surprised and astonished the honest cockneys. The diversion was, however, exclaimed against by persons in London and in other places as low and vulgar."

This brief, rare account from the point of view of an early football spectator demonstrates that the game was still considered a novelty. The "honest cockneys" were curious bystanders, "surprised and astonished" at the scene they were witnessing. They probably had no connection with the men from Cumberland and Westmorland, and no affiliation with either team. Nor, most likely, did they have a clear understanding of whatever rules the match was played by. Yet they were curious enough to attend, and interested enough to watch, and – for those who did not consider it "low and vulgar" – perhaps entertained enough to make a mental note to further explore the game of "foot-ball".

Other early football clubs included Edinburgh's aptly-named Foot-Ball Club, which was formed around 1824 by 17-year-old trainee lawyer John Hope. The club played on various parks around Edinburgh, and at one point had 85 members – mostly young professionals. For this type of early club, the distinction between player and supporter was blurred, and the majority of the 85 members were probably both. The club existed until at least 1841, and proved to be influential, with its rule book adopted by another club, the Surrey Foot-Ball Club, formed in 1849. Surrey's members all belonged to cricket clubs that played at the Oval.

On Christmas Day 1841, Lancashire clubs the Body Guards and the Fearnoughts played a 12-a-side match for a cash prize and a barrel of gin. The Body Guards were a pub team based at the Grapes Inn in Rochdale. It was intended that the first team to score two goals would win. However, with the game still goalless, the illegal intervention of a spectator brought it an early end. A Body Guards player, feeling tired, asked a spectator "not connected with the game" to come on to the field and "kick for him". The umpire decided this was foul play, and awarded the game, and the prizes, to the Fear-noughts.

By the early 1860s, as Sheffield FC and Hallam were establishing themselves in Sheffield, the clubs that would go on to form the Football Association were doing likewise in London. Barnes, the club of FA founding father Ebenezer Cobb Morley, played at Barn Elms Park, described as "a pretty and suitable spot", located on the south bank of the Thames (directly opposite the present location of Fulham's Craven Cottage ground). In November 1862, Barnes, "having been in existence only a short time, but already numbering a great many members", defeated Richmond in front of a large crowd.

When Barnes played the influential Forest club in 1863, *Bell's Life* said the skilful play of star players Morley of Barnes and CW Alcock of Forest "elicited great applause from the spectators, of whom there were a great number". Forest (later renamed Wanderers) played on parkland in Leytonstone. The *Bell's* report suggested an idyllic scene, describing the ground as "a large field with a noble avenue of trees running through it, which afforded a pleasant promenade for the spectators, of whom there was a goodly muster, including many of the fair sex, who added to the attractions of the sport".

The presence of "the fair sex" is notable, if not unusual, and, as women weren't yet playing organised football, makes clear that the appeal of watching the game extended beyond those who played it. These early matches were social occasions, and opportunities for family, friends and communi-ties to come together. But the football was more than just a sideshow – it was a valued entertainment. At a Forest match against the NNs (No Names) of Kilburn, the spectators "showed by their applause a keen appreciation of the play". And at a subsequent match against Thompson's Eleven, "the spectators, of whom there were a goodly array, justly acknowledged it to be the finest match they had seen for a long time".

The attraction of this newly-emerging game of football over other entertainments isn't difficult to fathom – particularly as there were few other entertainments available. Newspapers in the 1860s advertised occasional boxing and wrestling matches, plus the odd athletics contest, particularly involving the popular competitive walking sport of pedestrianism, which could draw huge crowds. Cricket was played in the summer months, but its wickets were removed for the winter. Tennis and cycling wouldn't become popular spectator sports for another couple of decades.

Away from sports, newspapers carried notices for theatrical shows and music concerts, but this type of entertainment wasn't really accessible to the masses. The more accessible and inclusive music hall theatres would become popular over the next couple of decades, but for the time being most people made their own entertainment, either at home or in their local watering holes. As far as popular entertainment went, football was the most attractive alternative to the pub.

At this point it's worth recalling the original purpose of a football club, which can easily be forgotten in the modern era. A club is an organisation formed for the benefit of its members, in order for them to pursue a particular activity. The likes of Sheffield, Hallam, Barnes and Forest were formed in order for their members to play football. But not all members could play in every game – perhaps due to numbers, ability, injury or age – so some would spectate. These non-playing members became the club's first supporters.

Then came the friends and relatives of playing and non-playing members. They attended matches by recommendation or persuasion, and became supporters by association. And then came others – from the local community, its workplaces, schools, churches and other institutions – not necessarily associated with the club, but curious of the spectacle they had heard about, or literally heard from a distance. Drawn by yells and thuds of leather on leather, these curious spectators found themselves watching football – and enjoying it. In the midst of other supporters, they became supporters themselves.

The emergence of clubs was a crucial development in the evolution of the football fan. Affiliation with clubs gave supporters a sense of belonging, and gave them a stake in the game, which increased interest – and often enjoyment. If their club won, they shared in the reward. "They won" became "we won". Supporters could bask in reflected glory, and a win for their club could make them feel better about themselves.

This tendency to bask in reflected glory, defined as "BIRG", was the subject of an influential study carried out by Robert Cialdini in 1976. Cialdini noted that individuals associated themselves with successful teams, even though they had not caused the team's success. He also found that individuals were more likely to refer to a successful team using the pronoun "we". Basking in reflected glory was found to boost self-esteem. But no scientific study could hope to fully explain the connection between fans and their clubs.

As clubs grew, their fan bases expanded, from reserve players and ex-players, to friends and family, to neighbours and workmates, to folk from all around the town and its surrounding area. All of them now belonged to the club, and the club now belonged to all of them. They were different, but they shared a connection with the club, and they all wanted their club to win.

But the growth of clubs and their supporter bases was restricted by a problem that had already been recognised by the football-playing public schools. Incompatible rulebooks meant that, for example, clubs from London couldn't necessarily play clubs from Sheffield, just as teams from Eton couldn't necessarily play teams from Charterhouse. What was needed was a universal set of rules. After a series of debates, conducted largely by public school old boys via newspaper columns, a meeting was held on 26 October 1863 at the Freemason's Tavern in London, "for the purpose of forming an association with the object of establishing a definite code of rules for the regulation of football".

The Football Association was duly formed, and its members drew up the Laws of the Game. The template was set for modern "association" football, although there was still a fair way to go. The initial Laws of the Game were rudimentary and problematic, and the FA spent decades refining and promoting them for universal adoption. None of the leading public schools joined the FA, and several founding member clubs quit to form the Rugby Football Union. The Sheffield teams continued to play by their own rules until 1877. In truth, it would take pretty much the full remainder of the 19th century for football to become properly codified and shaped into the game that would captivate fans for generations to come.

The formation of the FA and the publication of the Laws of the Game did make it easier to arrange and play matches. New clubs emerged, fixture lists expanded, and there were more opportunities for people to watch football. Notices of upcoming matches began to appear in local shop windows, and this duly led to increased attendances. Newspaper match reports from the 1860s do mention large crowds, although rarely qualify that with any numbers. While some games were played at established cricket grounds, many of the earliest football games were played on public fields, with no gates or turnstiles. A box might be passed around to collect a few pennies from spectators, but there was no accurate way of determining an attendance.

Where attendances were recorded for London matches in the 1860s, they rarely exceeded a few hundred. Attendances were higher in Sheffield, where the first football tournament outside of the public schools was played in 1867. The Youdan Cup final, between Hallam and Norfolk, was watched by 3,000 spectators – an attendance figure five times larger than that recorded at the Sheffield-Hallam derby of 1861. Hallam won the final by two rouges to nil in a match played under Sheffield Rules. The relatively high attendance indicated that competitive matches could be a bigger draw than friendlies, and gave notice of football's potential to attract spectators. Once the Association game caught up with the Sheffield game, there would be no stopping its rise in popularity.

3

Popular favour

On Saturday, 5 March 1870, hundreds of enthusiasts descended on the Kennington Oval to watch a first international football match between England and Scotland. They arrived at the famous cricket ground on foot and in brake carriages, some crossing the old Vauxhall Bridge, where folk stood to watch hot air balloon flights lift from Vauxhall Gardens into the late-winter sky. London's horse-drawn tram service had recently been extended to Kennington, and match-goers disembarked from double-decker carriages in anticipation of the big event. This was to be an unprecedented exhibition of football, and it generated much excitement among supporters.

"No better proof can be adduced of the extensive popularity enjoyed by the game of football in the vicinity of London, and indeed in all the southern districts of England, than the intense interest in which the preliminaries incidental to the great International Football Match gave rise," commented the *Glasgow Herald*. This was something special – a grand occasion of the kind football fans had not seen before. It was, without doubt, the most high-profile match that had ever been played.

The match had been arranged by FA secretary CW Alcock, whose influential Forest club had recently relocated to the Oval, and renamed itself "Wanderers". The England and Scotland teams were drawn from established London clubs such as Barnes, the No Names and Wanderers, plus more recently-formed "old boys" clubs such as Old Etonians, Old

Harrovians and Old Carthusians. Among the players were some of the most prominent and well-known gentlemen of the time, including two serving members of parliament – William Henry Gladstone (the son of Prime Minister William Ewart Gladstone) and John Wingfield Malcolm.

"For weeks prior," said the *Herald*, "the members of the various clubs situated in the neighbourhood of the English metropolis had been on the alert to glean any authoritative news on the subject of the players who had been selected to do battle for the interested of the two countries." The match had been postponed from its original date two weeks earlier due to a frozen pitch. "The delay only intensified the excitement," continued the paper, "producing an assemblage of spectators at the Oval such as is rarely seen on the occasion of a football match."

The size of the "assemblage", however, was relatively small, certainly in comparison to attendances at major cricket matches at the same venue, and at some big football matches in Sheffield and elsewhere. One newspaper reported that it was "computed to number upwards of 400 persons". The reason the excitement didn't really extend beyond club members to the wider public is that the "great International Football Match" was actually a pretty insular affair, played for the benefit of a narrow community of clubs from the London area. Both sides were made up exclusively of players from these clubs, and the Scottish side contained only one player who had been born in Scotland. As a result, the match is not regarded in modern records as an official international. This and four subsequent "unofficial" matches have become known as the "Alcock internationals". Nevertheless, it was of great interest to those attached to the local clubs, and generated the biggest football crowd that had so far been seen in London.

The supporters entered the Oval in bright sunshine, and took their positions on the pavilion and around the roped-off football pitch. There was plenty of room for the 400 spectators. Two years earlier, a cricket match between Surrey and a visiting Aboriginal Australian team had drawn 20,000 to the Oval. A pair of large gas holders stood over the north end of the ground – the Gasometer End. The south end was the Crown Baths End. A strong wind blew from one end to the other, and two days of heavy rain had made the pitch very slippery. Scotland won the coin-toss, and chose to kick with the wind at their backs – a decision that delighted the Scottish fans, who "represented no small portion of the spectators".

After 45 minutes, and with no goals scored, the teams changed ends, in accordance with a new rule recently introduced by the FA. Previously, teams had changed ends after each goal, with no requirement for a half-time switch. Despite the fact they were now playing into the wind, Scotland scored a goal, courtesy of a "lucky long kick" from Robert Crawford, "in the reprehensible absence of England's goalkeeper". This led to "vociferous applause from the 'canny Scots'". Then, in the very last minute, England's Alfred Baker ended a fine run by booting the ball into the Scottish goal, "to the enthusiastic plaudits of the spectators". The "most interesting and exciting" match ended 1-1.

A second Alcock international was played in the following November, again at the Oval, in front of "a gallery rarely seen on such occasions", numbering around 650 people. This time England won 1-0, but the jubilant "home" supporters appreciated the efforts of both teams. "It would be unjust to say that the result of the contest was not hailed with considerable satisfaction by the spectators," said the *Herald*, "but it is equally certain that there was an equal expression of praise for the gallant manner in which the Scotch struggled against the superior forces of the victors, who, it must be remembered, have a far greater selection of players at their disposal than the northerners."

Three more unofficial internationals followed, although none attracted more than 500 or so spectators, having failed to engage the interest of many beyond the memberships of the London clubs, or beyond London. According to one newspaper, the matches were regarded in the north "in the light of a mere farce". The England team was unrepresentative of that country as a whole, and the "London Scottish" team certainly didn't represent Scotland. Even CW Alcock admitted that the Scottish team was "counterfeit". There was little for supporters outside of the London clubs to get behind, but Alcock would soon make that right.

In 1871, he established the first national knock-out cup competition, the FA Challenge Cup. Alcock recalled the old "match for cock" competitions from his school days, and recognised that a competitive, knock-out format could generate more interest and excitement. All 50 of the FA's member clubs were invited to compete, although only 15 accepted. Of those, only two were from outside of London – Lincolnshire's Donington School and, most significantly, Glasgow's Queen's Park. Scotland generally preferred the rugby game over the association one, and there were few prominent Scottish association clubs. Queen's Park, formed in 1867, was an exception, and the club's plucky run to the cup semi-final – where they were eliminated only because they couldn't afford to travel for a replay – ignited interest in association football in Scotland.

The first FA Cup final, between Wanderers and Old Etonians, was played at the Oval on 16 March 1872, and was watched by a crowd of 2,000 spectators. Tents were erected for the "many ladies" in attendance, to keep them out of the sun, and it was stated that "there were several open landaus on the ground", landaus being luxury carriages, which perhaps gives an indication of the social status of some of those present. The attendance was much higher than for the

Alcock internationals, although it could perhaps have been higher. *Bell's Life* suggested that many potential match-goers had been put off by the decision to charge the relatively high admission fee of a shilling. A typical football admission fee at the time was threepence.

The first *official* international match took place later that year, on 30 November 1872. Alcock was once again the instigator, but he was assisted this time by the Queen's Park committee, and it was agreed that the match would be played in Glasgow, at Hamilton Crescent, the West of Scotland Cricket Club ground. "This was the first occasion on which an Association team from England played on Scotch soil, and the event was consequently looked forward to, and created an unusual amount of interest in Scotland," explained the *Sporting Gazette*. The England team was drawn from nine different clubs, including The Wednesday (later renamed Sheffield Wednesday) and Notts County, so it was no longer an exclusively London team. The Scotland players were drawn from only one club – all of them played for Queen's Park – but at least they were Scottish, which was something of an improvement over the Alcock internationals.

Unfortunately, the weather was "somewhat unfavourable", but several thousand spectators still made their way to Glasgow's west end, with special buses running from the city centre to the ground. Exactly how many thousands of spectators is unclear. According to the *Gazette*, the attendance figure was somewhere between 4,000 and 5,000, but the *Graphic* newspaper said only 2,500 spectators were present. Examination of the reported takings suggests that not many more than 2,000 paid to watch the match, although ladies were admitted free, so could have contributed to a higher attendance.

The first proper international ended as a rather anticlimactic 0-0 draw, although it was apparently a "most exciting and satisfactory match". Certainly, those in attendance seem to have enjoyed it, particularly the Scottish fans. "They applauded enthusiastically, but, owing to their strong national feeling, not altogether impartially," said the *Graphic*. Nevertheless, the paper said, "perfect order was observed".

Illustrations of the international, published in the *Graphic*, offered a glimpse at what those who attended the match looked like. Smartly dressed in shirts, cravats and overcoats, they wore top hats and billycock bowlers, and crowded right up against the rope that cordoned the pitch. The illustrations depicted a wintry scene, and the spectators crowded closely together, hands pushed into pockets. Smokers were puffing on pipes and cigarillos, and there was lots of fashionable facial hair on display. In one illustration, an errant ball had flown over the rope and struck a spectator on the nose. The fact that those present appeared well-to-do was likely related to the fact that tickets for the international again cost a shilling rather than a threepenny bit.

While tickets were sold in advance for the international, spectators were also admitted via a cash gate, which caused some debate in the local press. A correspondent to the *Glasgow Herald* complained that allowing ticketless fans to pay on the gate led to excessive crowds, which he said had spoiled previous matches. "A good and fair game is of more importance than large receipts," he wrote, "and it is impossible that the former can be properly under control if the admission of onlookers is not."

However, another correspondent disagreed, saying that cash gates were essential as he had not been able to secure a ticket in advance, and "it would be too bad if I had my journey for nothing". This was an early example of football fans having their say on aspects of the game via the media – a practice that would become much more prevalent over subsequent decades.

The first proper international was a success, regardless of its attendance, generating a huge amount of interest that extended way beyond those who had watched the match. International matches would be played annually between England and Scotland, and then, once Wales and Ireland had established teams, between the four home nations. But it was the FA Cup that really gave football the popularity and public awareness boost it needed. Here were matches worth winning, with something at stake – whether progression to the next round, or, eventually, the silver cup itself. The inclusive, knock-out competition proved hugely popular, and encouraged more clubs to join the FA and adopt the association rules. Participation increased from 15 clubs in 1871-72 to 32 in 1875-76, and 54 in 1879-80. The FA Cup would become the most famous and longest-running cup competition in the world, beloved of football fans for generations.

Still, though, football remained more popular outside of London, in places such as Sheffield and Glasgow. In 1873, a London representative team travelled to Bramall Lane (then the home of Sheffield FC and now the home of Sheffield United) to play a Sheffield representative side, and were met by a huge crowd. "On arrival at the ground the Londoners must have been surprised to see the number of spectators who had mustered, there being no less than 5,000," reported the *Sheffield Independent*.

An even bigger crowd of around 10,000 attended Hampden Park in Glasgow in 1875 to watch Queen's Park play London's Wanderers. Queen's Park's recent participation in the FA Cup had ignited a football craze in Scotland. As a result, in the hours before kick-off, the streets around the ground were thronged with pedestrians and "heavy-laden buses and cabs". Queen's Park raced to a 3-0 half-time lead, and eventually won 5-0, much to the delight of the vast majority of the crowd. "The enthusiasm was unbounded," reported the

Glasgow Herald. "Many of the onlookers, not content with cheering and waving their hats, tossed their headgear into the air in the ecstasy of their admiration."

Newspaper accounts of the match at Sheffield gave an indication of the facilities provided for early football fans at one of the country's best-developed grounds. Bramall Lane had opened as a cricket ground in 1855, before hosting Sheffield FC from 1862. "Bramall Lane is favourably adapted for football matches, both as regards the playing portion and the accommodation of spectators," said the *Independent.*

The wooden stand at the north end of the ground had been built in the previous year, and accomodated 1,500 spectators. At the west side of the ground, next to the Bramall Lane road, were "a succession of terraces" known as the sixpence pit. According to a description in the *Athletic News*, the terraces were "safely and securely railed off", and the terraces were racked, "so giving everybody an opportunity of seeing what is going on". On the other sides of the ground were "earthwork" terraces and refreshment booths. A gallery over the booths apparently afforded "a capital view".

One can only speculate whether the Bramall Lane refreshment booths sold Bovril, which was marketed in the 1870s, rather unappetisingly, as "Johnston's Fluid Beef". Certainly, however, the Bramall Lane facilities were advanced at a time when duckboards placed over muddy ground were considered a luxury. After an 1874 FA Cup tie between Old Etonians and Swifts, *Bell's* reported: "There was a pretty good number of visitors who were accommodated with boards to stand upon, an example which might be judiciously followed at other grounds, especially where a charge is made for admission."

One facility that Victorian football grounds didn't have was floodlighting, although there were several experiments in illuminating the game by electric light. One such experiment took place at Bramall Lane in 1878, arranged in part to promote the local Tasker electrical company. Lights were fixed to temporary wooden stands, 30 feet in the air, behind each goal, and the rare exhibition of night-time football drew a huge crowd.

"The match was announced to commence at half-past seven o'clock, and considerably before that hour the roads to Bramall Lane were completely besieged," reported the *Sheffield Independent*. "The wonder was where all the people came from. There seemed no end to the ever-coming stream, and the crowd of excited people outside the gates struggling to pass in at the turnstiles created a scene of great animation. The vast enclosure - extensive as it is - appeared quite crowded, so large was the assembly, and there must have been a considerable number who failed to get a fair view of the play, as it was quite impossible to see over the heads of the dense masses of humanity, all craning their necks towards the debatable territory."

The unusual experiment was not entirely successful. The lights didn't cover the whole of the pitch, and couldn't be moved quickly enough to keep up with play. The bright light dazzled the players and "caused some strange blunders", and when the ball moved into unlit areas of the pitch, the spectators were literally left in the dark. "It was difficult to follow the players with anything like certainty," said the *Independent*. Subsequent experiments, in London and elsewhere, also failed to impress, and floodlights weren't properly introduced to football for another 70 years. Until then, football matches would need to finish before the sun went down, which eventually led to the adoption of the traditional kick-off time of 3pm.

Even in the absence of floodlights, it was clear to see that a growing number of fans were watching football. In 1873, the *Penny Illustrated* reported on the increasing public interest in the game. "Football has enjoyed a more rapid rise in popular favour that even its most sanguine supporters could have ventured to anticipate a dozen years ago," the paper commented. "There are as many matches to be seen on any Saturday afternoon as there were players then."

This rapid rise in popularity really was phenomenal. Association football had only been created in 1863 – just a decade before the *Penny Illustrated* article was published. Within those ten years, aided by refined rules and better organisation, football had found a large and enthusiastic audience. It's perhaps difficult to appreciate in the football-saturated modern era that the game was once something novel and new. Many spectators going to watch matches in the 1860s and 1870s were experiencing football for the very first time, and a lot of them became hooked.

High profile cup matches and internationals served as football exhibitions, promoting the game to an ever-widening audience. But why did football find this broad audience, while other sports maintained only niche popularity – or found no popularity at all? The most obvious and entirely sensible answer is that football is completely brilliant, and is far better than any other rival sport. In the 1870s it was already beginning to outshine cricket, pedestrianism, rowing and other popular Victorian spectator sports. In the modern era it continues to eclipse cricket, rugby, basketball, US football, hockey, tennis, golf, baseball and anything else involving ball, bat, stick, club or racquet. Football is the best sport.

There is actually a scientific theory that can support this claim. Writing in *Nature* in 1996, Professor Nicholas Christenfeld stated that, in order to survive and attract fans, sports must provide "some combination of grace, strength, brilliance, violence and excitement". Football ticks all of those boxes. Christenfeld went on to say that the most satisfying sports for fans are those that involve a "finely calibrated mix" of skill and chance. Sports involving too much chance are, the Professor said, "pointless". But those involving too little chance offer no suspense, and "will never catch on". Football provided a perfect mix of skill and chance, so was deeply satisfying for fans, and swiftly caught on.

"As with natural selection," wrote Christenfeld, "it need not be the case that sports deliberately strike this balance, but rather those that do succeed." It seems doubtful that any of the game's founders considered the mix of skill and chance when they codified football, and it was more by accident than design that football evolved into a satisfying and successful sport. Nevertheless, satisfying and successful it became, providing much-craved entertainment for a growing number of Victorians.

Setting scientific theories aside, the secret to football's success, and its ability to satisfy fans, can be boiled down to one key attribute – its simplicity. Football is a game that can be understood and enjoyed almost instantly. A first-time spectator can almost immediately recognise that there are two teams, competing for a ball, and attempting to kick that ball between two sets of posts. Further nuances can be picked up as the game progresses – although in the 1870s there were few further nuances to worry about. It was entirely possible to turn up at the Oval or Hamilton Crescent or Bramall Lane with no prior knowledge of football and thoroughly enjoy the game. Those who did enjoy one game were keen to enjoy another. Football's simplicity meant it could be easily spread. The 1873 *Penny Illustrated* article recognised that the spread of the game had not been confined to London. "In the north of England, at Manchester, Liverpool, Hull, Doncaster and Rochdale, numerous important clubs have been started and are now flourishing," said the paper.

It was notable that the game's popularity was growing in the north, where there was a particular link between football and the working class. Social shifts meant workers had more money in their pockets and more time off to spend it. There was a growing demand for entertainment, and there were relatively few options available. Workers wanted something cheap, accessible and engaging to fill their Saturday afternoons. The association game was the perfect fit. Football was about to become the working-class game.

4

Extraordinary interest

The West End streets of London wore quite a holiday look on Saturday morning," reported the *Pall Mall Gazette* on the Monday after the 1888 FA Cup final. "There was the crowd of sprucely-dressed young gentlemen from the universities, attired in the tallest of collars, the glossiest of hats, and the shiniest of patent leathers, who were up for the Boat Race. There was the crowd of gentlemen, not quite so spruce, from the provinces, who were visiting the metropolis to shout for their men at the Oval."

The sprucely-dressed gents in the glossiest of hats were supporters of the Oxford University and Cambridge University boat crews, and the not quite so spruce gents, in non-glossy caps, were supporters of the West Bromwich Albion and Preston North End football teams. It wasn't uncommon for the University Boat Race and the FA Cup final to take place on the same day, but the contrast between rowing fans and football fans had rarely been more conspicuous. The first ten cup finals, from 1872 through to 1882, were won by gentlemen's sides comprised almost exclusively of public school old boys. At that time there was little distinction between those attending the boat race and the cup final. But, during the 1880s, things began to change.

In 1882, Blackburn Rovers became the first working-class club to play in the final. They were supported by "some hundreds of their local friends", who travelled down on special trains, and "cheered lustily" during the match. Then, in 1883, Blackburn Olympic became the first working-class club to win the final. Around 300 Olympic fans saw their team beat Old Etonians 2-1, and then thousands more welcomed the victors home with "such a reception as was never before accorded to any football team". The Olympic players – millworkers, plumbers and publicans – were driven through the packed streets of Blackburn in four waggonettes, their slow procession preceded by pipe bands. "Many flags were displayed in some streets, and fireworks were discharged," reported one newspaper. "The wildest enthusiasm prevailed among a vast crowd, who cheered repeatedly as the procession passed." A working-class club had beaten a team of public school old boys, and the old boys' hold on association football was at an end.

By 1888, the FA Cup – and football in general – was dominated by working-class clubs from the north and the midlands. Not unrelatedly, football was enjoying a surge of popular appeal. Cup final attendances had risen from around 2,000 in 1872, to 8,000 in 1883, and to around 20,000 in 1888. By contrast, although the 1888 Boat Race was watched by large crowds, it was reported that the attendance of spectators along the Thames had in recent years "gradually fallen off" and public interest had "appreciably lessened". "In the great world of athletics the final fight for the silver trophy of the Football Association is yearly increasing in interest," said the *Pall Mall*. "While the boat race is a pretext for a picnic, the football match offers a most inspiriting form of entertainment."

Nineteen Victorian FA Cup finals were played at the Oval, on a cordoned-off section of the ground in front of the cricket pavilion. A replacement pavilion – which still stands today – was built in 1888. By then, the Oval was far better equipped for football than it had been back in 1872. An account in Charles Dickens' *All The Year Round* periodical described the scene: "The enclosure railed off for the football play is surrounded by a dense array of spectators, rising in tiers head over head, ranged on the temporary wooden seats, or packed behind the railings. A fine sight it is... the green turf chalked out with the boundaries of play, the goalposts at either end... the great multitudes round about, a chequered mass... And the pavilion, too, is black as an ant-hill with its human throng. The enormous gasometers that tower over the cricket field bound the view, grim and silent reminders of the great wilderness of streets and houses that encloses this oasis of green turf."

At three o'clock on 24 March 1888, 30 minutes ahead of kick-off time, the Oval's gates were shut, with the ground full to capacity. "The spectacle of those solid banks of human beings, rising row above row, on the four sides of the square was a remarkable tribute to the extraordinary interest in the result," said the *Pall Mall*, adding that the extraordinary interest extended way beyond the Oval, with the 20,000 people in the ground being a "mere drop in the ocean" compared to the "countless thousands" who were waiting for the result in Preston and Birmingham "and in dozens of murky towns in Lancashire, Yorkshire and the Midlands, to say nothing of Scotland".

As kick-off approached, 20,000 voices joined in a communal sing-song, belting out music hall number *Two Lovely Black Eyes* ("*Two lovely black eyes! / Oh! What a surprise! / Only for telling a man he was wrong / Two lovely black eyes!*"), patriotic anthem *Rule Britannia*, and "other ditties". Communal singing was becoming common ahead of big matches, and the singing of the hymn *Abide With Me* would remain a longstanding FA Cup final tradition. Then the players took to the field, in their long-sleeved jerseys, knee-length knickerbocker shorts and whalebone shinpads. The original FA Cup, the "little tin idol", was placed on a table by the pitch. Then the referee appeared, and, with a peep on his whistle, the game was underway.

What followed was a fast, end-to-end game, with both teams hurling themselves into an exciting struggle, "in the face of much earnestness and savage enthusiasm". "Every fine bit of dribbling, every pass, every run, every shot at goal, was the signal for a deafening roar," explained the *Pall Mall.* West Brom scored first, after 20 minutes, "amidst tremendous cheering". Both teams were "mightily encouraged by the support of their friends and admirers". Shortly after half time, Preston equalised through Fred Dewhurst. Preston also hit the woodwork twice, and their fans yelled, "*Hard lines!*" But, ten minutes from time, West Brom captain Jem Bayliss headed into the goal to give his side a 2-1 win.

The West Brom fans were jubilant, but the Preston fans were devastated, with the latter realising something that subsequent generations of football supporters would also come to know – that defeat in a big match feels like the worst thing in the world. "When, after a gallant fight, the Prestonians were beaten, the looks on the faces of their supporters were suicidal," said the *Pall Mall*, while suggesting they might have sought solace in a drink or two. "If they drowned their sorrows in the flowing bowl, let us forgive them. Preston on Saturday evening must have been a town of mourning."

In Preston, supporters had gathered in great numbers to await the telegraphed result. Before the invention of radio, supporters relied on updates sent by telegraph, or by carrier pigeon, and posted in newspaper office windows. By the time the result arrived, there were "not less than five or six thousand anxious waiters" in front of the newspaper offices. At West Bromwich, the high street was lined with thousands of similarly nervous supporters. "The first intelligence of Albion registering a goal caused the liveliest satisfaction," said one report, "and when the final score arrived a scene of the wildest enthusiasm ensued, and for a time the street was almost impassable."

It had been a great cup final, and the "savage enthusiasm" of the fans had been as notable as the efforts of the players. Certainly it provided further evidence that football had now attained what the *Pall Mall* called "a degree of popularity that no other English pastime ever enjoyed". The game had obtained a hold on the public, and matches were attended by an "immense" number of people. "It is no uncommon thing to see from 15,000 to 20,000 spectators assembled at a single match, braving the inclemencies of the winter weather, and putting their health to extraordinary risks for the sake of the sport," the paper reported. "Sometimes the game is watched through a cloud of mist and drizzle, sometimes with the snow blowing in your teeth; but no matter what the weather may be, so long as it is not a hard frost, when play is impossible, the people will turn out in their thousands to shout for their football champions."

Association football was now in its third decade, and a generation of young fans had grown up watching the game. It was now the popular game of the masses, and was beginning to challenge cricket for the title of Britain's national game. Cricket had been widely played since at least the 17th century, and its laws set out in the mid-to-late 18th century, a hundred years before football was properly codified. And cricket is still regarded by some today as England's (if not Britain's) national game. Yet, in the 1880s, football was already winning the popular vote. The *Pall Mall* said cricket had been "completely eclipsed by football", and anyone who remained immune to the charms of football faced scorn: "For several months of the year, football is the chief, and in some circles the only, topic of conversation, and those who hold themselves aloof are looked upon as little better than milksops."

The increased popularity of football and the rise of the football fan were aided by two major pieces of legislation. First, the various Factory Acts implemented through the mid to late 1800s reduced working hours and ordered that all work should end on a Saturday by 2pm. Gradually, through the 1870s and 1880s, workers in different regions and occupations came to have Saturday afternoons off. Second, the Education Acts implemented between 1870 and 1880 required that all children be given an elementary education and be taught to read and write. Workers had Saturday afternoons free to watch football, and a growing audience could read about the game.

The newfound freedom on Saturday afternoons had a profound effect on the popularity of football in industrial towns. Workers had their pay in their pockets, and were keen to enjoy spending it. Football provided a welcome means of escape from working life, and represented an exciting and entertaining alternative to the pub. "Long days or arduous labour in the mill or the foundry leave little time for pleasure," said the *Pall Mall*, "and the manufacturing town presents few amusements for its inhabitants. So it is not difficult to understand the enormous popularity of football."

The football boom ran hand in hand with the newspaper boom. Up until the mid-1880s, the coverage afforded to football by national newspapers could be accurately described as sparse. Horse racing filled much of the sports columns, and football vied for attention in the remaining space with the likes of rowing, pedestrianism and pigeon shooting. The *Times* and the *Daily News* covered selected FA Cup ties and international matches, and weeklies such as the lengthily-named *Bell's Life in London and Sporting Chronicle* and the Manchester-based *Athletic News* provided more comprehensive coverage of other high-profile matches, but, in general, supporters relied on their regional papers for regular up-to-date coverage of their teams' fortunes.

It was in the regional papers that the first football columnists emerged, writing under pen names, such as White

Rose in the *Leeds Mercury*, Spectator in the *Liverpool Mercury*, and Tityrus in the *Nottingham Daily Guardian*. (Tityrus was the pseudonym of Jimmy Catton, an influential and respected football journalist of the Victorian and Edwardian eras, who would later become the editor of *Athletic News*.) These columnists introduced insight and opinion to football coverage, offering criticism and praise, and inviting correspondence from supporters. Correspondence was a major feature of football columns, which became valuable forums for supporters to air their views on the game. Rules were debated, best practice was deliberated, and arguments were settled, with football columnists becoming unofficial arbitrators of football-related disputes.

The Darlington-based *Northern Echo*'s football column, *Football Notes by Off-Side*, became a vital driver of sales for one of the country's leading regional newspapers, and expanded in length and in frequency during the late-1880s. Football coverage was vital to a paper seeking to meet the needs of its many working-class readers. Writing in the column, Off-Side celebrated "the increased interest which has been evoked by the game among the masses – it is always the masses". "The cause for this is not far to seek, and that is the great encouragement given to the game by the local press," he wrote. "It is the same all over the country. The contagion – if one may be allowed to use the word – is growing."

The realisation that football boosted sales led many papers to expand their football coverage across the sports columns and into Saturday night football specials. While early football reporters had submitted match reports via carrier pigeon, the installation of telegraph poles at grounds from the mid-1880s meant reports could be filed more quickly, allowing regional papers to issue their football specials, the first of which was *Saturday Night*, a halfpenny paper launched in Birmingham in 1882. By the end of the 1880s, many British towns had their own football specials. By the end of the 1890s it had become common for them to be printed on coloured paper stock, and they were subsequently given suitably colourful names, such as the *Green 'Un* or the *Football Pink*.

Football's rapid growth had been fostered in the regions, and local newspapers and their football writers played an important role. When, during the 1886-87 season, the *Times* published a leader reflecting upon "how immensely the game has grown in public favour in late years", it felt out-of-date and ill-informed, speaking of the game's popularity in the public schools and universities, when the real story was happening in working towns around the country.

A review published during the same season in the *Northern Echo* painted a more accurate picture of the state of the association game: "A few years since, football was almost confined to a particular class, and the games only proved of interest to the players and their own friends. Now, however, all classes are represented by the players, and the games afford amusement to countless thousands of spectators throughout the country."

It was during this rapid period of growth for the game that many of modern football's biggest clubs were founded. Most of them emerged from institutions – workplaces, churches, cricket clubs – that provided ready-made pockets of support. Manchester United were formed in 1878 as Newton Heath LYR by workers at a Lancashire and Yorkshire Railway depot. Manchester City were originally St Mark's, formed in 1880 by the rector of a church in West Gorton. Arsenal were Dial Square, a works team formed in 1886 at the Royal Armaments Factory in Woolwich. Gradually, these clubs expanded beyond their institutions and began to represent their respective communities.

In order to attract supporters, emergent clubs placed posters in shop windows and ads in newspapers. One ad from

1882 promoted a match between Nottingham Forest and Small Heath Alliance (now Birmingham City):

> *"FOOTBALL! – OPENING MATCH.*
> *Notts Forest [sic] v Small Heath Alliance.*
> *On Saturday next, September 23, 1882.*
> *Kick-off at 4pm prompt.*
> *Admission 3d. Reserve 2d extra.*
> *Omnibuses to the ground every ten minutes."*

In 1881, for a match between Blackburn Rovers and Scottish pioneers Queen's Park at Blackburn's recently-opened Leamington Road ground, the *Blackburn Standard* said the players "were received by at least 15,000 persons". Many supporters had arrived several hours early, and such was the demand that the ticket booths and gates were closed long before kick-off. "Not only was the field crowded," said the paper, "but the fields adjoining were invaded by several thousand enthusiastic football supporters, and even the top of the grandstand was for a considerable time occupied, every place of vantage being taken up." Pressure from the crowd caused the boundary ropes around the pitch to be broken. However the *Standard* noted that, despite the "immense" number present, "good order was preserved".

That game finished as a 2-2 draw, but the influence a large crowd could have on the performance of their team and the result of a match was now being recognised. Writing to the *Yorkshire Post* in 1882, a correspondent requested to draw readers' attention to what he called the "power of the spectators". "Apart from the sympathy of enthusiasm – which has a strong vein of prejudice and partiality running through it – there is a spirit manifested by onlookers generally which recognises and applauds the playing of the game," wrote the correspondent. "This vast concourse of spectators is in possession of a great power which, when wielded with wise discretion, may produce incalculable benefit." Spectators could, he wrote, "exercise an essential influence" over the game, and cheer their team to victory with "a long and prolonged ring of *huzzahs*". The ability of fans to influence games led to the crowd being referred to as "the 12th man".

Large crowds brought another – perhaps more tangible – benefit, in that they generated valuable takings. Although football was still an amateur pursuit, clubs had expenses that increased as they grew. They had to pay for ground rent and maintenance, goal posts and corner flags, leather balls and team kits, transport to away matches and other outgoings. Initially, costs were paid from membership subscriptions – and that would remain the case for hundreds of smaller clubs. But clubs that could attract respectable crowds became funded by their supporters, and came to rely on gate receipts.

Some clubs struggled to generate enough money from gates, but others turned over large profits. In 1883, a match between Blackburn Rovers and crosstown rivals Blackburn Olympic at Leamington Road saw the relatively huge sum of £150 taken in sixpences and threepences at the gate. The crowd of more than 10,000 included hundreds of season ticket holders – common at most clubs by the 1880s. Paying in advance for a season ticket was a natural progression from paying for membership subscriptions, as support expanded beyond core club members and out into the wider community.

The growing commercialism of football was ramped up considerably in the mid-1880s following the legalisation of professionalism. Clubs had been illicitly paying signing-on bonuses and match fees to players for years, and such enticements and rewards were regarded by many within the FA as "serious evils" and "abuses". But the power and popularity of clubs that embraced professionalism couldn't be ignored. Football was now a business, and players were a commodity. In a series of heated meetings, FA secretary CW Alcock attempted to convince his colleagues that it was no longer possible to operate football "on strictly amateur lines". Eventually, in July 1885, a begrudging agreement was reached. Football was changed forever.

Clubs could now legally pay their players - and pay to sign new players - but to do so they needed to attract a sizeable number of supporters. High attendances became critical. Large "gates" allowed clubs to pay higher wages and attract better players. And, of course, better players drew more supporters. Clubs began to sign talented players from outside of their usual catchment areas. In particular, English clubs raided Scotland for proponents of the attractive passing game that was popular north of the border. The arrival of the professional footballer meant that teams were no longer comprised entirely of local men, but this didn't affect the tribal nature of football support.

The vast majority of early fans supported their local clubs, but they also appreciated other high-profile teams. Queen's Park and Corinthian FC toured Britain as exhibition sides, and attracted big crowds wherever they played. And successful teams like Preston's "Invincibles", the unbeaten league and cup winners of 1888-89, could add several thousand to the gate of any ground they visited. Star individuals, like Nevill "Nuts" Cobbold and Gilbert "GO" Smith of Corinthians, also attracted big crowds. Supporters were no longer only inclined to cheer local men who they recognised from the streets and pubs of their own towns.

By the time the Football League was founded in 1888, the typical admission fee for a football match was sixpence, which wasn't cheap considering the average weekly wage for a general labourer was only 13 shillings (with two sixpences in a shilling). In fact, despite modern complaints about the cost of football tickets, admission was proportionately almost as expensive then as it is in the modern era. According to BBC and ONS figures from the 2014-15 season, the average price of a football ticket across England's top four divisions was £21.49, and the average weekly wage was £460, with the ticket price representing around 4.7% of the weekly wage in 2015, compared to 4.3% in 1888.

In 1889, Newcastle's East End FC, the club that later became Newcastle United, reduced their admission fee in an attempt to increase attendance. It didn't work. "In the East End and Middlesbrough match, the former club tried a threepenny gate by way of experiment," reported the *Northern Echo*, "with the result that it was considerably less than half the amount taken at the sixpenny admission when the Darlington team played." The experiment suggested that the sixpence admission fee was not necessarily a barrier to entry for football supporters, and that the same number would attend whether the admission fee was sixpence or threepence.

A year later, East End made a more successful move, issuing 1,600 shares to become a limited company. The shares, valued at ten shillings each, were sold in local pubs, and prospective shareholders could pay in two instalments – half on application and half on allocation. The aim was make the scheme as accessible as possible to the working classes, who the club realised made up the vast majority of the community. The club's share returns showed that every single shareholder lived within three miles of the club's home ground, and the majority were manual workers. As a result of the share issue, the club effectively became fan-owned, but they also banked a good deal of capital, allowing them to survive and ultimately thrive, while other clubs – including cross-town rivals Newcastle West End – folded due to financial difficulties.

East End were one of the first major football clubs to become a limited company, although many would follow suit over the following decade or so. In 1888, the *Athletic News* urged all clubs with a turnover of more than £10,000 to incorporate. The benefits were not just financial. Incorporation provided clubs with a stronger legal footing, and limited the individual liability of directors. The newspaper believed "more intelligent" supporters would become shareholders, suggesting, perhaps naively, they "would not allow any pique to upset their discretion in a purely business transaction".

Clubs such as Aston Villa and the then-named Royal Arsenal initially rejected incorporation. After a consultation in 1889, Villa's committee said such a move would be "against true sport". Instead, clubs looked for other ways to boost their finances. They held athletics meetings, dinner dances and music recitals. Nottingham Forest held a longstanding annual athletics meeting at Trent Bridge, which in 1888 attracted between 6,000 and 7,000 spectators to watch sprinting, distance running and safety bicycle racing, plus a closing "football race".

Some clubs held prize draws and raffles. In 1886, Blackburn Olympic held a huge draw with 100 prizes, the biggest of which was a "house of furniture" worth £50. Three thousand spectators watched the much-anticipated prize draw after a match against Blackpool club South Shore. The draw was held at the back of the Olympic ground, with winning tickets and associated prizes drawn from two large bowls by a pair of little girls. When the winner of the house of furniture was announced as Nathan Denham, a local stationer, the jealous crowd yelled, *"Be hanged!"*

Not to be outdone by their rivals, Blackburn Rovers held their own prize draw, "designed to help the club through difficulties occasioned by indifferent gates", and gave away a newly-built house named Rovers' Cottage. The house was won by 24-year-old gas meter inspector JT Barker, who was newly married, and lived with his father-in-law. According to the *Blackburn Standard*, Barker had bought three tickets but didn't expect anything in return "beyond the knowledge that he had helped a deserving football club". "The news of his luck was all the more welcome on that account," said the paper.

In January 1888, 27,000 spectators watched an FA Cup tie between Aston Villa and Preston North End at Villa's Perry Barr ground, generating receipts of £1,100, "by far the largest sum ever taken at a football match". It was clear that the way to maintain large crowds and high receipts was to arrange more regular matches between the country's top teams. Step forward Villa director William McGregor, who, for the 1888-89 season, instigated the Football League. The League was formed to benefit its member clubs by scheduling a regular series of first-class fixtures in order to guarantee a regular stream of income. League matches were nowhere near as attractive as cup ties, with the FA Cup remaining English football's most prestigious competition right up until the Premier League era. But supporters welcomed fixture lists of regular matches against top sides. Going to watch football became a weekly pursuit. It became a routine.

Hot on the heels of the Football League came the Northern League, the Southern League, and the Football Alliance – the latter integrated into the national Football League as a Second Division in 1892. The Scottish and Irish Football Leagues were both formed in 1890. England, Scotland, Ireland and Wales all had their own national FA cup competitions, and many counties had their own local FA competitions. Then there were exhibition matches against touring sides, and friendlies against teams from other leagues. And there were regular international matches, too, with the British Home Championship founded in 1883 as an annual round-robin contest between the four home nations. So there was a lot of football to watch – and there were a lot of fans watching it.

"No words of ours can adequately describe the present popularity of football with the public," wrote Montague

Shearman, in his book *Athletics and Football*. "It is no rare thing in the north and midlands for 10,000 people to pay money to witness an ordinary club match, or for half as many again to assemble for a cup tie. If Aston Villa meet Notts County at Trent Bridge, special trains have to be run from Birmingham to carry the spectators who go over to see the match. The enthusiasm and excitement which follow each move in the game are unbounded. The writer has heard the roar that followed the scoring of a goal from a distance of more than half a mile."

Shearman mentioned special trains, and the expansion of the railways was another key factor in the rise of football and the development of the football fan. New transport links – train, tram and omnibus – allowed the catchment areas of clubs to grow, and enabled fans to travel to away matches. Railway companies advertised football specials in local newspapers, and they were hugely popular. Previously, supporters who rarely left their home towns had relied on local newspapers for away results and match reports. Now they could embark on "cheap excursions" to faraway towns in order to support their heroes in person.

"When the town to be visited is very remote, the journey has, of course, to be begun very early," said the *Sheffield Independent*. "Aston Villa versus Sunderland, at Sunderland, means real hardship for the enthusiasts who start from Birmingham before daybreak. That stupendous jaunt may be made for a very few shillings, and if the window is not clouded with human breath all the way, the mere spectacle of so much of England's surface ought to be worth twice the money."

It was an anecdote that hinted at the romance of being a football fan, although romance was not always guaranteed. Football's growing popularity was changing the nature of the sport, turning it from a pleasant pastime into a high-stakes pursuit. The change was partly driven by professionalism and commercialism, which required that clubs be successful in order to generate finances. But it was also driven by partiality and fanaticism, which demanded that clubs be successful in order to satisfy their supporters. And supporters could be very demanding. Football was becoming a different beast, and football fans were becoming beastly.

5

Howling roughs

The sun shone brightly over Turf Moor ahead of the big match. It was 22 February 1890, and 8,000 fans filled the grandstand and thronged around the pitch in eager anticipation of a derby match between Burnley and Blackburn Rovers. As was often the case with local derbies, this football rivalry had been fuelled by an industrial rivalry, between the towns' cotton mills. (Burnley v Blackburn is still known as the Cotton Mills derby.) But the football rivalry was now fierce enough to stand on its own, having intensified over more than a decade of derby meetings. This was the fourth Football League match between the two clubs, and Blackburn had won the first three by big scores (7-1, 4-2 and another 7-1). Burnley were after revenge and, according to a reporter from the *Manchester Courier*, the match "aroused the feelings of the crowd to a height never before witnessed".

Blackburn arrived 15 minutes late, and the delayed kick-off caused the atmosphere to bubble towards boiling point. When the game began, it did so in explosive fashion. Straight from the kick-off, Burnley surged through the Blackburn defence, and Alec Stewart slotted the ball into the net. 1-0 to Burnley in the first minute, and the home fans celebrated wildly. And Burnley soon had the ball in the net again, when Jimmy Hill (not that one) knocked it past Blackburn keeper Johnny Horne. However, to the bafflement of players and fans alike, the goal was disallowed for a very dubious offside call. The Burnley fans were furious, and the sound of "hot and universal hooting" filled the air.

Their anger increased as a certain nugget of information began to spread through the crowd. The referee, one Richard Horne, was revealed to be the brother of Blackburn goal-keeper Johnny. Clearly, Richard was biased, and had disallowed the goal in an act of favouritism towards Johnny's team. *"Turn him off the field!"* yelled the Burnley fans, as more of their "hooting" filled the air. The home crowd's ire had barely abated when, towards the end of the first half, the visitors equalised through Nat Walton. Burnley fans thought they should have been 2-0 up, but at half time the score was actually 1-1.

In the second half Burnley had the best of the play, but Blackburn's forwards created several chances. "Both sides put in all they knew, and were fairly evenly matched," said the *Lancashire Evening Post*. The game was eventually decided by two more controversial incidents. First, the visitors had a goal disallowed for offside, "to the satisfaction of the clamorous spectators". Then, with eight minutes remaining, Blackburn's Billy Townley put the ball in the net – apparently with his hand. The ref, with his whistle to his lips, looked ready to blow for handball, but eventually allowed the goal to stand, "amid great disapprobation". Burnley's players and supporters appealed desperately, with the players arguing for a full five minutes, and the supporters urging them to leave the field in protest. It was to no avail.

"The home team, disheartened, fell to pieces," said the *Evening Post*. As the game slipped away from them, the Burnley fans turned on the referee, believing that his biased performance had robbed them of a win. Such was the veracity of their anger, the *Evening Post* reporter feared for the ref's safety. "It was evident from the hooting on all sides of the field which the referee visited and the threats that were made," wrote the reporter, "that the rougher element intended violence."

At the final whistle, with Burnley having lost 2-1, club officials raced onto the field to form a protective cordon around the ref. An invasion of thousands of aggrieved supporters followed, with the dozen-or-so policemen present incapable of stopping them. The officials pushed Mr Horne into the grandstand, out of the clutches of the baying mob. *"Go for him!"* fans yelled, as they attempted to force their way into the stand.

Burnley committee members attempted to pacify the huge crowd, without success. After half an hour, with the crowd unwilling to leave, officials managed to hurry Horne out of the back of the grandstand and into a neighbouring house, with reinforcements of police forming a cordon around the premises. The crowd swiftly followed, and began to surge towards the house, attempting to break through the police cordon. Eventually, the ref was bundled into a horse-drawn cab, and escorted slowly by police through the packed streets, "amid a hooting, running, stone-throwing mob".

A police sergeant who had climbed up onto the cab beside the driver was hit with a shower of rocks. The police responded by chasing the stone-throwers, and eventually succeeded in forcing the crowd back, and escorting the cab to the railway station, where Mr Horne's brother and the rest of the Blackburn party awaited. "The hunted referee joined his comrades, and got away from the town uninjured," reported the *Evening Post*. "If he had fallen into the hands of the mob, who were mad with frenzy, he must have been very badly treated."

A combination of mix-ups had led to Richard Horne refereeing a match involving his brother. A telegram from the Football League had incorrectly suggested that Johnny Horne would not play, and the Burnley committee subsequently selected Richard Horne as referee from a list of four candidates. Once it became apparent that Johnny *would* play,

Richard sent a telegram to Burnley advising that he would rather not referee the game, only to be told that he must, and that the Burnley committee had "every confidence in his impartiality".

Nevertheless, there was no excuse for the near-riot that ensued, and it was fortunate no one was badly injured. The Burnley fans were criticised in the press. "Their conduct was reprehensible in the extreme," said the *Evening Post*. "The scene was a disgrace to football."

"The unfairness of the Burnley people is notorious in the matter of football," wrote a correspondent from Blackburn.

"I quite agree that the habitual football spectators at Turf Moor are notoriously unfair," wrote another. "It is not much to be wondered at that a little spark of irritation and provocation by the referee... should have set on fire, as it were, the very worst passions of a menacing mob."

The Burnley "riot" was an early example of what would now be called football hooliganism – and it wasn't an isolated incident. In 1885, following a match between Aston Villa and Preston North End, Villa fans objected to their 5-0 defeat by chasing the Preston players from the field. According to one witness, the players were pursued for half a mile by "2,000 howling roughs". "Thicker and faster came the stones, showers of spittle covered us, and we were struck at with sticks and umbrellas," reported the witness.

In 1886, there was a "general fight" between spectators on the field during a match between the St Peter's and Brierfield clubs in "notorious" Burnley. "Unfortunately there is too much partiality displayed by football spectators," wrote a reporter for the *Burnley Express*. "They ought never to allow themselves to be carried away so far as to enter upon a general fight in the field."

In particular, there were a growing number of reports of referees being abused, threatened and assaulted by spectators who disagreed with their decisions. In 1887, referee John Reed described how a Cleveland Cup match he officiated between Yarm and North Skelton ended amid "the most blackguardly and disgraceful scenes ever witnessed on a football field". The final score was 8-3 to North Skelton, and the Yarm supporters blamed the referee. Reed was cursed and sworn at by spectators before being chased from the pitch by "a couple of hundred reckless hobbledehoys and half-drunken men" who intended to "put poor me into the river". "If I had no fear, I certainly had the wings that fear lends," said Reed. He outran the crowd and took safe refuge in a nearby house.

The *Manchester Courier* labelled such behaviour towards referees "disgraceful rowdyism and terrorism", and called for it to be dealt with by the "strong arm of the law". In response, a referee wrote to the paper to say, "Your remarks about the conduct of modern football spectators are clear and to the point. I am getting so disgusted with football that I am seriously thinking of throwing it up."

Football fans really joined the ranks of villains and rogues in 1897, when the *Illustrated Police News*, the popular sensationalist paper of the day, ran a story alongside its usual fare of murder and melodrama with the headline: "A Football Referee Mobbed and Shamefully Treated". A typically lively sketch showed the ref being grabbed, struck at, and pelted with eggs by a horde of moustachioed, top hat-wearing, cane-waving football fans. The referee, William Hay, was assaulted at the end of a Scottish cup match involving Moffat FC. Eight individuals were prosecuted and fined for threatening and attacking Hay – and one for attempting to pull his nose.

Such behaviour baffled observers. Why would individuals, the majority of whom might be entirely decent and peaceable in their ordinary lives, act so improperly and aggressively when part of a crowd? The behaviour and psychology of crowds had been studied in the pre-football era by Scottish journalist Charles MacKay, who published the book *Extraordinary Popular Delusions and the Madness of Crowds* in 1841. "Men, it has been well said, think in herds," wrote MacKay. "It will be seen that they go mad in herds, while they only recover their senses slowly, and one by one."

However, the most influential study of crowd psychology was Gustave Le Bon's *The Crowd: A Study of the Popular Mind*, published in 1895 – in the thick of football's boisterous boom. According to Le Bon, when individuals were submerged into a crowd they acquired "a sentiment of invincible power", causing them to lose their sense of personal responsibility and to act on instincts that they would normally restrain. Crowd behaviour was a "contagion", spreading between submerged individuals. But Le Bon's study was deeply problematic. For example, he wrote that the "special characteristics" of crowds ("impulsiveness, irritability, incapacity to reason, the absence of judgement") were usually observed in "inferior" beings – "in women, savages and children, for instance".

Le Bon's hypothesis was based on the false assumption that all crowd behaviour was irrational and destructive. It could not be fairly applied to football crowds, and would be dismissed by subsequent crowd psychologists. Le Bon had never attended a football match, and had no understanding of the mostly peaceable, agreeable nature of the football crowd. He was most likely writing from a position of ignorance and fear, with crowd behaviour representing a threat to his definition of social order. It was true that football crowds could be overly-boisterous, aggressive, and even violent. But such behaviour was not caused by any kind of collective madness. Instead, it was primarily caused by the influence of a minority of troublemakers, who were likely to exist within any large crowd.

Considering that football had evolved from a brutal mob game over just a few decades, the majority of early fans were extremely well-behaved. There was an argument that football prevented violence rather than encouraged it. "Since football became popular with all classes, there have been less wrenching off of knockers and boxing of the watch, and fewer free fights in the street," wrote Montague Shearman. "Wrenching off of knockers" meant stealing door-knockers, and "boxing the watch" involved trapping a night-watchman in his sentry box, then rolling the box down a hill.

Football was a release. It provided an opportunity for fans to let off steam and discharge pent-up emotions, and offered an avenue through which to channel frustration, anger and displeasure. Troubles at work and home could create bottled-up feelings that could not easily be let out in a relatively reserved society, where men in particular did not talk about their problems. Football, and the cheering and yelling that went with it, was thoroughly cathartic, allowing for (usually) an entirely harmless purging of the emotions. As Shearman wrote, "Football has its national uses quite apart from the cheap enjoyment it has given to thousands."

Alcohol also provided cheap enjoyment, and it played an important part in the early matchday experience. Drinking was a more well-established release, although not always a harmless one. In the context of football, though, alcohol was an enabler, loosening lips and inhibitions, and encouraging fans to join in with the jumping and shouting and to let off steam. Fans leaving work at lunchtime could quench their thirst by downing multiple cups of beer purchased from pushcarts outside their factories and workplaces. Pre-match drinking continued in pubs on the way to grounds. "Happy is the publican who is installed near the entrances to football fields," commented the *Sheffield Independent.*

Football betting also became prevalent as the game's popularity increased. Gambling on sports away from a race course was actually illegal, and remained so until 1960.

Nevertheless, from the 1880s, bookmakers were a common – if often unwelcome – sight at football grounds. "The betting mania is decidedly growing," wrote a correspondent to another newspaper, "and if it is allowed to go on, the popularity of football will soon decline." The correspondent described seeing a bookmaker "booted off the stand" for "daring to play his thievish vocation", and called on football committees to remove all bookmakers from football grounds, "otherwise respectable people will have to stay away".

Betting, of course, added an extra layer of interest to football's match-going experience. As if the emotional rewards weren't enough, betting added the prospect of financial rewards. So those fans who did not have an emotional investment in a particular match may have had a financial one. After a London football columnist commented that supporters attending football matches had a "practical connection with the game", a correspondent responded, "The practical connection most of them have is that they 'have money on it.'" "Listen to the talk of these crowds of onlookers," the correspondent wrote, "and you will learn why they get so excited over play. There is nothing in the air but bets."

But while betting was regarded as a problem, it seemed unlikely that many fans were attending football matches, as they might attend horse races, for the primary purpose of gambling. Football was too unpredictable, too involving, and too time consuming to attract those whose sole interest was winning wagers. It seemed much more likely that those who placed bets on football matches were doing so to add a secondary layer of interest. Even in the modern era, when matches can be followed at home, football betting appeals more to the casual punter, with the more clued-up gambler sticking to racing. But while football betting is now widely-accepted as a legitimate hobby, in the Victorian era it was illegal.

"Betting at football is undoubtedly a great evil," said FA President Francis Marindin in 1888. But, when asked if betting interest was the reason football matches drew large gates, he replied, "Hardly. Football is rapidly becoming such a popular game that it is drawing even larger gates than cricket."

In fact, football was becoming so popular that it was challenging and often outstripping all other forms of entertainment, sporting and otherwise. It could not have gained such popular appeal had it been patronised solely by violent, drunken gamblers. The vast majority of football fans were ordinary, law-abiding citizens, and football's match-going experience was becoming increasingly civilised. By the 1890s, the grounds of league teams had been developed and improved. Most had at least one grandstand, plus banked standing terraces that afforded spectators better views. Entry was gained by paying a gateman through a hole in a wall.

Once inside, fans packed right up against the touchlines, with those at the back needing to crane their necks above a sea of hats. There were no replica strips, or even football scarves, but some fans wore cardboard badges, featuring their team's colours, pushed into their hatbands. Communal singing was popular ahead of kick-off, and fans remained vocal throughout games, which were played to a soundtrack of cheers and roars. "*Play up!*" was a popular yell of encouragement. But negative aspects of the game would be met with "a hurricane of criticism" containing no little profanity.

Some critics seized upon the coarse vocabulary of the football fan as evidence of the degenerate nature of the game, which was surely only fit for the lowest of classes. "The multitude flock to the field in their workaday dirt, and with their workaday adjectives very loose on their tongues," wrote Charles Edwards in 1892. "It is really surprising what a number of emphatic and even mysterious expletives may be heard on these Saturday afternoons." According to Edwards, supporters "often forget themselves in the ferocity of their cries", some of which were "remarkably unpleasant and not fit for a lady's ears". He also highlighted some of the shouts "and even abuse" aimed at the players: *"'Down him!', 'Sit on his chest!', 'Knock their ribs in!'"*

Edwards hoped the players might be deaf to these types of yells, but of course they were not. Interviewed in 1895, Wolves captain Harry Wood described some of the types of fans likely to offer constructive criticism in games. "There's the spectator, for instance, who knows exactly how the ball should be played – and the unfortunate player who doesn't," said Wood, "[and] there's the eccentric season ticket holder who fancies he has a mortgage on every player in the club." This type of direct interaction with players was part and parcel of being a football fan, with praise and criticism given in equal measure. But some onlookers thought that dispensing any kind of criticism was unbecoming of so-called supporters.

In 1898, a Derby County fan wrote to the *Derby Mercury* requesting to point out the meaning of the word "supporter". "Now that the football team are doing rather badly," wrote the fan, "many so-called 'supporters' are ever ready at any and every opportunity to scoff instead of encouraging them and giving them credit for any good work they perform... I quite understand that it is disappointing to have the same poor results every week, but some team must win matches, and that cannot always be our own." The fan called on fellow Derby followers to "stick to their team and support it", and said they would surely soon see some improvement. "In conclusion," he wrote, "I may say that a most fitting time for a restoration in public favour would be against the Villa on Saturday, whom I would very much like to see humbled." Derby lost the match 7-1.

It would have been understandable if some Derby fans had offered criticism during that defeat, and, given they had paid their admission fee, they were surely entitled to do so. Chiefly, though, contemporary sources credit early fans with unrestrained enthusiasm, "How keenly the onlookers watch the game! How well they appreciate and note every little display of science!" wrote an anonymous ex-international in 1892. "A running fire of cheers accompanies a favourite player as he sprints and dodges down the line. The cries grow deeper as he nears the goal, and culminate in a very roar as he kicks the ball through it. I promise you it is worth going some distance to find such keen appreciation of a manly game."

A wonderful account of football fans appeared in the *Daily News* in 1892, wherein an anonymous reporter attended an unspecified league match in an unnamed "great northern town". "There is scarcely room for the spectators to move about," wrote the reporter, "and there must be quite eight or ten thousand people present." The most common shout is *"Play up!"*, exhorted in "voices of thunder". And when a goal is scored, the spectators "become wild with delight". "Hats are thrown in the air, sticks are flourished, and the partisans of the two teams enter into a noisy rivalry in appealing to their favourites," the reporter writes. "Nobody who witnesses a match between first class teams can wonder at the hold which football has obtained upon the affections of the people, and few would go away without having suddenly acquired an interest in the game. There is no other game which is capable of producing the eagerness and excitement that are noticeable at every good football match."

Watching football was no longer a passive form of entertainment. It was an engaging, emotional experience, with fans having developed a deep-rooted connection with their individual clubs and the overall game. "There is no mistake about it," wrote Charles Edwards in his 1892 article, "the exercise is a passion nowadays and not merely a recreation." The article was aptly titled *The New Football Mania*.

Edwards was a former footballer, and his contemporary Ernest Ensor was a former cricketer. In 1898, Ensor wrote a similarly-themed article titled *The Football Madness*. Ensor said the "astonishing increase" in the numbers of people watching football was due to "the dull monotony of life in our large towns". "It is the absolute necessity of some change, some interest outside the daily work, which has long since ceased to be interesting, that causes the large crowds at the weekly matches," he wrote. "Association football as it is now played commands more money and support than any other game the world has ever seen."

Responding to Ensor's article, the *London Standard* added that the press was also responsible for "a great deal of the extravagant excitement now displayed over football". Britain's growing audience of readers had created a newspaper boom, and football coverage increased along with the game's popularity. "By minutely discussing the merits and habits of individual players, and in other ways, some of the newspapers have fostered the interest in football until it has become nothing less than a mania," said the *Standard*. "In many of the great industrial centres football is the staple subject of daily conversation – in fact little else is spoken of."

The rise of the football fan and the growing popularity of the game during the late Victorian era can be tracked via FA Cup final attendance figures. From 2,000 in 1872, attendances increased to 6,500 in 1882, 15,000 in 1886, 32,800 in 1892, 48,800 in 1896, and 73,800 in 1899. League matches were relatively less well-attended, but by the end of the Victorian era top First Division clubs were attracting average crowds of around 20,000. Attendances would continue to climb through the Edwardian era and beyond. Football mania was here to stay.

6

Millions of them

In April 1901, the *Daily Mail* called for a tax to be placed on football fans. This followed a divisive parliamentary budget delivered by Sir Michael Hicks Beach, the chancellor of the exchequer, who responded to rising government expenditure and national debt – and the spiralling cost of the ongoing Boer War – by increasing the rate of income tax, and raising duties on beer, spirits and tobacco. "Why", asked the *Mail*, "did not [the chancellor] think of putting a tax on football spectators?" The newspaper's editorial may have been primarily intended as a criticism of the chancellor, but it reflected a widening opinion that the increasing popularity of football was placing a burden on society, and that the country's growing number of football fans were becoming unmanageable.

The *Mail*'s interest in football fans had been piqued by the remarkable attendance at the 1901 FA Cup final. The match, played between Tottenham Hotspur and Sheffield United at the Crystal Palace, was watched by 114,815 people, some 45,000 more than had seen the previous final. Increasing attendances around the country pointed to the growing proliferation of football fans.

"There must be millions of them," said the *Mail* in its editorial. A tax levied at the turnstiles, or in the form of "an annual licence to yell", would generate "an enormous revenue". And such a tax would not keep fans away from football any more than duties on beer, spirits and tobacco might stop drinkers and smokers. "Football enthusiasm evidently rises superior to any consideration of expense," said the paper, noting that many of those who attended the cup final had forfeited a day's wages, and paid for railway journeys and other expenses. "They would not have minded [paying] an extra few pence towards the cost of the war," it continued. "Besides, it would not matter if they did object – not to the government – for the majority of them do not seem to have votes."

At the time, around 40% of men – and 100% of women – were ineligible to vote. Many of those who could not vote were working class, and many of the working class were football fans. Certainly, the FA Cup final was of much more interest to them than the budget. "I think I may safely say that the budget suffers by comparison with the cup," wrote one newspaper reporter. "It is the one absorbing topic of the hour, and, go where you will, nothing else is talked of."

Observers had anticipated a record crowd at the final, given the huge rise in popularity of the game, and the fact that the match pitted together a team from London, generating much interest in the capital, and a team from the football hotbed of Sheffield, guaranteeing a huge influx from the north. Football's previous attendance record had been set two years earlier, at the 1899 cup final, when 73,833 people watched Sheffield United beat Derby County, indicating that Sheffield United were a big draw. And, although Tottenham Hotspur were not a Football League club (they played in the Southern League until 1908), they had amassed a large following. More than 45,000 had watched Spurs' semi-final win over West Brom, and their support would undoubtedly be swelled by tens of thousands of neutral Londoners keen to make the short trip to the Crystal Palace ground.

The Crystal Palace itself was a huge plate-glass exhibition hall, located in a large park at Sydenham Hill in South London. Its unusual football ground was set into a dry lake basin within the park. This natural bowl helped to form banked standing terraces around three sides of the field. Seated stands, with room for 12,000 posteriors, lined the fourth side. Refreshment tents and booths were enclosed within a ring of turnstiles and gates. The whole ground was surrounded by a curtain of trees, and overlooked by a wooden switchback railway rollercoaster ride, with the glinting glass of the Palace visible in the background.

"The great charm of the Crystal Palace was that it was so utterly unlike any other place where football was played," wrote journalist Jimmy Catton. "The sports arena at the Palace was not a building. It was just a space – sylvan, verdant, luscious – God's work." The ground's unusual charm and large capacity made it attractive to fans and football legislators. From 1895, the Crystal Palace replaced the Oval as the venue for cup finals and several international matches.

Ahead of the 1901 final, the *Sheffield Independent* considered the motives of the tens of thousands of Sheffield United fans who were expected to attend. "There is, in the first place, local patriotism – anxiety to see Sheffield at the top of the tree in football," explained the paper. "In the second place there is sporting keenness, and loyalty to the team which is bent on winning honours for the place with which it is associated; and thirdly there is the desire to spend a lively and interesting holiday in a lively and interesting city." So it was patriotism, loyalty, and the expectation of a good day out. In response to those who might "sneer at football enthusiasm", the paper said that these motives were worthy and "very human". The cup final, the paper said, would provide "a vivid illustration of the extent to which football enters into national life".

Around 30,000 to 40,000 fans travelled from Sheffield by train, many of them on "special trips", which included sightseeing tours, refreshments, and admission to the match. "It is possible to 'do' the city, see the match, and cover the railway journeys between Sheffield and London for an amount something less than £1," reported the *Sheffield Daily Telegraph*, "certainly a marvel of economy to those who know what trips to the metropolis usually run into." But the £1 special trips were still too expensive for many supporters, some of whom preferred transport-only "cheap trips" by rail or horse-drawn omnibus. Others, it was noted, "bunked" onto trains without paying, hiding under seats to avoid ticket inspectors.

The arrival of tens of thousands of northern football fans in the capital represented something of a culture clash, certainly as far as the London newspapers were concerned. Whenever northern teams reached the FA Cup final – which, during the Edwardian era, was every season – the newspapers published incredibly condescending articles about these provincial invaders. "The average Londoner does not pretend to understand the football excursionist from the North," read one example from the *Daily Mirror*. "On cup-tie day he is confirmed in his opinion that industrial England is a very strange place, containing an almost alien people. He cannot understand their language. He is openly amused at their clothing. Why do they all – every one of them – wear caps?"

The truth was that the northern fans of Sheffield United and the southern fans of Tottenham Hotspur were not that different, as was revealed when they were packed together on a stream of local trains carrying them the nine miles or so south from central London to Sydenham Hill. Railway compartments that were designed to hold six people were crammed with 20 or 25, some of whom stuck their heads out of the compartment windows for gulps of fresh air. Sheffield fans wore red and white rosettes, and Tottenham fans wore white hat bands with blue lettering spelling out: "Play up Hotspurs!"

These were not dry trains, and the rival supporters raised bottles of beer to their respective teams' good fortune. A *Daily News* reporter noted that Sheffield fans drank Guinness stout, while Spurs fans drank "foaming bitter". But, while "etiquette forbade complete friendship while we drank different drinks", the reporter wrote that, as the trains left the city for the suburbs, "rivalry faded away, and the joy of living and seeing others live took its place".

On arrival at the Crystal Palace, both sets of fans were struck by the sight of the green and pleasant ground. "Every one of us felt as proud as if we owned the place ourselves and were country squires," wrote the *Daily News* reporter. Admission prices for the final ranged from a shilling and sixpence for the standing terraces to five shillings for the covered seats. Many advance tickets had been snapped up by "speculators", who touted them outside the ground at four or five times their face value. Fans heading into the ground were also encouraged to purchase match cards that folded out to show the team line-ups. (Both teams went with 2-3-5 formations.)

Kick-off was at 3.30 in the afternoon, but the ground was busy by 11.30 in the morning. The attendance was boosted by magnificent weather, which attracted thousands of day-trippers unconnected with either competing club. Football was "the winter game", but it was much more enjoyable to watch in sunshine than in rain, particularly in the pleasant setting afforded at the Palace. "The weather attracted everyone who ever thought of going to a football match," said the *Sheffield Daily Telegraph*. However, the sheer size of the crowd sent some day-trippers away. "Many were so frightened at the numbers that they went back immediately on arrival," said the paper.

Inside the ground, a festival atmosphere prevailed. Brass bands played, sailors "danced with their lasses", women and children picnicked on the green, and the growing crowd sang and yelled and jostled around the roped-off field, attempting to find the best view of the pitch. Fans swarmed across the ground and sought every available vantage point, clambering on fences, shimmying up poles, and climbing into the trees that surrounded the ground. One reporter counted 36 people in a single elm tree, and said the ground's "layers of shade" were "thickened with people in every storey". Fans in the uncovered seats tied handkerchiefs around their necks to protect them from the sun. By kick-off, the ground presented "an extraordinary sight", the terraces and stands packed with "a rolling sea of colour and calmly excited humanity".

Amid such a remarkable scene, it was possible that the actual football could have been relegated to something of a sideshow. However, those present were treated to an entertaining – and controversial – match. These were two good sides. Tottenham were captained and managed by former Scotland international John Cameron, while Sheffield United's captain was the great Ernest "Nudger" Needham. And Sheffield's goalkeeper was one of football's biggest characters, William "Baby" Foulke, the larger-than-life star better known to some as "Fatty".

Sheffield scored first, through Fred Priest, and the huge contingent of United supporters celebrated with "ringing shouts". ("*Phut!* Up goes a carrier pigeon to bear the good news to Sheffield," said the *Daily News*.) "But London out-yelled the visitors when Tottenham equalised," reported the *Sheffield Telegraph*, "and the closely-packed ranks of spectators broke out into a delirium of waving hands and handkerchiefs, of tossed hats and twirling sticks." Tottenham took the lead five minutes into the second half. But the Spurs fans had "hardly ceased cheering" when Sheffield United's Walter Bennett equalised with a header that Tottenham keeper George Crawley – and many observers – claimed had not crossed the goal line. Referee Arthur Kingscott ignored the Spurs protests and allowed the goal. The game finished 2-2, but the supporters weren't too disappointed.

"One could not but wonder whether the crowds who had travelled all night would have done so if a draw had been a certainty, and we felt somehow that they would," wrote the *Daily News* reporter. "The scene at the famous Palace arena will not be forgotten by those who were present. The patch of turf was surrounded by a vast sea of faces, the trees, the roofs of buildings, and every point giving a glimpse of the play being utilised. It was an orderly and good-tempered throng, and although some resentment was shown at the decision of the referee with regard to Sheffield's second goal, matters passed off very pleasantly."

As the big crowd dispersed, travelling back into the city centre via train and omnibus, one little red-haired chap in Sheffield United colours asked the *Daily News* reporter how many of the capital's sights he could see before boarding his train home. "I don't want to waste any part of my six hours in London," said the chap, "as I have got to work sixteen hours on a stretch to make up for this holiday." "Sixteen hours on end to see a football match!" exclaimed the reporter. "If that little red-headed man wasn't a sportsman – *hang it!* – who is?"

Newspapers celebrated the record-breaking 114,815-strong crowd, and several ran pieces tracing the evolution of football attendances, from 2,000 at the first FA Cup final in 1872, through the surge of Victorian growth, and into an explosion of Edwardian popularity. The *Mail*, however, continued to gripe: "It would be better, no doubt, for the physical well-being of England if 114,000 people could play football and only 22 look on, instead of the numerical proportions being reversed."

The cup final replay was played at Bolton's Burnden Park, where transport problems and league fixture clashes resulted in a relatively low attendance of only 20,470. Tottenham won the replay 3-1, and returned to London with the FA Cup. They were the first "non-league" club to win the cup since the formation of the Football League, and the first southern club to win it since the dethroning of the public school old boys in the 1880s. Crucially, Spurs' win gave London football fans something to celebrate, and gave an indication that London, like Sheffield, Nottingham, Manchester and elsewhere, could become a hotbed of football fanaticism. As journalist and FA administrator William Pickford wrote: "On their return to the south they received a welcome which meant that at last the people of the metropolis had taken football to their hearts."

It's worth noting that more than 20,470 did get to see some of the action from the 1901 FA Cup final replay, as it was filmed by Robert W Paul's Animatograph Works company. Paul's flickering, silent footage shows the two teams running out past top-hatted and flat-capped officials and supporters, and a helmet-wearing policeman. The camera pans along a large open terrace packed with expectant spectators, clapping and smoking. Then it shows a few brief moments of action, framed against Burnden Park's roofed stand, which looks similarly packed. Paul's film catalogue promoted *The Football Final* as "the finest football film extant", which may well be true, although it fails to capture any of the match's key incidents. As a record of the match it can hardly be compared to a modern highlights package, but the film and others like it do provide rare insight into the early match-going experience.

Robert Paul is thought to have shot the first ever football film, *A Football Match at Newcastle-on-Tyne*, in October 1896, although unfortunately that film no longer survives. The Lumière Brothers' camera operator Alexandre Promio shot a film called *Football*, in London in 1897, which does survive, but doesn't show a match or spectators, instead showing a training kickabout between a group of players. The earliest surviving film of a football match with spectators is a very short, scratched and damaged clip of a First Division game between Blackburn and West Brom, shot by Wales-based filmmaker Arthur Cheetham on 24 September 1898. Filmed from an elevated position behind one of the goals, the footage shows the players ghosting around the pitch and, at the far end of the ground, a bank of supporters packed behind a fence and framed against a row of terraced houses.

The best football films from this turn-of-the-century era were made by the Mitchell and Kenyon company. Sagar Mitchell and James Kenyon were topical filmmakers who documented early 20th century Britain using hand-cranked cameras. Hundreds of Mitchell and Kenyon films were found in the basement of an old toy shop in Blackburn in 1994. Among them were scores of football films, comprising a remarkable historical archive. The Mitchell and Kenyon films place a particular focus on football fans, and represent the nearest it's possible to get without a time machine to experiencing life as an Edwardian football fan.

One of the earliest examples is Mitchell and Kenyon's film shot at a Newcastle v Liverpool match on 23 November 1901. The silent, flickering footage is grey and scratchy, but remarkably clear given its age, placing the viewer inside the Edwardian St James' Park, surrounded by a living, breathing mass of fans. It was one of the biggest games of the season, but the focus isn't on the match action, and instead almost half of the seven-minute film is devoted to the crowd, panning across packed terraces filled with smiling, waving fans in flat caps and bowler hats, all keen to be recorded for posterity. It was difficult to film the match action, as the heavy cameras couldn't be moved quickly enough to follow the ball. And Mitchell and Kenyon wanted to get as many fans as possible on camera in the knowledge that people would pay to see themselves and their friends on screen.

After being shot at St James' Park in the afternoon, the film was screened at a Newcastle theatre in the evening. So rather than going home to watch *Match of the Day* like their modern equivalents, Edwardian fans could have crowded into their local theatres and watched Mitchell and Kenyon football films, no doubt in awe, as their faces appeared onscreen. Moving pictures were new and exciting. Many of those present would never have seen themselves in a still photograph, so to see themselves in a moving picture must have seemed like a magical experience.

Technological improvements and the advent of newsreel would see the quality of football films improve through the 1910s and 1920s, but it remained difficult to properly capture match action. Goals and other important incidents were often missed, so emphasis remained on conveying a flavour of the atmosphere, and cameras remained focused on fans. The earliest football films are fascinating pieces of social history, but they're of little use if you want to see goals. Robert Paul's film of the four-goal 1901 FA Cup final replay was entirely goalless. Fans could read about the match action in newspapers, but the only ones who knew what any of the goals actually looked like were the people who went to the match.

Twelve months later, Sheffield United returned to the Crystal Palace to play the 1902 FA Cup final against another Southern League side, Southampton. The match finished 1-1, and a replay, also at the Palace, was won 2-1 by Sheffield United. The attendances, 76,914 for the initial match and 33,068 for the replay, were large, but even combined could not match the 114,815 attendance from the previous year. There were several reasons for this. First, there was no London side involved, reducing local interest. Second, London was suffering from a severe outbreak of smallpox, causing many travellers to avoid the capital. The semi-final match between Southampton and Nottingham Forest had been played at Tottenham's White Hart Lane ground, and fewer than 200 Forest fans had attended, "owing to the fear of mixing freely with a London crowd".

Not everyone thought a smallpox outbreak should affect football attendances. "Football is too important a matter to take serious account of such a trifle as disease," said the *Coventry Herald* in an apparently sincere editorial. "Smallpox may be brought back by some of the exuberant spectators of the final to towns hitherto immune, but football must not be interfered with; it must be allowed to pursue the even tenor of its way, notwithstanding smallpox or any other dread occurrences, to the end of the season."

The third reason for the drop in attendance was that football fans – and society in general – had been rocked by a terrible tragedy. Just two weeks prior to the final, 25 fans were killed and more than 500 injured in what has come to be regarded as football's first stadium disaster.

The Ibrox Park disaster occurred on 5 April 1902, during a Scotland v England home international. The match had been expected to be played at Celtic's 60,000-capacity Parkhead, but was switched to Ibrox after Rangers insisted that their expensively-expanded ground could hold 80,000. "There was a general feeling that they should be, other things being equal, given the chance to prove their statements and to partly recoup themselves for their lavish expenditure," reported the *Edinburgh Evening News*, adding that "a considerable number of SFA committee men did not subscribe to this idea, but the Rangers influence happens to be in the ascendancy".

The Ibrox pitch was surrounded by a cycle track, with covered seating stands at the north and south ends, and standing terraces at the east and west. The west terrace, built under the supervision of famed Glasgow architect Archibald Leitch, consisted of racked wooden floor beams, supported by a steel frame, on concrete foundations. The beams at the back of the terrace were suspended 40 feet above the ground. Entrance to the terrace was gained via access points to the lower levels, or via wooden stairs to the upper levels.

Despite heavy rain that had fallen incessantly for a day or so, great interest in the game attracted around 74,000 spectators, who came wrapped in overcoats and mackintoshes and wearing flat caps and bowler hats. The attendance figure represented a huge increase over that for the previous season's England v Scotland match, when only 18,250 fans had rattled around the Crystal Palace. Internationals were much better attended in Scotland than in England. 63,000 had watched Scotland play England at Celtic Park in 1900. Such high attendances in Glasgow reflected the popularity of football in Scotland, and also the enthusiasm for football in the north of England. Football fans from Manchester and other northern cities could travel to Glasgow just as easily as they could travel to London.

Ibrox was rammed full a good 30 minutes before kick-off. A witness quoted in the *Scotsman* described "an ocean of faces [that] appeared to monopolise every available foot of vantage", and said many thousands more were streaming into the ground, "leaving behind them five miles of main road still alive with pedestrians and laden vehicles of all descriptions". Stewards began to put up "full" signs at the lower-level terrace entrances, diverting the surging crowd towards the upper levels. By kick-off time, there was "much inexplicable swaying and scrimmaging" and the terracing "was showing eloquent signs of the unprecedented strain to which it was being subjected".

The terrible disaster occurred around nine minutes into the game. A shot on goal caused great excitement in the stands, but it seems likely that sheer pressure of weight caused what happened next. Those present at the back of the west terrace heard an ominous creaking sound. Then a row of wooden beams gave way and a small section of the terrace collapsed. Several hundred people fell through the steel framework and 40 feet to the ground.

Remarkably, few spectators away from the immediate vicinity were aware of the catastrophe. "So great was the buzz of excitement at the time of the disaster that the crash of the timbers was unheard by those in close proximity," said the witness. All that could be seen by the majority of those present was a cloud of dust that rose high into the air. A surge away from the collapsed area caused fans at the front of the terrace to spill onto the pitch. The game was temporarily stopped, and the players were ushered into their pavilion. But, once mounted police had cleared spectators from the pitch, the players came back out and the game resumed. "To have stopped the match would have been to make the situation tenfold more dangerous," said the *Scotsman*'s witness. "Panic would have been created if the extent of the disaster had been realised."

And the extent of the disaster was truly shocking. Underneath the collapsed section of terracing, hundreds of people lay in a pile of bodies that was described as being four feet deep. A few had been killed instantly, but most were suffering from serious injuries, ranging from broken limbs to fractured skulls. Many were stuck under other bodies, and some were trapped under fallen beams. Others were hanging precariously from the steel framework, some 20 or 30 feet in the air. Latecomers who had been unable to get onto the terracing were the first on the scene, helping to "disentangle writhing human forms from the awful mixture of stricken timbers and men". Police and doctors arrived, and injured fans were carried to ambulance wagons and taken to the infirmary. The dead were taken in police carriages to the mortuary.

Meanwhile, the match continued. "Overhead were the cheering multitudes, delighted with some favourite's cleverness," said the witness. "Beneath were hundreds of poor mortals, some dead, many dying, still more wounded and maimed for life. Surely pleasure and sorrow have seldom been brought together in more ghastly contrast." It was only after the match, which ended as a 1-1 draw (a result subsequently excised from official records), that the majority of the crowd realised the extent of the disaster. Those passing the west stand on their way home could see a "yawning hole" in the terrace, a line of ambulance wagons, a pile of broken beams, and a heap of caps and hats, "some of them blood spattered, a few crushed flat as if they had borne the brunt of their owners' fall".

An inquest found that heavy rain had weakened the wooden beams, which collapsed under the weight of overcrowding. The timber merchant and contractor who supplied the wood was arrested and charged with culpable homicide, but later acquitted by a jury. Newspaper editorials shared the opinion that the tragedy could not be blamed on the construction of the stadium or the size of the crowd. Even the *Daily Mail* said that the disaster had been "beyond the power of man to prevent".

Nevertheless, there were calls for increased safety measures at football matches. "The warning is clear," said the *Daily Telegraph*. "Throughout the football season vast assemblies aggregating many thousands come together every Saturday afternoon. The margin of safety cannot be made too wide, for a swaying crowd is a blind mass, devoid of reason."

The disaster cast a black cloud over football that would take some time to lift. After decades of remarkable growth, the game's explosive popularity had apparently become dangerous. "One question which arises is whether the popular craze for football has not really attained uncontrollable dimensions," said the *Sportsman*. Had football become too popular for its own good? Had fans become unmanageable?

Attendance figures were slightly subdued in the aftermath of the Ibrox disaster, but they soon recovered. Very large crowds were once again able to attend matches without incident. 101,117 spectators watched Aston Villa beat Newcastle in the FA Cup final at the Crystal Palace in 1905. And 121,452 watched Scotland beat England in a home international at Hampden Park in 1906. The average FA Cup final attendance during the Edwardian era (excluding replays) was more than 80,000. England v Scotland home internationals attracted an average of more than 52,000 spectators. The biggest Football League clubs had average home attendances of more than 30,000.

So football fans had not become unmanageable, and huge crowds only added to the spectacle and appeal of the game. However, there were always going to be potential dangers associated with large gatherings of people, and necessary measures and precautions needed to be taken. Unfortunately, safety warnings issued in the aftermath of the Ibrox Park disaster were not sufficiently heeded. It would not be the last tragedy to occur at a football stadium, nor even the last at Ibrox. For football fans, there was worse suffering to come.

7

Lost enthusiasm

On Christmas Day 1914, football fans arriving at Goodison Park to watch Everton play Bradford City were handed a census postcard. The aim of the census was determine why these football fans had not enlisted in the armed services. Christmas Day football was a longstanding and popular tradition, and attendances were generally very large. Previous Christmas Day matches at Goodison had attracted crowds of around 40,000. Today's crowd was half that size, and the mood was very subdued. On the Western Front, soldiers were playing football in the no-man's land between the trenches during a brief Christmas truce. At home, the Football League season was continuing without interruption or apparent consideration for the growing crisis. Britain was at war with Germany, and football was at war with itself.

When war was declared in August 1914, it was widely believed that the conflict would be short-lived. As a result, the 1914-15 football season began pretty much as usual (and would be allowed to run its course). However, within weeks it became clear that the war would be much more protracted and consequential than initially thought.

By September, Lord Kitchener's iconic "Wants You" recruitment campaign had encouraged more than 500,000 volunteers to enlist in the armed services. While many fans volunteered for service, footballers were prevented from doing so under the terms of their contracts. As casualties began to mount, football faced strong criticism. Some observers claimed football was an unwelcome obstruction to the war effort, while others said it was a welcome distraction from the horrors abroad.

"Football is an excellent thing, even in times of war," wrote respected historian AF Pollard in a letter to the *Times*. "But there is no excuse in diverting from the front thousands of athletes in order to feast the eyes of crowds of inactive spectators." Those spectators were either unfit to fight or "unfit to be fought for", Pollard said. Every club that paid a professional player was "bribing" a potential recruit to avoid enlistment, and every spectator who paid his gate money was "contributing so much towards a German victory".

But the sporting newspaper *Athletic News* defended football, saying the "whole agitation" was "nothing less than an attempt by the ruling classes to stop the recreation on one day in the week of the masses". "What do they care for the poor man's sport?" asked the paper. "The poor are giving their lives for this country in thousands." Many others were unable to fight because they had to stay at home to work in jobs that were important to the war effort, and, the paper said, there were precious few entertainments left available to them. "These should, according to a small clique of virulent snobs, be deprived of the one distraction that they have had for over 30 years."

One of football's most influential critics was Sir Arthur Conan Doyle. The author had served as a volunteer doctor during the Boer War, and had also played football, as a goalkeeper for amateur side Portsmouth AFC. He felt strongly that eligible players and supporters should abandon football and enlist in the armed forces. "There is a time for games," said Conan Doyle during a speech at a recruitment rally. "There is a time for everything. But there is only time for one thing now, and that is war."

Another high profile critic of football during the early months of the war was TC Fry, the dean of Lincoln, who called for all players' contracts to be cancelled and for all supporters under 40 years of age to be barred from attending matches in an effort to encourage more footballers and fans to enlist. In response, FA secretary FJ Wall said that football clubs had been given dispensation to release any player who wished to enlist, and that football matches were being used as recruitment rallies for supporters.

In September, the FA issued a notice, which was to be posted at football grounds around the country, appealing to "the patriotism of all who are interested in the game to support the nation in the present serious emergency, and to those who are able to do so to render personal service in the Army or the Royal Navy, which are so gallantly upholding our national honour." Two months later, a further notice was issued, attributed to FJ Wall, and headed: "An appeal to good sportsmen". "The need for more recruits for our Army is very urgent," said the notice. "Appeals should not be necessary. Every man must know his duty to himself and his country. There are approximately three millions of men with no family responsibility playing in and watching football matches. I ask these to show they are good sportsmen and to enlist now, and help other good sportsmen who are so bravely fighting England's battle against the world's enemy."

By Christmas, almost 1.2 million volunteers had enlisted. Severely reduced attendances at football matches indicated that many fans had chosen to serve their country. However, suspicion remained that many of those still attending matches were shirking their national duty. The Christmas census was intended to remove that suspicion. It was proposed by Lord Derby, the former mayor of Liverpool. The idea was to distribute census postcards at the Everton match on Christmas Day, and then at the Liverpool match on Boxing Day. The aim was to prove that the majority of football fans at these matches were ineligible for enlistment, either on the grounds of health or age, or because they were employed in reserved or protected professions, such as mining or munitions work. The cards asked fans to sign a commitment to join the Liverpool Reserve Regiment, or to provide a reason why they could not do so. Fans who refused the census cards, or did not return them, would be counted as "against enlistment without satisfactory excuse".

Lord Derby insisted that he had proposed the census not because he was against football, but "the very opposite", and stated that he had the "hearty co-operation" of both Everton and Liverpool football clubs. Everton chairman WR Clayton said his club would do everything it could to assist, although he pointed out that substantially reduced attendances demonstrated that a good number of Everton fans had already enlisted. "During the past few weeks we have made a careful examination of the individuals constituting our audiences," said Clayton, "and we find that only a very negligible percentage thereof consist of young fellows who apparently are eligible for enlistment."

On Christmas Day at a frost-bound Goodison, 20,296 fans turned up to watch the Everton v Bradford match, and 10,375 census cards were issued by recruitment officers to "suitable candidates". However, there were voices of dissent, with supporters questioning why the authorities, "after slanging players, spectators and the game for months... should suddenly find out that we have reasons for not joining, and desire to know them". There were also concerns that the census required the names and addresses of employers, and was being carried out via postcard, which "could hardly be a guarantee of the 'confidential'".

Lord Derby was present at the match, and saw Everton come back from a goal down to draw 1-1 on an icy pitch. The highlight of the day was deemed to be a "novel and really funny" half-time interlude, when "a wounded Tommy and a sailor" dribbled across the pitch, to great cheers from the crowd.

On the following day, at an also-icy Anfield, Liverpool drew 1-1 with bottom-of-the-table Manchester United. The attendance was 27,015, including 3,044 boys, and 1,453 soldiers – the latter group admitted free of charge. "We do not hear of theatres, picturedomes and other entertainments opening their doors free to soldiers," noted the *Liverpool Echo*. 6,075 census cards were issued to potential recruits.

A few days after the Everton and Liverpool Christmas matches, the *Echo* reported that census cards were coming in steadily, but that "the response has so far not been good". "Have you sent in your card yet?" the paper asked. "If not, do, please, at once." Despite this and other appeals, of the 16,450 cards issued, only 1,034 were returned. Of the respondents, 206 committed to enlist, 31 were already enlisted, 335 were unfit for service, 144 were prevented from enlisting by their employment, 129 were too old, and 35 were too young. Of the remainder, the majority cited domestic obligations for their inability to enlist, while 24 responses were spoiled with "abusive" messages. A disappointed Lord Derby refrained from personal comment, but newspapers called the return "very unsatisfactory".

"Lord Derby's scheme was intended to be a vindication of the good name of football, and that it should have failed is a disappointment," said the *Liverpool Daily Post*. "Not one man in 16 of those who were handed a postcard returned it." The poor return rendered the results fairly unrepresentative. However, of those who did return their cards, only 15% were unwilling to enlist and unable to provide an acceptable reason, suggesting that the majority of football fans were being unfairly criticised. And the census did generate 206 new enlistees, all of whom received a personal acknowledgement from Lord Derby.

The 1914-15 season limped to a conclusion, with Everton winning the league, and Sheffield United winning the FA Cup. The "War Final" was played at Old Trafford, as the Crystal Palace was being used for training purposes by the navy. The cup was presented by Lord Derby. The gate was given as 50,000, with takings of £4,012, and newspaper reports suggested that as many as 20,000 soldiers may have been admitted free of charge.

"The dominant note was khaki," said one report, "for the crowd contained a big proportion of the men of Britain's army, while the pathetic spectacle of sorely-wounded soldiers hobbling painfully into the seats provided for them brought home the grim reality... It was hard to realise that this match was really the crowning battle of the football campaign." Three months later, in July 1915, it was finally announced that, while football would continue, the Football League and FA Cup competitions would be suspended.

That September, the *Manchester Courier* described a "vastly different crowd" at Manchester City's Hyde Road ground than had been seen during the previous season. "The country had not realised the full import and gravity of the crisis in which it found itself involved," wrote the paper's reporter, "and the majority of those who follow the winter pastime seemed disposed to cry: 'Football as usual.'" Now, however, football fans had gained "a sense of proportion", and this season would not be like the previous one. "Football is to be played," wrote the reporter, "but not at the expense of national interests." So, the paper asked, "What sort of crowd was it that hurried in trams and taxis, or plodded along on foot, to watch 22 men kicking a bit of leather in these days of Armageddon?"

This was Manchester City v Stockport County, the opening game of the Lancashire Section of the War League. It was effectively a friendly tournament, with teams made up of amateur players and former professionals who were ineligible for armed service, and none of whom were being paid. Around 40% of professional footballers had enlisted in the armed forces. Others, with their playing contracts suspended, had found work in protected professions. Despite the scratch nature of the teams, the standard of play was described as very good – "so much so that those who came to sneer remained to praise". Nevertheless, the *Courier*'s report – published adjacent to a long list of casualties from Gallipoli – ran under the heading "Lost enthusiasm".

The attendance was 12,000, compared to 30,000 at Manchester City's opening home game of the last pre-war season. "They were deeply interested in the game," wrote the *Courier* reporter, "but there was not that effervescing enthusiasm, that ebullition of partisan feeling, that one associated with even the most unimportant football matches." The reporter studied the crowd in an effort to determine how many of them might have been eligible for enlistment. "The proportion did not seem large," he concluded. Many wore exemption badges, indicating that they were on war service in protected professions. "On their faces was a tired look, as of men who had been working at high pressure, and for long hours at a stretch, on tasks having peculiar significance," he wrote. Many others wore khaki uniforms, some bearing the wounds of war. No-one enjoyed the match more than the soldiers, the reporter noted, and they cheered good play "as doubtless as they would cheer when charging a German trench".

Manchester City won the match 3-1, and went on to win the Lancashire Section, although those results were unimportant in the grand scheme of things. But football itself did play an important role during the war. A big part of football's great popularity, particularly among the working class, stemmed from the fact that the game offered an escape from often tough lives. During wartime, such escapism became even more valuable and – perhaps – vital. The *Courier* concluded that wartime football was healthy and exhilarating, "and gives the minds of the people a rest from war thoughts". "The idea of 'football as usual' has long been abandoned as something unworthy," wrote the reporter. "Perhaps a suitable substitute would be: 'Some football and a few hours' forgetfulness.'"

The lack of professional football during the war did give rise to another popular attraction – "ladies' football". The women's game had attracted a brief flurry of interest during the 1880s and 1890s, although it had been regarded as a novelty, and even a travesty. In 1881, a pair of matches designated as Scotland v England were played in Edinburgh and Glasgow in front of 2,000 and 5,000 spectators respectively. Many of those present treated the players with disdain, offering "loud guffaws" and "sarcastic or personal remarks". During the second game, hundreds of spectators charged onto the pitch and "roughly jostled" the players, sending them fleeing back to their omnibus. Thankfully, the players escaped with "nothing more than serious fright".

Women's football hit the newspapers again in 1895, when 10,000 spectators gathered at Crouch End, London, to watch the first public match of the British Ladies' Football Club, which had been formed a few months earlier by the wonderfully-named Miss Nettie J Honeyball. The *Daily Sketch* described "an astonishing sight" as, on the afternoon of the match, "train-loads of excited people journeyed over from all parts, and the respectable array of carriages, cabs, and other vehicles marked a record in the history of football."

Unfortunately, the large crowd was again dismissive of the women's game. Spectators jeered the players, and many decided to leave before the final whistle. Nevertheless, the match was a commercial success, and Honeyball took her team on a lengthy tour that saw them play around 100 exhibition matches over the next two years. However, women's football would not be allowed to flourish. The FA banned women from playing football on first-class grounds, and the game fizzled out.

The ban was lifted during the 1916-17 season, when teams of female munitions workers began playing fundraising matches to support the war effort. The most prominent "munitions girls' football" team was Dick, Kerr Ladies, representing the Preston-based Dick, Kerr & Co railway works. Dick, Kerr's played their first match on Christmas Day 1917 against a team from the Arundel Coulthard lawnmower factory. 10,000 spectators packed Preston's Deepdale ground, and the *Lancashire Evening Post* said "the appearance of the historic enclosure was quite like the old times".

"After the Christmas dinner, the crowd were in the right humour for enjoying this distinctly wartime novelty," said the *Post*. Dick, Kerr's won the match 4-0, and the skills of Dick, Kerr's and the efforts of Coulthard's were greatly appreciated by the crowd. "At first the spectators were inclined to treat the game with a little too much levity, and they found amusement in almost anything," said the paper. "But when they saw that the ladies meant business, and were 'playing the game', they readily took up the correct attitude, and impartially cheered and encouraged each side."

The match takings, combining gate money with collections taken by wounded soldiers and donations from the two factories, totalled more than £488, which was donated to the local hospital. This success prompted a series of further games against other munitions girls' teams from around the country. Dick, Kerr's continued to play through the war and beyond. In 1920, they played a French team, in what was billed as the first ladies' international. After that, Dick, Kerr's were widely featured in newspapers and newsreels, and fan-favourites such as goal-scoring captain Alice Kell and teenage forward Lily Parr became celebrities.

At Christmas 1920, 53,000 fans packed Everton's Goodison Park to see Dick, Kerr Ladies beat St Helens Ladies, raising £3,065 for local ex-servicemen. However, in December 1921, the FA reinstated its ban on women's football, ostensibly regarding the "appropriation of receipts" and the "inadequate percentage devoted to charitable objects". The FA resolution also stated that "the game of football is quite unsuitable for females and ought not to be encouraged". It was estimated that Dick, Kerr's had raised around £50,000 for charity.

The sidelining of women's football coincided with the return of men's professional football, which resumed in 1919-20. Some commentators believed the FA ban was reinstated because women's football had become too popular, and was a threat to the men's game. While 53,000 watched Dick, Kerr's play St Helens at Goodison on 28 December 1920, only 35,000 had watched Everton play Arsenal at the same ground on Christmas Day. That Dick, Kerr's crowd was bigger than the 1920 FA Cup final crowd, with "only" 50,018 watching Aston Villa beat Huddersfield Town at Stamford Bridge.

The capacity of Stamford Bridge was given at the time as 85,000, and newspapers questioned the decision to switch from the Crystal Palace as "it is evident there will not be room for all". In the event, the capacity wasn't tested. The minimum admission fee of half a crown (two shillings and sixpence) may have kept some fans away, particularly given post-war austerity.

After the devastation of the war, with around a million Britons dead and another 200,000 wounded, the country had other things on its mind. But football remained important, as a distraction and an escape. Crowds returned, and their enthusiasm was regained. Then, in a rush of footballing optimism, the FA announced plans to build a new national stadium – "probably the finest stadium in the world".

8

Jumbles of men

It wasn't until 5am on the morning of the match that the last turnstile was installed and the new stadium was finally completed. Workers in flat caps and dust coats packed up tools, folded away stepladders, and swept up sawdust and loose nails. At the same time, around the country, football fans were waking up, pinning on their coloured rosettes, and boarding trains and motor coaches. The date was 28 April 1923, and the weather was bright and clear. It was the day of the FA Cup final between Bolton Wanderers and West Ham United – the first football match to be played at Wembley Stadium.

The Empire Stadium, as it was also known, was built for the 1923 British Empire Exhibition at Wembley Park over a period of 300 days at a cost of £750,000. The idea was that it would replace the Crystal Palace (and, latterly, Stamford Bridge) as the regular venue for the cup final, and – in an unrealised plan – that it would become the permanent home ground of a First Division club. For a few hours that morning the great stadium stood silent and empty: 25,000 tons of concrete, 40 miles of terracing and 300 square feet of turf, overlooked by a pair of 115-feet tall twin towers. The official capacity was 125,000. It was the biggest stadium in the world, but it wasn't nearly big enough.

The 1923 match is popularly remembered as the White Horse Final due to famous photographs and newsreel footage from the day showing a single white police horse and its rider attempting to clear the Wembley pitch of tens of thousands of spectators. In fact, the single white horse, Billy, was a grey, and was one of ten police horses on the pitch that day. The light-coloured horse appeared white in monochrome images, standing out among the mass of spectators, and becoming the focus of media attention. Billy's rider, PC George Scorey (despite his goal-getting name) was not a football fan. After being singled out as a hero in the aftermath of the match, Scorey was presented with complimentary tickets to subsequent cup finals, but did not use them. (After Billy died in 1930, Scorey was presented with another unsought gift – an inkwell made from one of Billy's hooves.)

The images of the "white horse" among a swarming crowd are striking, but they only tell part of the story. While Billy and PC Scorey received due praise for helping to clear the pitch, allowing the match to be played, fans who had encroached on the playing area were vilified in Parliament as "hooligans". They were painted as delinquent pitch invaders, but in fact they had been forced onto the pitch by the pressure of the huge crowd that had built up behind them. There were so many people in attendance that they could not be counted, and could not be contained within the biggest stadium in the world. It was only the good nature and patience of these fans that prevented a terrible tragedy.

It was clear in advance that the 1923 cup final would attract a very large attendance. Enthusiasm for football had only increased since the end of the war, and the game was once again stirring up a frenzy of passionate obsession. A writer in the *Scotsman* newspaper commented that the devotion of football fans was "scarcely to be distinguished from monomania", a relic of 19th century psychology referring to a form of partial insanity in which otherwise sound minds were gripped by a kind of irresistible frenzy. The less-than-subtle implication was that football fans were completely mad.

As had been demonstrated at the 1901 final, a big team from the north would bring tens of thousands of fans, and a London team would generate huge interest in the capital. But it was Wembley itself that was the biggest draw, with neutral fans keen to see the opening of this new home of football. "The wish to see the widely-advertised stadium, the natural desire to cheer a London club on to victory, and the belief that there would be room for everyone attracted a far larger crowd than has ever been compressed into a similar space," noted the *Times*.

Elaborate transport plans were put into place to convey the predicted large number of fans to the stadium. 120 trains were expected from "the provinces", carrying 40,000 fans, and a non-stop fleet of local trains would run from central London to Wembley. The expanding London Underground service would run an augmented service, and the London General Omnibus Company added extra routes and services. Special road regulations were put into place, and arrangements were made for the parking of two thousand cars at the stadium.

Ironically, the well-planned transport arrangements may have contributed to the overcrowding problems that later occurred, allowing smooth travel to Wembley for an unprecedented number of people. The first trains began to arrive at London stations as early as 3am, carrying "jumbles of men from the north". "Some of the Bolton enthusiasts looked a bit tired, but they soon woke up," reported the *Yorkshire Evening Post*, adding that many had brought large quantities of beer with them. "At Euston, a wag sat astride a barrel of beer that was being wheeled along in a hand-cart," said the paper. "A dozen pals cheered him until the roof of the station well-nigh quivered."

At Wembley, there were hundreds of fans gathered at the gates by 8.30am, and a sea of thousands by 11.30am, when the turnstiles finally opened. "All the men in Britain seemed to be converging on the stadium," said the *Evening Post*. Such was the flow of people that to attempt to go against it would have been "like a straw trying to float against the Niagara". Once through the turnstiles, fans ran and trotted towards the stands and terraces, "except for an occasional old man who hobbled forward as fast as he could".

Most spectators were smartly dressed in suits with ties and waistcoats, as was the fashion at the time, but many wore or carried extravagant embellishments. One photo taken on the day showed a group of ten or so West Ham fans sprinting into the ground led by a man in a sailor's cap who was yelling and ringing a bell. These fans wore rosettes and cardboard flowers in their buttonholes, and team-coloured top hats and party crowns on their heads. They carried football rattles, emblem-bearing standard poles, cardboard FA Cups, and giant hammers or irons. Another photo showed a Bolton fan carrying an umbrella emblazoned with the words, "Play up the Trotters!"

Newsreel footage of fans entering the stadium was captured by Pathé News cameraman Jack Cotter, although the fans may not have been aware they were being filmed. That's because Cotter was undercover, and his movie camera was hidden inside a giant hammer with "Play Up West Ham!" written on the side. Another newsreel company, Topical Budget, had paid £1,000 for exclusive rights to film the final, but their rivals went to great lengths to obtain "pirate" footage. As gleefully revealed in the finished Pathé News film, Cotter disguised himself as a West Ham fan, complete with button-hole rosette and stick-on moustache. Pulling a crank handle from his pocket and attaching it to his "hammer" he was able to film footage of the crowd and the game from the stands.

From the time the Wembley gates opened through to around 1pm the influx of spectators into the stadium was described as "steady". After that, though, pressure began to build. By 1.45, with the standing terraces full, the decision was made to close the gates. Telephone calls were made to Scotland Yard to request police reinforcements, and to transport hubs to request that they stopped ferrying fans to the stadium. Still, though, tens of thousands continued to arrive by bus, train and tram. Some fans climbed over the turnstiles. Others shinned up drainpipes and over the stadium walls. At 2.15, the pressure of the crowd caused the gates to break open. With around 125,000 people already inside, up to 100,000 more surged into the stadium. Barriers collapsed, seats were broken, and spectators were forced from the terraces and stands onto the running track and all across the pitch.

"We expected nothing like this at the new stadium," wrote a reporter for the *Sheffield Independent*. "Everything became a mixture of stampede and pandemonium. Women shrieked, and men shouted hoarsely to those in the rear. But onward still came the rush, and everyone in the worst-affected areas had to fight for his or her own safety. It swarmed into the stands, leaving those down below no option but to push forward and crash onto the playing area. The oval patch of new green was quickly peopled by a mass of frenzied, struggling humanity." Unseen by the reporter but later shown in photographs were scores of fans who had somehow climbed up onto the peak of Wembley's roof, and were surveying the scene against a backdrop of the stadium's twin towers.

Sir Frank Swettenham, a 73-year-old former British colonial official, was carried into the stadium on a "tidal wave" of supporters, and found the pitch entirely covered with people. "No grass was visible, only the tops of the goal posts," he wrote in a letter to the *Times*, describing how the small number of police "struggled rather aimlessly with an elusive crowd of thousands". His most striking memory occurred following the arrival of King George V shortly before the supposed kick-off time of 3pm. "Surely no monarch has ever before been greeted by such a wild burst of cheering from such a throng," wrote Swettenham. "It was so marvellously impressive in its intensity."

The arrival of the King indicated that the match would go ahead, and encouraged those on the pitch to attempt to move back towards the stands. The *Times* praised the "amazing good humour and patience" of the fans, and emphasised that there was "no hooliganism, no wanton disorder". "Probably no other crowd in the world would have behaved so well under circumstances which looked as if they would make the playing of the match an impossibility," said the paper. After standing to attention to sing *God Save the King*, fans began a slow retreat. Billy and PC Scorey and their colleagues – assisted by the Bolton and West Ham players – were eventually, after 40 minutes or so, able to push the crowd back behind the touchlines, leaving the pitch "defiled with orange peel and papers and refuse", but suitably playable.

The match kicked off at 3.45pm and, despite a ten-minute interruption when the crowd once again spilled onto the pitch, was played to a conclusion. However, the massed crowd that was pressed right up against the touchline did interfere with play. Bolton took the lead within two minutes through David Jack, his thunderous shot striking a spectator stood in the goal net, and apparently knocking the chap out. There were regular incursions onto the field, as fans accidentally and not-so-accidentally overstepped the touchline.

In the second half, Bolton's Jack Smith hit a shot that appeared to come back off the woodwork. The referee, however, decided that the ball had hit a fan on the goal line, and awarded a goal. Bolton won the match 2-0, but any controversy over the scoreline was swiftly forgotten as explanations were sought for the overcrowding.

It was initially reported that up to a thousand fans had been injured at the match, although this was "somewhat exaggerated". According to a statement made in the House of Commons by home secretary William Bridgeman, the majority of injuries were very minor, and only 22 fans were taken to hospital, including three with serious injuries. All of those injured at the ground recovered. In addition to those injured at Wembley, several fans were injured in a road accident on the way to the ground. A packed omnibus swerved to avoid a tram, hit a post box, and overturned. Passengers on the upper deck were thrown into the road, and those in the lower deck were trapped inside. Fifteen passengers were taken to hospital, although only two were said to be seriously injured.

In response to the home secretary's statement, Oswald Mosley, MP for Harrow and future fascist leader, denounced the Wembley crowd as hooligans, eliciting jeers from the House. "What steps does the right honourable gentleman propose to take to protect Wembley from hooliganism?" Mosley asked. But Jack Jones, MP for Silvertown and a West Ham supporter, said the crowd had been "good-humoured", and Mosley had "no right to talk about hooliganism". The House cheered, and the Speaker of the House chastised Mosley. The latter's attempt to respond was interrupted by cries of "*Sit down!*" It would not be the last time football fans would be slighted in such a manner in parliament.

The FA deflected all blame for the incident onto the Wembley Stadium authorities, who they said were fully responsible for the event. Wembley officials subsequently issued a statement saying that the cause was simply "the altogether unexpected size of the crowd", which had been twice as big as anticipated. "The plain fact is that the largest sports arena in the world proved inadequate for the largest football crowd ever assembled," read the statement, adding that means would need to be devised to "ration" the number of fans who could attend future matches. The means devised seems obvious in hindsight – subsequent FA Cup finals would be all-ticket affairs.

In the aftermath of the match, an official from the BBC said that the huge Wembley crowd could have been better controlled via loudspeakers, which the corporation had offered to install. The BBC had requested to broadcast entertainment from its experimental London radio station, 2LO, to the crowd via loudspeakers, but permission was refused. Had permission been granted, the official explained, it would have been possible to address the crowd through 2LO and via the loudspeakers "with, no doubt, salutary effect". Loudspeakers would be installed at Wembley in the following year, without the assistance of the BBC.

At the time, the nascent British Broadcasting Corporation was expanding its radio coverage, with transmitters in London, Manchester, Birmingham, Newcastle, Cardiff and Glasgow. But the transmitters were relatively low-powered, and only those listeners in close proximity could pick up signals on their crystal sets or two-valve radios. The earliest football programme featured in the BBC's *Radio Times* listing magazine was *Humours of Football*, a talk by Arsenal director Charles Doland Crisp, broadcast from London to all stations at 9.05pm on 20 October 1923.

In subsequent months, regular league football round-ups began to be broadcast, nationally and regionally. The installation of a chain of relay transmitters extended the BBC's reach, and by 1925 the majority of fans around the country were able to receive football programming via radio – if they could afford to own a radio set, which cost around £7 for a crystal set or upwards of £12 for a two-valve set, and a radio licence, which cost 10 shillings per year.

The first live running commentary on a football match was broadcast on 22 January 1927. The match was Arsenal v

Sheffield United at Highbury, and the broadcast was arranged at such short notice that it was not billed in advance in the *Radio Times*, although the morning's newspapers did list community singing from Highbury at 2.05pm followed by the match "broadcast by wireless link" at 2.45. This first association football commentary followed an experimental rugby football commentary, England v Wales, which had been broadcast from Twickenham on the previous Saturday. The commentator for both games was Teddy Wakelam, a former Harlequins rugby player. Later described as "one of the giants of broadcasting", Wakelam was Britain's first sports commentator, covering football, rugby, cricket and tennis through to the start of the second world war. Unfortunately, his career got off to an inauspicious start. Wakelam's first rugby broadcast was described by the *Observer* as a "fiasco".

"With regard to the commentaries, the official responsible for this part of the broadcast had no idea of what I call dictating a narrative of the progress of the struggle," commented the paper. "His remarks were rather a series of ejaculations." A reviewer in the *Yorkshire Post* wrote that "most listeners would not be able to visualise the play from the announcer's story". However, a correspondent in that paper's letters column disagreed. "I found it easy to follow the course of the game," wrote the correspondent. "I actually felt something of the excitement of a real spectator."

The correspondent recommended that listeners should write down the names of the players from both teams on a sheet of paper, and "follow the game with the squared diagram provided". This squared diagram, which divided the playing pitch into eight numbered sections to be referred to in commentary, was printed in newspapers and the *Radio Times*. It would also be used in association football broadcasts, with the intention that the commentator could advise listeners, for example, "*Arsenal have the ball in square one, and move forward to square four...*" The squared diagram system is said, possibly apocryphally, to be the basis for the idiom "back to square one".

The Arsenal v Sheffield United broadcast – the first *proper* football commentary – received mixed reviews. There was particular interest in Sheffield, where United fans had the unprecedented experience of being able to follow an away match, being played 150 miles away, from the comfort of their own homes. The *Sheffield Independent*'s wireless correspondent wrote that the match was not ideal for broadcasting, as there were few goals, and poor weather conditions made it difficult for the commentator to distinguish between the players. "It was easier to form an idea of how the game was going by the ebb and flow of the cheers than by the comments of the narrator," wrote the correspondent. "Whenever the Arsenal were pressing, the cheering was terrific, and there were plenty of noises when the play was at the other end."

The writer thought the idea of dividing the pitch into eight sections was a good one, although "the ball passed so quickly from section to section that often the narrator had no time to describe the play, and merely called the numbers of the sections". And Wakelam's rather bland comments ("*Those Sheffield United fellows are clever with their heads!*", "*Isn't Green's backheel play pretty?*", "*Well played, Harris!*") were regarded as "really the remarks of one spectator to another" rather than the expert insights that were expected. However, the audible noise from the fans led the wireless correspondent to think the football broadcast experiment worthy of repeating: "In the background the cheers of the crowd – and the jeers when they disagreed with the referee, the stamping of spectators in the grandstand, and occasionally the referee's whistle, gave a splendid idea of the atmosphere of a big soccer match."

In the following week, a live football commentary was broadcast from Nottingham Forest's City Ground, and commentaries became regular features in the radio listings. However, football clubs soon began to object, arguing that radio broadcasts had a negative effect on gates. "Directors believe that in wet weather many supporters would rather 'listen' to the match rather than go and see it," explained the *Yorkshire Post*. But some fans listened to matches because they were unable to go and see them. This included several fans, represented in newspapers, who had been blinded or otherwise injured in the war.

After Nottingham Forest decided not to allow any further commentaries, the aggrieved wife of one Forest fan wrote to the local paper. "My husband, when he was able to get about, was a regular patron of football matches," wrote the correspondent. "He is now paralysed, and the recent broadcast of Nottingham Forest was a godsend to him. Now he is to be denied a similar privilege, so far as the Forest are concerned, because they think that they might miss a shilling or two."

In February 1927, the *Radio Times* listings included a Liverpool v Newcastle match from Anfield, with commentary by Ernest "Bee" Edwards, the *Liverpool Echo*'s football columnist. However, the commentary was not broadcast, as Liverpool refused to give the BBC the necessary permissions, stating that the club "did not feel disposed to be placed in the position of creating a league precedent". Everton, however, did give permission, and their match in the following month against Leeds United was broadcast on the radio, with commentary by Bee.

The *Liverpool Post* described the experience of listening to the Everton v Leeds match at home, and provided snippets of example commentary ("*Did you hear that roar?*", "*That was a real Dixie effort!*", "*Weldon has been kicked. I won't say where.*"), suggesting that Bee was a more colourful commentator than Teddy Wakelam. Everton came from a goal down to equalise, and then – "*Weldon has done it! Everton 2, Leeds 1!*" "The crowd roars out of the loudspeaker," wrote the *Post* reporter. "But this is when we learn the danger of broadcasting football matches to drawing rooms. Well enough to cry out and wave your arms on the stand at Goodison Park. But regard what has happened here at the news of Everton's goal. An Everton supporter has risen. He has scattered the cake stand with one exulting arm, and in an ecstasy of relief he has given his wife a hail-fellow-well-done slap."

Exactly how many football fans were gathering in their drawing rooms around their radio sets and cake stands to listen to match commentaries was unknown. There does seem to have been some resentment among radio connoisseurs of the fact that this shiny new technology was being used to broadcast sport rather than more highbrow programming such as music recitals or lectures. One newspaper wireless columnist, "Ohmic", described football broadcasts as "a mistake", and said they were unlikely to appeal to urban types or women. "One can quite understand a football enthusiast in a remote village enjoying a broadcast description of a football match, but it is not likely to appeal to listeners in towns and cities," wrote the columnist. "Football matches usually take place in the afternoon, and the majority of listeners at this time are women. Not many will bother to tune in."

Other columnists pointed out that a radio commentary would never be able to compete with the match-going experience. "Football at the fireside, of course, is not likely to be anything but a poor substitute for the drama and thrills of the real thing," wrote a correspondent in the *Falkirk Herald*. "It will be a long time, if ever, before second-hand sport empties the football grounds." Another columnist, "Radio Rex", agreed: "The most vivid description of a game appeals rather as an interesting curiosity than as a substitute for the real thing, and no genuine football 'fan' who could by any possibility reach the ground is likely to prefer his armchair and his headphones."

It was true that radio commentaries could not quite replicate the experience of actually going to matches, but they were nevertheless entirely valid and entertaining broadcasts. And they were a real gift for football fans who couldn't attend matches, including those who couldn't travel to away games. As a result, football on the radio swiftly became a very popular form of entertainment. As the *Radio Times* commented in 1927, "Nothing that the BBC has done has aroused more interest and given more pleasure than the series of sporting broadcasts that began only this year." Over the next few seasons, radio commentaries began to be broadcast on an almost-weekly basis, with the BBC covering league matches and FA Cup ties, including cup finals. Football fans would continue to listen to football on the radio, despite the emergence of another very popular medium.

Back in February 1924, even before the arrival of football on the radio, the *Daily Chronicle* had printed a remarkably prescient letter suggesting that "in a few years hence half a million will see the cup final quite easily by means of television". "The Football Association will sell the rights of transmission," wrote the unnamed correspondent, "and the football fan will get the whole thing in comfort at his own fireside. There seems to be no reason why, when the whole thing has been reduced to televisionary form, the winning goal should not be repeated any number of times." The correspondent also suggested that "slow motion effects" could be used for "educational purposes". It would take several decades, but television would entirely change the experience of being a football fan.

9

Amazing scenes

On 30 July 1930, Uruguay played Argentina in one of the most significant matches in the whole of football history. It was the final match of the inaugural Campeonato Mundial de Fútbol, or Football World Championship. It was the first World Cup final. Up to 100,000 fans watched the match at the newly-built Estadio Centenario in Montevideo, and much of South America was gripped by a remarkable football frenzy.

Yet in Britain the first World Cup passed virtually unnoticed, and few British football fans were even aware of its existence. No British newspaper covered the earlier rounds, and only a handful published a short Press Association report of the final that dismissively referred to the tournament as "the so-called World's Association Football Championship". *The Times*, regarded as Britain's newspaper of record, ignored the first World Cup entirely. The reasoning was simple: No British teams were involved, so it could hardly be considered a legitimate World Championship, could it?

Britain had invented association football, and was keen to send its Laws of the Game rulebook around the world. During the Victorian era, British immigrants spread the association game throughout Europe and across South America. Football was introduced to Uruguay by English teacher Henry Castle Ayre, and to Argentina by Scottish teacher Alexander Watson Hutton. Britain was happy to share its game, but less happy to cede control of it. The four British nations were not members of FIFA, the Paris-based international football governing body, having withdrawn following a disagreement over payments to amateur players. So, although FIFA did send a letter of invitation to the English FA, none of the British nations competed in the first FIFA World Cup.

The host nation, Uruguay, were the winners of the previous two Olympic football tournaments and the nearest football had to reigning world champions. Uruguay had beaten Argentina in the 1928 Olympic final in Amsterdam, in front of a capacity crowd and "amid amazing scenes", so Europe had a hint of what South American football and its fans could offer. At the World Cup, Uruguay would compete with 12 other teams – six from South America, two from North America, and four from Europe.

According to the accounts that exist, the 1930 World Cup was a competitive and entertaining tournament that was particularly notable for the manner in which it grabbed the attention of the watching public. When further details eventually trickled through from Uruguay, the British press seemed surprised by the evident popularity of football on far-flung shores. As noted in one brief British newspaper report, published a full month after the final had been played, "The enthusiasm of football crowds in this country is mild in comparison with that of South American spectators."

Britain had been offered a glimpse of the South American football fan in the previous year, when Chelsea toured Argentina, Brazil and Uruguay. While the South American players were said to be "masters of the game", the fans were regarded as being rather unsporting. As Chelsea full-back Leslie Odell wrote in a letter home, "The spectators here are separated from us by a fence of barbed wire, so you can tell what sort of people they are." Opposition teams were likely to be pelted with orange peel, and worse, and it seemed "a commonplace thing" to throw bottles or other missiles at the referee if he gave a decision that did not suit the opinion of the crowd.

After Chelsea beat an Argentina XI 1-0 in front of 60,000 fans in Buenos Aires, the final whistle triggered a "barrage of hooting and booing". In a second match in Buenos Aires, after Chelsea captain George Rodger shoulder-charged an opponent (a fair challenge in England, but frowned upon in Argentina), a spectator ran from the stands and slapped Rodger in the face. Then Argentina captain and notorious hard man Luis Monti kicked Rodger "in the groin" with such force that the big Scottish half-back fainted and had to be carried from the field, to the unanimous cheers of the crowd. "It is unpleasant to record that the Argentine footballing public are lacking in the sportsmanship to be found amongst the crowds in other countries," noted the English-language *Buenos Aires Standard*.

So British footballers might not have been keen to make the long sea journey to Uruguay, and in any case they were left at home, most likely oblivious, as the World Cup finals got underway and progressed through a four-group stage, then semi-finals, to the hugely-anticipated final at the Estadio Centenario. The whole tournament had been scheduled to be played at the newly-built Centenario, but construction delays meant that eight of the tournament's 18 games had to be played in smaller local stadiums. Described by FIFA president Jules Rimet as a "temple to football", the 90,000-capacity Centenario was – and remains – a broad, uncovered concrete bowl, with a distinctive 100-metre tower reaching up into the sky above the main Olympic Tribune stand. It was the biggest football stadium outside of Britain.

A remarkable aerial photograph taken on the day of the final showed ant-like swarms of fans congregating on the stadium, lining up at the turnstiles, climbing staircases, and filling the stands. Another photo, taken in the surrounding streets, showed groups of fans in fedoras, wide-lapelled jackets, open-necked shirts and high-waisted slacks, bustling their way past motor cars towards the stadium.

The turnstiles had opened at 8am, some six hours before kick-off. Fleets of special trains and planes brought fans from all over Uruguay to Montevideo. Newspaper reports said some fans had set out three days earlier in order to get there on time. The city came to a standstill, with all of the city's shops and offices closed. The Press Association reported that among the first fans to arrive were 50 members of the Uruguayan parliament. Ships carried fans from Argentina over the River Plate. (One ship, packed with 1,800 fans, never arrived due to fog.) On landing, fans were searched and made to surrender their weapons. Conflicting reports said the Uruguayan authorities confiscated somewhere between 1,500 and 5,000 revolvers. "They take great care of the referee in that part of the world," remarked one newspaper.

The first World Cup final was played amid "scenes exceeding in enthusiasm even those of an English cup final", according to the Press Association report. That report omitted any details of the actual match, other than the final score. For the record, Uruguay scored first through Pablo Dorado, and newsreel footage showed banks of cheering fans waving their hands in the air. But Argentina equalised, then took the lead before half time. The second half, though, belonged to Uruguay. They scored a second goal to equalise, then a third to lead 3-2. Fans around the stadium waved newspapers and handkerchiefs, and those near the pitch bounded up and down like kangaroos. Scores of fans ran onto the pitch to celebrate with the players. Uruguay scored again, through an 89th minute header from Hector Castro, to win 4-2.

The victorious Uruguayan team paraded around the pitch with a large symbolic cup, trailed by enthusiastic supporters, while fans in the stands waved their fedoras in the air. (The actual World Cup – the Jules Rimet trophy – was presented to the president of the Uruguayan FA at a post-match banquet.) The players were hoisted onto shoulders and carried from the field. Uruguay was so proud of its team's achievement that it would declare a national holiday.

Alongside these celebratory scenes were some rather unsavoury ones. After the match, according to one report, thousands of aggrieved Argentinians began throwing "bombs and things" at "every Uruguayan in sight". And over in Argentina there were several "minor riots". Crowds of cheering Uruguayan fans paraded through the streets of Buenos Aires, and gathered at the offices of the *La Critica* newspaper, where the match result was posted on a sign for all to see. Amid the celebrations, several gunshots were heard, and the police were called on to disperse the crowd. No casualties were reported. Then a group of Argentinian fans responded by marching on the Uruguayan consulate and pelting it with stones. "It seems that people in South America get fairly excited over football," commented one British newspaper. "If all this happens over football, goodness knows what their military manoeuvres are like."

The Press Association's World Cup final report gave the attendance as 100,000. The official attendance was subsequently recorded as 68,346 but, with reports claiming that many thousands were turned away from a 90,000 capacity stadium, the 100,000 figure might be more accurate. In any case, the attendance for the biggest football match that had ever been played was not quite as big as had been seen at cup finals and home internationals in Britain. And those attendances continued to grow through the 1930s, reaching unprecedented sizes. Numerically, at least, Britain could still claim to be the world's hotbed of football fandom.

The official attendance for the 1934 World Cup final, at the National Fascist Party Stadium in Rome, was 55,000 (although initial reports said 40,000). Hosts Italy came back from a goal down against Czechoslovakia, and the game went to extra time. "So great was the excitement that it was feared at one time that one of the stands would collapse under the strain of countless stamping feet," said one report, syndicated to several British newspapers. That might have been an exaggeration. After Italy scored an extra-time winner and were presented with the Jules Rimet trophy, the report said the "gold championship cup" was "so big that it took four men to carry it". Whether or not the 55,000 figure was also exaggerated, perhaps for propaganda reasons, the tournament was well-attended, proving that there was a big appetite for football in Europe, as well as in South America. But Britain remained the hotbed, and the attendances in Buenos Aires in 1930 and Rome in 1934 were dwarfed by an attendance in Glasgow in 1937. This was British football's biggest-ever crowd.

The date was Saturday 17 April 1937, and the match was Scotland v England at Hampden Park. It was the first all-ticket international. The official attendance figure was given after the game as 149,407. (Some later sources give the figure as 149,547.) Once non-ticketed guests, reporters, stewards and police were taken into account, newspapers agreed that the attendance must have been close to, or in excess of, 150,000. Even judging by the lower official figure of 149,407, this was a world record attendance. It remains a British and European record.

Hampden Park was the biggest football ground in the world in 1937, and it would remain so until the opening of Rio's Maracanã for the 1950 World Cup finals. Hampden already held the football attendance record, set in 1933 when 136,259 went through the turnstiles for another Scotland-England international. Reconstruction ahead of the 1937 match was supposed to increase the ground's capacity to 180,000. In fact, a safety inspection by Glasgow's Master of Works assessed the expanded capacity to be 149,969, with 14,269 seats and 135,700 standing places.

By comparison, the capacity at Wembley in 1937 was 93,000, having been slashed following the chaos of the 1923 FA Cup final. Hampden, though, was relatively accustomed to handling crowds of 100,000 and more for international matches and Scottish Cup finals. The ground had been regularly expanded and improved since its opening in 1903, and the 1937 redevelopment was regarded as essential in order to meet the demand to attend internationals and finals. (League matches involving tenants Queen's Park, meanwhile, saw only around 4,000 spectators rattling around Hampden.)

The huge attendance for the 1937 international was particularly astonishing given the fact that the match was effectively a friendly – a dead rubber in a home international championship that had already been won by Wales. Consider also the economic climate of the 1930s, when few football fans had much disposable income. Britain was still dealing with the effects of the Great Depression, and unemployment remained a major problem. (The Jarrow March had taken place just a few months earlier, in October 1936.)

There were also other distractions. Britain was consumed with preparations for the coronation of George VI, with rehearsals for parades and processions taking place across the nation. Yet the Scotland v England international retained utmost importance among football fans on both sides of the border. Internationals were traditionally an opportunity to see star players who could otherwise only be read about in newspapers or glimpsed in occasional newsreels. As the *Times* noted in the build-up to the game, "The association match between England and Scotland has an appeal which is quite independent of goals and points, and not even the FA Cup final at Wembley can surpass it in pageantry and excitement."

The scramble for tickets (or "briefs") began in January, with fans advised to apply via their local clubs. Tickets for the ordinary terracing cost two shillings. The only way to follow the game live was to be there in person, as it wasn't being broadcast on the radio due to a dispute between the BBC and the SFA over the payment of a fee. "We are very sorry that you who cannot go to Hampden Park that day, but would like to listen to a commentary, are unable to follow the match in this way," said BBC director Melville Dinwiddie. (The recently-launched BBC TV channel, meanwhile, would instead be airing "a demonstration of locomotives".)

In addition to well over 100,000 fans from all over Scotland, up to 50,000 were expected to travel from England in what was described as a "greater-than-ever English invasion". Necessary preparations were made to feed and water visiting fans. Restaurant and pub owners applied for extended licences, and civic halls were turned into mass feeding stations. Newspapers estimated that 250,000 meals would be served to match-goers. As for alcohol, according to the *Dundee Courier*, "The tonic taken if Scotland win will be sufficient to float a battleship."

A huge police operation was planned to deal with the crowd. 700 "stalwarts of the force" would be on duty in and around the ground, and detectives and plainclothes constables would mingle with the crowd to watch for pickpockets. It was publicised that the police would be "directed by radio" – an experimental method of communication at the time.

There were fears that the reconstructed Hampden Park might not be ready in time, with steelworkers threatening strike action over a delayed pay rise. But by the beginning of April it was announced that work was complete. The expanded ground had 117 turnstiles, each of which, it was estimated, could cope with 40 admissions a minute, or 2,400 an hour. As the big day approached, newspapers printed instructions for match-goers. "Remember your brief!" advised the *Dundee Courier*. "The enthusiast who arrives at Hampden without a ticket will be right out of luck." Fans were instructed to arrive early ("a crowd of 150,000 cannot be accommodated in comfort if there is a last-minute rush"), and to wear a "bunnet" – a flat cap rather than a taller hat so as not to block the view of those behind.

On the morning of the match, newspapers on both sides of the border anticipated a record-breaking occasion. "Soccer crowds invade Scotland!" reported one English paper, while the *Scotsman* heralded "football's biggest day", and predicted that the noise produced by the unprecedented crowd would hand a huge advantage to the Scottish team. "Now for the loudest-ever Hampden Howl," said the *Dundee Courier*, adding that the match promised to be "the greatest spectacle of a sporting lifetime".

England fans began to arrive in Glasgow in great numbers from the early hours, "before even the milkmen had started their rounds". They arrived in trains decorated with the colours of St George, and marched into the city through heavy rain. Many wore white roses in their buttonholes. One large group was led through the streets by a man carrying aloft a stuffed lion. Queues formed outside restaurants, with many opening as early as 5am to serve the visitors with breakfasts.

By noon, tens of thousands of Scotland fans were arriving from all around the country, many of them via 150 special trains. After arriving at Glasgow Central, fans took a tram – or a walk – across the Clyde and a south to Mount Florida, where Hampden Park is located. The route was lined with street vendors selling hats and buttonholes, yelling "All the colours!" Vendors also sold match programmes, with a cover featuring a sketch of Scottish and English players battling for a lace-up ball, at a cost of 3d. Also on the streets were hundreds of apprentice shipbuilders and other engineers from the Clyde, who were seeking support during deadlocked industrial action by making a collection and selling strike bulletins to match-goers.

At Hampden, the preparations made to ensure smooth access to the ground appeared to be successful. A correspondent from the *Motherwell Times* noted that he was able to enter the ground an hour before kick-off without standing in a queue. "Hampden Park with its throng of humanity was something to remember," he wrote. "Accents heard ranged from Caithness to Devon, from Lincoln to the Western Isles. Roses, thistles, white emblems and tartan favours made a brave show. Bowler hats, thanks to the official request, were few and far between and the humble hooker-doon had a field day."

"Hooker-doon" caps provided some protection from the rain, which continued to drizzle as fans took their places on the terraces. One chap raised an umbrella, but was swiftly "told all about it", his umbrella having to withstand a barrage of orange peels and "other ammunition". Short shrift was also given to the aeroplanes that circled above Hampden, trailing adverts for Cuticura medicated soap and Bile Beans laxatives. When the planes flew too low, the crowd gave them "the bird" – an early example of the use of the middle-finger gesture.

As kick-off approached, the crowd was treated to a programme of music involving a Scottish pipe band, and community singing led by Elliot Dobie, a popular music hall and radio singer. Spectators joined together to sing *Bonnie Banks o' Loch Lomond*, *Hail Caledonia* and, with a nod to the forthcoming coronation, *God Save the King*. The music and singing continued as the teams entered the field, greeted by "driving rain and ear-splitting cheers".

England came out first, led by captain George Male, to *Heart of Oak* (the official march of the Royal Navy). Next came Scotland, led by Jimmy Simpson, to the more familiar *Scotland the Brave*. Then came a voluminous wall of "shattering noise" – the Hampden Howl. "Starting on the embankment opposite the pavilion," said the *Scotsman*, "the famous cheer spread round the lofty terracing until the huge bowl echoed and re-echoed with the heartening roar that is perhaps the most notable demonstration known of enthusiasm and sporting patriotism."

Male won the toss, and allowed Scotland to kick-off, accompanied by what the *Dundee Courier* called "the mightiest roar in international history". England had the better of the first half, and scored through Freddie Steele. But Scotland improved in the second half, and equalised when Tommy Walker beat the English defence and squared the ball to Frank O'Donnell for a tap-in. The reaction was described by the *Courier* as "absolute bedlam in the most amazing crowd ring in football!" "The Hampden Howl might have been heard in the centre of the city," said the paper. "The Englishmen might well have taken fright."

The Hampden Howl did frighten the English players – a fact confirmed by Stanley Matthews. "If ever a match was won and lost by a roar, it was this one," Matthews later wrote. "I had, of course, heard about this war-cry of the Scottish football fan, but had never previously experienced it. Those who have never heard the roar cannot appreciate the effect it has on a player. It shook me and my colleagues in the England team." With the immense crowd roaring them on, Scotland took the lead through Bob McPhail. And McPhail made it 3-1 in the dying minutes, scoring with a header from a free-kick. The vast majority of the crowd celebrated in a raucous frenzy. "Hampden's first all-ticket international must remain a happy memory," said the *Dundee Courier*.

Newspapers were quick to confirm that the official attendance of 149,407 was a world record. (They also revealed that the revenue generated from ticket sales was £12,373.) The *Motherwell Times*, however, launched a tongue-in-cheek search for "the missing 593". "According to the SFA, 150,000 tickets were issued," said the paper. "According to the official returns, 149,407 people were present. What happened to the 593? We leave the question to engage those of an inquisitive mind."

Whatever the answer to that question, the huge attendance figure was the high watermark of a remarkable period of football fanaticism. A full English league programme was played on the same day, and there was no discernible effect on attendances. A week later, 146,433 turned up at Hampden for the Scottish Cup final between Celtic and Aberdeen.

The timing of the record British attendance coincided with arrival of football on television. The BBC had launched its television service in November 1936. Initial broadcasts were experimental, lasted only an hour or so per day, and could only be received by a small number of viewers in close proximity to the transmitter at Alexandra Palace.

The transmitter could be seen from nearby Highbury, and it was the Arsenal Stadium that hosted television's first football broadcast on 16 September 1937. This wasn't a full match, only a 15-minute demonstration of shooting, dribbling and goalkeeping by members of the Arsenal first team and reserves, introduced by George Allison, the Arsenal manager and popular radio commentator. The BBC's mobile television unit used three cameras - one on the stand "to give a comprehensive view of the ground", and two near the goals "to give close-ups of the play and players, and visual interviews". Newspapers proclaimed that history would be made, which was true, although the actual broadcast was somewhat disappointing.

"Bad light yesterday spoiled the first football television broadcast to be made in this country," said one review. "As a prelude to a rainstorm, the sky grew steadily blacker and the television picture became duller as the broadcast continued." Nevertheless, it did serve as a useful rehearsal for the planned broadcast of full matches. The BBC had already been informed by the Football League that it would not be allowed to broadcast league matches on television, but, in early 1938, the corporation announced that it would broadcast a Wembley international and the FA Cup final.

The first full football match broadcast on TV was England v Scotland on 9 April 1938. Scotland won 1-0, and the scorer of the first goal on television was Tommy Walker. A single commentary for radio and TV broadcasts was provided by George Allison. The broadcast was described as "a triumph", at least from a technical standpoint, with the play clearly visible on screen, although relatively few football fans were able to watch, as reception remained limited to within a 30-mile radius of Alexandra Palace.

Three weeks later, the FA Cup final between Preston North End and Huddersfield Town was also televised. The broadcast began with community singing and the presentation of the teams, and was introduced by Ivan Sharpe, the journalist and former amateur footballer. George Allison commentated on the first half, and former Royal Navy officer Thomas Woodrooffe commentated on the second. Woodrooffe also commentated on extra time, and, with the score 0-0 and just a minute left to play, announced, "If there's a goal scored now, I'll eat my hat!" Preston promptly won a penalty, and George Mutch scored the winner. Woodrooffe subsequently ate a hat-shaped cake in penance.

Other than a loss of sound during the community singing ("Please bear with us – we are doing our best," said an apologetic announcer), the cup final broadcast was a success, with sound and picture described as "perfect". "No football enthusiast today has any excuse for not knowing something about the atmosphere at Wembley on cup final day," said the *Lancashire Evening Post*. "Those who have not seen the North End win the cup have had the game described to them in the press and on the wireless. Some have seen it televised."

By the time the 1939 Cup final between Wolves and Portsmouth was televised, the signal was said to be receivable within an expanded 50-mile radius of Alexandra Palace (although an enthusiast named Arthur Haslehurst claimed to have watched it on his specially-modified TV at his home in Derby, some 100 miles from the transmitter). Some fans within the radius who did not own televisions watched the game in TV dealers' showrooms. At the Griffin Brothers' showroom in Leighton Buzzard around 70 fans crowded around three televisions. "The sets gave excellent pictures, only slightly marred by crackling due to motor cars passing in the High Street," reported the local newspaper. "The general impression gained was that as good a view of the game was obtained as would have been gained from the stands."

Football fandom was all set to enter a brand new era, in which it was possible to watch a game without actually going to the match. Watching football on television was a very different experience to watching in a stadium, and it couldn't properly convey the communal atmosphere and excitement that had helped make the game such a draw. But television offered the opportunity to watch football without travelling long distances or braving bad weather, and it greatly expanded the game's potential audience. Far from being restricted to within a small radius of Alexandra Palace, television would eventually make football accessible to fans around the world. However, in September 1939 the television transmitters were switched off. Britain was once again at war.

10

Much-needed escapism

On Saturday 2 September 1939, Blackpool defeated Wolves 2-1 in front of 20,000 fans to move to the top of the First Division table. On the following day, Sunday 3 September, Britain declared war on Nazi Germany. All places of entertainment and outdoor sporting meetings were closed, and all football was cancelled. "In accordance with the proclamation by His Majesty's Government," the FA announced, "all football under the jurisdiction of the Football Association is entirely suspended until official notice is given to the contrary." There would be no league football for seven long years.

However, within days of the start of the war, and with bombs yet to fall, it was decided at a meeting of the FA and the Football League that a modified form of wartime football could provide some much-needed recreation and boost the morale of anxious citizens. This was football in reduced circumstances, with teams organised into ten regional mini-leagues. The most interesting feature of these wartime leagues was that the players, freed from their contracts, were allowed to make guest appearances for any club of their choosing. For example, Stanley Matthews played for Manchester United, Stan Cullis played for Liverpool, and Joe Mercer played for Aldershot Town.

Despite the involvement of guest players, wartime matches were essentially scratch-standard friendlies, played by makeshift sides that were often cobbled together at the last minute. Attendances were relatively low – in part because gates were restricted for safety reasons. It was forbidden for large crowds to gather in congested areas, and football clubs were required to obtain permission from their local police force before they could open their grounds to spectators. Restrictions were placed on clubs in congested areas (in major towns and cities) that limited attendances to a maximum of 5,000 spectators. This limit was later increased to 8,000, and to 15,000 or 50% of the capacity of the grounds in some areas of the country.

The wartime leagues proved to be popular enough that they continued throughout the war, even after the Luftwaffe commenced its aerial bombardment of Britain. Some of football's most famous grounds were severely damaged by bombs. Old Trafford was virtually demolished in two separate air raids in 1940 and 1941. The ground wouldn't reopen until 1949, and Manchester United were forced to take up temporary residence alongside Manchester City at Maine Road. Sheffield United's Bramall Lane was severely damaged during the Sheffield Blitz in 1940, and Chelsea's Stamford Bridge and Sunderland's Roker Park were also heavily bombed. Birmingham City's St Andrew's ground suffered 20 direct hits, and the grandstand burnt down after a fireman accidentally tried to dampen down a fire with petrol.

Despite all of this, and the terrible toll that was being inflicted away from football, fans still turned up in limit-testing numbers. In April 1941, with bomb sites still smouldering, 8,000 people watched Sheffield Wednesday beat Sheffield United, and 7,500 saw Chelsea beat Arsenal in wartime league games. Then in May, for a wartime international between Scotland and England at Hampden Park, the attendance limit was set at 75,000 (50% of the stadium's capacity), and was a complete sell-out. Thc size of this wartime crowd was all the more remarkable given that Glasgow, and particularly its shipbuilding works along the Clyde, was a key target for Nazi bombers. The match was described by the *Aberdeen Journal* as "ersatz", with play "far below classic standard". But the mass communal experience provided some much-needed relief for beleaguered fans. One reporter wrote that the revived "great Hampden Park roar" emitted by the blitz-defying crowd was "like sweet music in the ears".

A couple of weeks later, more than 60,000 fans attended Hampden to watch a Scottish wartime league cup final between Hearts and Rangers. And, at Wembley, 60,000 watched a wartime cup final between Arsenal and Preston. Tickets for the Wembley final cost one shilling and a penny, the penny being a tax levied on public entertainments to assist the war effort. As had happened during the first world war, football matches served dual functions as fundraising events for wartime charities and as recruitment drives for the armed forces.

Primarily, though, football provided a distraction from the realities of life in wartime Britain, even if the necessarily reduced circumstances meant the quality of entertainment on show was not particularly good. "Wartime football was no substitute for the real thing but it did serve a purpose," wrote Preston and England centre-forward Tom Finney in his autobiography. "Football provided the country with some much-needed escapism and it was thoroughly enjoyable – despite the bombs."

Football eventually emerged from the fog of war into a world that would never be the same. Air raid sirens were silent and gas masks could be set aside, but the conflict had left an indelible mark on all who had lived through it. Loved ones had been killed, homes had been destroyed and unforgettable horrors had been experienced. The country was crippled with war debt, and its citizens were slaves to their ration books. Life in post-war Britain was austere and difficult. Football was just a sport, an amusement, a frivolity. Could there be any place for football in this changed new world?

In January 1946, the Football League announced that the full league programme would be restored for the following season. "The public stood gallantly by us during the war and they shall be repaid for that loyalty as soon as possible," said one administrator. But football couldn't simply pick up where it had left off seven years earlier. Wartime football had been little more than a pantomime, and fans could be forgiven for having become disillusioned with the game. Clubs had been starved of proper income for the duration of the war, and some were in great financial difficulties. Every team in the league needed to be rebuilt, as did many league grounds, and that wouldn't be easy.

Clubs still held pre-war player registrations, but some players had been killed or seriously injured, some remained in military or Essential Works service, and others had simply grown too old during the seven-year gap to resume their football careers. New stars had emerged via the wartime leagues, including young coal miners Nat Lofthouse at Bolton and Jackie Milburn at Newcastle, but there was still a shortage of players. To make matters worse, the Players' Union was threatening a strike, over a rescinded promise to increase the maximum weekly wage following seven years of lost earnings. "Football strikes! What next?" wrote a fan named Arthur Turner in a letter to the *Liverpool Evening Express*. "Suppose the spectators went on strike. What then?"

Many grounds were in a sorry state of disrepair after being requisitioned for the war effort or pummelled by the Luftwaffe, and plenty of rebuilding was required. A shortage of cash and materials meant repairs weren't always easy to come by. Some grounds had been requisitioned for use as physical training centres, ARP (Air Raid Precautions) stations or storage depots, and were now slowly returned to their proper use. Highbury had been requisitioned *and* bombed during the war, and Arsenal had played their wartime matches at White Hart Lane. (It was a returned favour on behalf of Spurs – they had played at Highbury during the first world war.) Many grounds had been stripped of railings and other metal fixtures and fittings in order to assist the war effort, so some clubs welcomed fans back without any gates or turnstiles.

As an appetiser for the full 1946-47 season, the FA sanctioned an FA Cup competition, the first post-war competitive football tournament, which ran from November 1945 through to April 1946. Unusually, rounds prior to the semi-finals were contested over two legs, with the aim of providing additional revenue for cash-strapped clubs. Huge crowds of football-starved fans attended many ties, and this deluge of interest in the game's return – combined with the unsuitability of many war-damaged and neglected grounds – led to one of British football's worst-ever disasters. At a sixth round tie between Bolton Wanderers and Stoke City on 9 March 1946 up to 80,000 fans were crammed into Burnden Park, leading to a crush that killed 33 people.

The details of the Burnden Park disaster are horrific, and many of them are chillingly similar to those of another football disaster that would occur 43 years later. The ground's supposed capacity was 69,500, but alterations and disrepair caused by years of wartime requisition meant that it could not hold anywhere near that number of people. The biggest attendance the ground had been able to accommodate since the war had been 43,000. The Burnden Stand was out of commission as it was still being used as a Ministry of Supply storage depot, and – most crucially – the turnstiles that provided access to the Railway End embankment terrace at the Burnden Stand side of the ground were closed. This meant the embankment terrace, which held more than 28,000 people, could only be accessed via turnstiles at the congested Manchester Road side.

The match was due to kick-off at 3pm, but the ground was "fairly well filled" an hour before that. A reporter from the *Lancashire Evening Post*, attending the match as a spectator, wrote that at 2.15pm "there was tremendous confusion inside and outside the ground". Crowds at the turnstiles were so tightly packed that the reporter was swept against his will into the ground and onto the embankment terrace, which was already rammed full. "Individual movement was impossible," he wrote. "I could not even drop a cigarette end to the ground."

The gates were eventually closed at 2.45pm, with around 65,000 fans having gone through the turnstiles, and more than 15,000 locked outside. Thousands of those who were locked out, according to a police statement, realised that they would not get to see the match and went home. Others gained entry via a gate that was opened from the inside by people attempting to escape the crush. And some climbed over onto the adjacent railway line, then climbed over fences into the ground and onto the embankment terrace, which was already dangerously overcrowded.

Then, at around the kick-off time of 3pm, two of the terrace's steel crush barriers collapsed, causing the crowd to surge forward over scores of trapped fans. "When the crowd began to move forward, I felt as if my ribs were being crushed and I gradually lost consciousness," said witness Christopher Stone. "When I recovered I found myself being carried over piles of people about four deep."

"I was lifted off my feet and flung onto the heads of those in front," said another (unnamed) witness. "I saw people on the ground and others sweeping over them."

"Somewhere under the feet of the crowd were the unfortunate victims," recalled the *Lancashire Evening Post* reporter. "Life must have been crushed from most of them within a minute."

Thirty-three people died in the crush, mostly of asphyxiation, and around 500 were injured. The disaster could have been even worse had the wooden fences around the pitch not been quickly pulled down with the assistance of police and St John Ambulance volunteers, allowing fans to spill out onto the playing field. Remarkably, the match continued for around 15 minutes, until a police inspector walked onto the pitch and asked the referee to halt play. But, as at the Ibrox disaster 44 years earlier, it was felt that abandoning the game might have made the situation even more dangerous. The match was suspended for 26 minutes while the casualties were removed. It then resumed and was played to a conclusion.

Many of those in attendance were unaware there had been fatalities. That evening, the *Lancashire Evening Post*'s headline was "Crowd Mishap Delays Cup-tie at Bolton". Buried within a report on the match, the paper said play had been temporarily halted amid "amazing scenes" of spectators wandering onto the pitch and crowding into the goalmouths. Although "the hubbub was hushed" when it was realised that people had been hurt, the paper reported that the crowd cheered the resumption of the game, even as casualties were being loaded into ambulances. There was no further indication at this time of the scale of the disaster.

That had changed by the following morning, when newspapers confirmed that 33 people had died in "the worst football crowd tragedy in British history". Blame was very quickly placed on fans who had "broken in" to the ground after the gates had been closed. Bolton's Chief Constable, WJ Howard, claimed that 15,000 fans had overwhelmed police in a rush to break down fences.

In the *Bolton Evening News*, football columnist Olympian wrote of "the increasing violence that great crowds of people are ready to use nowadays". "The crowd is a lower organism than the individual, and in many ways the most frightening aspect of all this business is the sub-human vitality that seems to have possessed Saturday's concourse," he pontificated. "Apart from illegal breaking and entering, they were guilty of wilful destruction of property in their frenzy to catch a glimpse of the match... Obviously, if the public interests are to be the first consideration, then it is unsafe to let such people loose. A stricter control will have to be organised to protect the community as a whole."

Olympian should perhaps have examined his own role in creating the circumstances that led to the disaster. Three days before the match, and with all tickets already sold, he had written a column under the heading "Plenty of Room for Spectators without Tickets", and had stated that "most of the ground" would be available for fans turning up on the day to pay at the turnstiles.

An inquiry was launched two days after the disaster, led by lawyer Moelwyn Hughes, and its findings were published in early July. The inquiry found that the main causes of the disaster were the unanticipated size of the crowd and the unsuitability of the ground. Too many fans were admitted to the embankment terrace, exceeding safety limits, and the action taken to control admission was insufficient. If the gates had been closed ten minutes earlier, the inquiry stated, the disaster would not have occurred. The fans, including those who had allegedly broken in to the ground, were exonerated. Unauthorised entry was not a major factor in causing the disaster, and the actions of fans who had gained entry to the ground after the gates were closed were largely "irrelevant".

The inquiry recommended that all football grounds should be licenced by their local authorities, and should be expertly surveyed to ensure their safety and to determine their capacities. New legislation would make it an offence to exceed those capacities. Grounds should install "mechanical means" to accurately count admissions, allowing gates to be closed when capacities were reached, and fans should be directed to other parts of the grounds, or "peaceably dispersed". (English football's first "electronically operated indicator system", which monitored crowd numbers admitted at each section of the ground, was installed at Burnden Park in 1950.) Compliance with the recommendations would cost money, said Moelwyn Hughes in his inquiry report, and would mean a drop in attendances for many clubs. However, Hughes said clubs would willingly pay the money, and would welcome measures that increased public safety. Otherwise, he warned, "the disaster at Bolton might easily be repeated at 20 or 30 other grounds".

There would, of course, be further football disasters, but the recommendations of the Burnden Park disaster inquiry most likely prevented several others. Association football was now more than 80 years old, and was showing its age. Many of its grounds were relics of the Victorian era, and hadn't been improved since the first flushes of football's popularity. Relatively little consideration had been given to the safety of football fans. The response to the increase in the number of fans attending matches had generally been to endeavour to pack as many of them as possible into decrepit grounds that had perhaps not had so much as a lick of paint in half a century. It was not entirely a coincidence that the Burnden Park disaster occurred upon the resumption of football after the war. The wartime dereliction of grounds – and a post-war rush to make up for lost gate money – no doubt contributed to the tragedy. It served as an important reminder that football could not continue as it had before the war, and that a new start was required for a new era. In many ways, this new post-war era would come to be the golden age of the football fan.

When league football resumed in August 1946, fans returned in unprecedented numbers. In an effort to welcome fans back to matches, the League had ordered that standard admission prices should be reduced. However, some clubs limited the number of "standard" admissions that were available and increased other admission prices in order to avoid losing gate money. Fans complained, but still turned up in greater numbers than ever before. Despite torrential rain, almost a million people attended the 43 opening day matches. Five of the 11 First Division matches attracted 50,000-plus gates. The biggest opening day crowd was at Stamford Bridge, where 61,484 saw Chelsea defeat Bolton. "If the sun did not welcome footballers in the traditional manner," reported the *Times*, "enthusiasm for this new and most important of seasons was greater than ever."

The long gap between league seasons meant some fans had forgotten which teams were in which division. The likes of Grimsby and Brentford were in the First Division, while Manchester City and Spurs were in the Second. As the *Times* noted: "Nobody could be expected to remember that sort of thing for seven years, and the rediscovery involved several mild shocks." Opening day match programmes from around the country showed unfamiliar line-ups containing new and unknown names. Widespread team reconstruction would lead to an uneven and unpredictable season. Reigning champions Everton would finish in mid-table, Arsenal would slide into the bottom half, and unfancied pre-war strugglers Manchester United and Liverpool would end up challenging for the title.

High attendances continued throughout the season, despite the arrival of a brutally cold winter that decimated the fixture list and extended the season by eight weeks into mid-June. The total Football League attendance figure for 1946-47 was 35.6m, substantially higher than the pre-war total for 1938-39 of 27m. Second Division Newcastle were the best-supported side of 1946-47. "Newcastle could probably fill their ground whatever price they cared to charge for admission," remarked one commentator, "and Liverpool could do so if they were playing the blind school at water polo." Liverpool eventually won the First Division by a single point. But, in the end, match results and league standings almost didn't matter. The most important thing was that football was back.

11

Rosettes and rattles

The 1950 FA Cup final, between Liverpool and Arsenal, was among the most colourful of a black and white era. The match, at Wembley, was a 100,000 all-ticket sell-out, with 40,000 fans expected from Merseyside, a similar number from North London, plus thousands of neutrals from all over England and beyond. But what was particularly notable about the crowd for this first 1950s cup final was not its size but its vivid display of support.

The traditional dark suits and overcoats that had been worn by generations of previous fans were now accompanied or adorned with colourful hats, scarves, rosettes, ribbons and other football "favours". London was a sea of red and white, with tens of thousands of fans displaying their team colours. (Both Liverpool and Arsenal usually wore red shirts and white shorts, although for this particular final both teams wore change kits – white shirts and black shorts for Liverpool, and yellow shirts and white shorts for Arsenal.)

It was quite a spectacle, and drew plenty of media coverage. Under the headline "Rosettes and rattles", one newspaper described the fans as "bursting with confidence and good cheer, wearing their team colours in rosettes of all sizes, their carriages and coaches be-ribboned, and armed with rattles, bells and trumpets". Special attention was paid to fans who had made an extra effort to stand out. One particular Liverpool fan, said to be unsatisfied with the normal-sized rosettes worn by his companions, wore a pair of foot-wide "monster rosettes" pinned to each side of his coat.

Rosettes had been around since the turn of the century, initially resembling a relatively elaborate paper rose before evolving into a flat circular badge during the 1950s. They were sold by street hawkers around football grounds. The hawkers, competing with programme sellers and newspaper vendors, would display their wares on a board and yell, "Buy a favour?"

Yorkshire Post columnist Eric Stanger wrote about the increased colour and noise of football crowds, describing "colours flying, rattles racketing in the air, bugles blowing, klaxons hooting, and even saucepan lids clashing together – anything to make a din". Supporters, he wrote, wore "rosettes as big as tea plates, fancy hats, and garments like those in which the Pied Piper astonished the town fathers of Hamelin". There had not been this "parading of partisanship" before the war. "Rosettes by the thousand, yes, and the rattles, but not the fancy hats, berets, scarves with players' initials embroidered on, and the complete coloured dress we see today." Stanger put the spread of the scarf and beret down to the "feminine influx" of young girls, who he said jostled and jockeyed with men on the terraces, and had contributed greatly to rising attendances in this burgeoning golden age.

For the 1950 final, many Liverpool fans wore coloured scarves – the most enduring of football favours. One fan wore a "gaudily-painted" red and white bowler hat decorated with the names of the Liverpool players. ("The men who are going to win the cup today," he confidently told a reporter.) Other fans wore various combinations of homemade bonnets, striped bow-ties, embroidered jackets, and customised boots, all illustrating their support for their team. But, according to one report, no fan could match a young boy who had "gone to the extent" of wearing a "vivid" red football shirt. Replica shirts didn't really exist in 1950, although it was possible to buy football jerseys in the colours of favourite teams – often from the same outfitters that supplied the players.

Unfortunately, all manner of football favours were soaked by heavy rain, which fell throughout the day of the final. Liverpool fans who had arrived in London in the morning sheltered in cafes and huddled in doorways. Some visited St Paul's Cathedral and the National Gallery, and others took bus rides "just to keep dry". Red and white scarves were spotted all around the city, and Merseyside accents could be heard "echoing around the streets". Another sound that filled the air ahead of the final was the incessant clacking of football rattles. Thousands of fans twirled painted wooden rattles, and some waved one in each hand. There were songs and shouts *("Play up, the Arsenal!")*, too, but the loud clatter of rattles could drown out all other sounds.

Football rattles have an unusual provenance, having evolved from rook-scarers, which were twirled by farmers to protect crops. Rattles were subsequently used as alarm signals by the police (before being replaced with the police whistle in the 1880s), and to drum up business at coconut shy stalls and other fairground attractions. They were also issued to troops during the first world war to imitate machine gun fire. These ear-piercing "machine gun" rattles were brought home from the war and taken to football matches, before being banned in the early 1920s because they frightened the players.

Great interest in the sold-out cup final brought out an unprecedented number of ticket touts, who swarmed around railway and bus stations, and surrounded arriving coaches in the hope of snapping up spare tickets, accosting fans from the moment they set foot on London's pavements. The touts offered more than ten times face value, offering 40 shillings for standard three shilling terrace tickets, and up to £10 for the best seats in the house. "Clearly they had clients willing to pay much more than those amounts waiting," noted one newspaper reporter. "Some people were prepared to pay fantastic prices for tickets to get into the match at all costs."

Touts didn't just offer cash. Under the headline "Nylons Offered for Tickets", it was reported that, in a Euston cafe, a "black marketeer" had attempted to obtain tickets by producing a box of American tights. "Another temptingly opened a suitcase full of bottles of Scotch whisky," said the report. Liverpool fans leaving the National Gallery were offered boxes of cigarettes for their tickets. But, to the disappointment of the touts, "they found very few people willing to sell".

One group of entrepreneurs doing a bustling trade were hawkers selling plastic headscarves and rain hoods. Some fans sheltered under red and white umbrellas, and others made do with soggy newspapers on their heads. But the clear plastic headscarves, tied under chins, and the dark rain hoods, buttoned around necks, were visible all over Wembley as fans took their positions. One of the reasons this disposable headgear was such a good seller was that fewer football fans were wearing hats. A "hat census" conducted in 1947 by a men's outfitters found that almost half of all football fans at a particular match were "hatless". Among those who did wear hats, soft-brimmed hats or caps were most popular. Bowler hats had clearly fallen out of favour – the census counted only five bowlers among the entire crowd, "all worn by middle-aged men". Certainly the emerging trend was to eschew headgear, as the census found that 99% of "younger" fans did not wear hats. "According to the outfitters," remarked one newspaper, "that is nothing to throw your hat up about!"

The 1950 cup final has become known as the Compton final, as Arsenal had Dennis and Leslie Compton in their side, although it was Ray Lewis who scored once in each half to give the Gunners a 2-0 win. Fans waved handkerchiefs, programmes and newspapers in the air, in what the Movietone News report called a "fearful state of frenzy". Curiously, the Movietone announcer chose to mimic supporters' voices during his commentary. A cap-wearing fan pictured licking his lips was made to say, *"Yes sir, it's thirsty work this watching."* And after Arsenal scored their second goal, the announcer had a rattle-bearing fan in a Liverpool hat say, *"Proper terrible, isn't it? Well fancy that, would you believe it?"*

The match was broadcast live on BBC television with commentary from Raymond Glendenning, a former chartered accountant and *Children's Hour* presenter. It was the first cup final to be televised outside of London and the south east, although there were still only a minority of households that had televisions. Many viewers watched it at communal gatherings, in clubs and shops and factory canteens. Some watched in pubs, which were given special permission to open during the afternoon. 500 people watched the match on TVs at Kensington Town Hall in West London, and 1,200 watched it on a big screen at the Odeon cinema in Penge in South East London – an experimental screening for radio and television experts and enthusiasts.

Even taking into account such communal gatherings, it's likely that fewer fans watched the match on television than watched it at Wembley. Nevertheless, one newspaper made a bold prediction: "Within the next few years, as television reaches out all over England and becomes normal entertainment in every home, it is estimated that something approaching 20 million will be able to watch the cup final from the comfort of their armchairs."

That prediction would not be too far off the mark, although it was not football but the coronation of Elizabeth II in 1953 that really drove the mass-adoption of television across Britain. After that, millions could watch the cup final, although league matches remained off-limits to the TV cameras. The rise of television would eventually have an effect of football attendances, even if there wasn't much football on the schedules. TV was an alternative form of entertainment, and some fans would prefer to stay at home and watch *Come Dancing* or *Muffin the Mule* rather than go out to see a match.

Football's post-war golden age saw attendances peak at an all-time high, then gradually decline. The aggregate attendance for Football League games in the 1948-49 season was 41,271,424 – an increase of more than a million compared to the previous season. On one particular match day, 16 October 1948, a total of 1,167,446 people had attended the 44 league games, which was a football record. The average attendance in the First Division in the 1948-49 season was 38,792, the highest in history, and an average that has never quite been topped, even in the Premier League era. The average attendance across all four divisions was 22,318, another all-time record that has never been beaten. (By comparison, the average attendance in 2015-16 in the Premier League was 36,452, and across all four divisions it was 14,768.) Despite the growing distraction of television, attendances remained high into the early 1950s, as football fans gained a public profile that made them hard to ignore and, inevitably, provoked some resentment.

Writing in his "Speaking Frankly" column in the *Sunderland Echo* in 1950, Frank Roffe called football fans "soccer-suckers" who "inflict themselves on we sane people". "Suggest to them they look a bit odd with rosettes, rattles and red noses as they bawl blithely through the streets, and they look at you as if you were a madman with a head as empty as a football," wrote Roffe. He marvelled at fans who would "grouse bitterly" if it rained while they were at work during the week, but were happy to be "sodden victims of mass hysteria" if it rained during a match on Saturday afternoons. And he suggested that the time and money spent on football would be better spent "taking the kids into the country for a day", otherwise the kids would grow up "just like father" as slaves to football.

Having criticised football fans, Roffe wrote that he expected to be inundated with letters to the editor, and several responses were published in the following days, although not all of them disagreed with his point of view. "Grateful thanks to Frank Roffe," wrote a correspondent identified as "Common Sense". "If only these men who grin, shout and wave their hands in ecstasy like little children because a big dirty ball happens to find its way between the goalposts saw themselves as they really are!"

"May I congratulate Frank Roffe," wrote WB Greener. "In condemning the stupidity of the football-crazy thousands he did a very brave thing. To my mind the majority of people who go to big football matches do not go out of a pure love of the sport and a keen desire to see the best team win, but merely to be stimulated by the mass hysteria which overcomes the crowd during the time of play." Football, wrote Greener, was "one of the veritable evils of our time".

In the following week, though, correspondent Peter Aslett dismissed this stance as "facetious poppycock". "Football as an evil exists only in the minds of some irresponsible prudes who spend their entire lives in a moral fog," wrote Aslett. "Every red-blooded person loves a sport of some kind, and football easily outstrips all others in the number of its followers." Responding to Greener's comment about "mass hysteria", Aslett wrote, "Would he prefer the kind of mass hysteria which existed in Germany before the war? I say this merely to show that if every nation could become as interested in sport as we Britons are in our football the world would be a far more comfortable place to live in."

What Peter Aslett possibly didn't realise was that many nations were just as interested in sport and in football as Britain, and that fact would be highlighted during the 1950 World Cup finals in Brazil. Once again, British media coverage of the international tournament was sparse, despite the participation, for the first time, of England. (Scotland had also "qualified" for the tournament by virtue of finishing second in the British Home Championships, but the Scottish FA declined to participate.) Newspapers relied upon short news agency dispatches, and radio provided only brief reports of England's matches, presented by Charles Buchan, the former England centre-forward. There was no television coverage.

After England's 0-1 defeat to the USA in Belo Horizonte, the *Times* published a short Reuters report that called the result a "sensation" and described how at the final whistle the 20,000-strong crowd went "wild with enthusiasm", with many fans rushing from the stands to congratulate the American players and carry them shoulder-high from the pitch, while others waved burning pieces of paper in celebration. Media interest waned further following England's elimination. The *Times* dedicated only seven lines and fewer than 50 words to the deciding match of the tournament – effectively the World Cup final – between Uruguay and Brazil.

The match was played on 16 July 1950 at Rio's newly-built Maracanã stadium, the design of which incorporated a moat around the pitch "to protect players from crowds". The Maracanã had surpassed Hampden Park to become the biggest football ground in the world, and had also beaten Hampden's 149,407 attendance world record after 152,722 fans had paid to see Brazil defeat Spain in the previous round. And that record was beaten again in the final, when 173,850 saw Brazil lose to Uruguay. It was estimated that the actual attendance for the decisive final game, taking into account officials, journalists, police, and ticketless fans, could have been as high as 200,000. But it is the official figure of 173,850 that is recognised by Guinness as the world record, while Hampden's 149,407 remains the British and European record.

Tickets for the final match were sold from one of Rio's biggest department stores, and were gone within a few hours, with touts buying them in large blocks. Queues of fans who had missed out became enraged and began to riot, smashing windows and looting the store. This was despite the fact that, due to the huge demand, control of ticket sales had been taken over by Rio's police. The police did subsequently "swoop" on touts and seize back 14,000 tickets, which were resold at face value to fans.

Brazil were firm favourites to win, and it was reported that their fans, some of whom had written and recorded a "victory samba", "had not entertained a thought of defeat". Brazilian newspaper *O Mundo* had proclaimed Brazil as world champions on the morning before the match was played. And Brazil did take the lead early in the second half, only for Uruguay to hit back with an equaliser and then silence the crowd with a winner, scored by Alcides Ghiggia in the 79th minute.

The result, according to newspaper reports, "left the world record crowd of nearly 200,000 Brazilian fans completely dumbfounded and bewildered". Many fans openly wept, while others were "silent and depressed". Some fainted, and there were several cases of "fits and hysteria". The Maracanã's medical officer said that 169 fans required treatment in the stadium, and six were taken to hospital, three of whom were in critical condition. Away from the ground, it was reported that at least one man – and possibly as many as three – had died from shock while listening to the match on the radio. Overall, according to the *New York Times*, eight fans died during or after the match.

The fact that the *New York Times* gave more coverage than the London *Times* to the 1950 World Cup was perhaps due to the US team's notable victory over England, although North America remained relatively immune to the contagion of football fandom that had spread over South America and Europe. However, in 1951, the American photographic news magazine *Life* published a major feature on British football, which it called "the great spectator sport".

"Crowds are football's most overwhelming feature," said the magazine. "In Great Britain some two million people, carrying fish and chips and thermos jugs, flock into stadiums each week." Alongside some wonderfully evocative photographs showing crowds of fans passing fog-draped pubs, steel mills and shipyards, the magazine emphasised the working-class appeal of the game, and explained how football's popularity stretched well beyond those who filled its grounds, stating that one in three Britons was a "football pools addict".

The popularity of football pools had been highlighted by a 1951 government report into gambling, which stated that around 14 million people took part in football pools betting, staking £4 to £5 each per year. "Even those who do not win a prize have the satisfaction of knowing that at least they have forecast some of the matches correctly," said the report. Inevitably, given the popularity of football pools, there were calls for it to be banned. But, rather than finding it to be a danger, the report found that the amusement obtained from pools was "as innocent as the amusement to be found in solving chess problems or crossword puzzles".

Football pools had been popularised by Liverpool bookmaker Littlewoods, which was founded in 1923 by wireless telegraph operator John Moores. "Littlewood's Football Pool", as it was originally called, spread in popularity across Liverpool and Manchester, and then around the country. By the early 1930s Moores was a millionaire. Rivals inevitably emerged, but Littlewoods, "the biggest and safest pool in England", remained top dog. Moores went on to set up the Littlewoods mail order and department stores, and by 1950 had handed over the running of the pools business to his brother, Cecil. By then, the company had 10,000 employees, many of whom were tasked with manually checking the seven or eight million coupons that were submitted each week. During the 1950-51 season, the biggest Littlewoods pools winner, who requested to remain anonymous, won £104,000.

Another football-related pursuit that began to boom in the 1950s was programme collecting. Previous generations of fans had collected football cards, and also player autographs. But collecting match programmes was relatively new, with requests and offers beginning to appear in exchange and mart columns of sports newspapers. "You may think your club programme modest value for twopence or threepence, but to some boy it is a pearl beyond price," wrote Eric Stanger in the *Yorkshire Post*. "It explains why on coming away from several games this season I have been sought out by boys with the request, 'Programme mister, please?'" The sports exchange and mart columns also allowed the swapping of other items. Stanger highlighted the example of one young boy who was offering a stack of comics and penny dreadfuls in exchange for "one full-sized football rattle".

An essential football purchase for boys of all ages was *Charles Buchan's Football Monthly*, a heavily-illustrated magazine published and edited by the former Sunderland, Arsenal and England footballer, who had become a popular journalist and commentator. The first issue was published in September 1951, and featured a full-colour image of Stanley Matthews on the cover. Inside Buchan announced, "Our object is to provide a publication that will be worthy of our national game and the grand sportsmen who play and watch it." Alongside full-page photos of star players and teams, the first issue included articles by contributors as diverse as Raich Carter, JB Priestley and the Marquess of Londonderry. There were cartoons, a pools column and a readers' letters page.

Buchan intended his *Football Monthly* to fill a gap in the market for an intelligently-written football publication that he believed had existed since the closure of *Athletic News* some

20 years earlier. According to Buchan, football, unlike other sports, had not been the subject of much good literature, although he noted that the likes of JB Priestley and Arnold Bennett had included football in their novels. "Surely the game is popular enough to be worthy of the attention of our leading writers," Buchan reasoned.

The JB Priestley piece included in the first issue of *Football Monthly* was a reprint of a wonderfully evocative description of the football fan experience, from the 1929 novel *The Good Companions*. Priestley wrote about a match between the fictional Bruddersford United and non-fictional Bolton Wanderers, and presented a romantic vision of the communal escapism provided by football in exchange for a hard-earned shilling. That shilling, Priestley said, offered spectators conflict and art, turned them into critics and partisans, and made them members of a new community, "all brothers together for an hour and a half".

"Not only had you escaped from the clanking machinery of this lesser life," wrote Priestley, "but you had escaped with most of your mates and your neighbours, with half the town, and there you were, cheering together, thumping one another on the shoulders, swopping judgements like lords of the earth, having pushed your way through a turnstile into another and altogether more splendid kind of life."

Among the advertisements in the first *Football Monthly* was one for the National Federation of Football Supporters Clubs, which in 1951 was protesting a proposed rise in the Football League's minimum admission charge from 1s 3d to 1s 6d. "Supporters receive scant respect and consideration for their loyalty," said Federation secretary Leslie Davis. "Any attempt to raise the prices of admission should be opposed." In the *Yorkshire Post*, Eric Stanger wrote that an increase in the admission charge could have a negative effect on attendances. "The Football League clubs would do well to think things over seriously," he wrote. "There is such a thing as killing the goose which lays their golden eggs."

But the minimum admission charge was raised to 1s 6d in 1951, and then to 1s 9d in 1953, and 2s in 1955. The latter raise was proposed by West Bromwich Albion, and supported by the majority of clubs, although Sunderland opposed it, saying it was "not the way to attract people to the game, particularly with the severe competition coming from broadcasting and television". In a Football League meeting in June 1955 it was revealed that the aggregate attendance for the 1954-55 season was just over 34 million, a drop of more than two million compared to the previous season – and a drop of seven million compared to the record-breaking season of 1948-49.

Still, despite prices rises and the distraction of television, people continued to go to football in big numbers, with their rattles and scarves and rosettes. But the evident enthusiasm of these golden age fans did not always translate into positive support, and could just as easily generate a barrage of criticism. "There is a hardening of that core of people who attend football matches and can't seem to enjoy themselves unless they're yelling at the tops of their voices rotten lousy abuse," observed football official Sid Burgess. Naturally, much of this "rotten lousy abuse" was directed at the referee.

"It is an amazing game, football," wrote World Cup ref Arthur Ellis in 1954. "A man leaves his home on a Saturday afternoon to enjoy 90 minutes of the greatest game on earth. When he leaves home he is a happy family man, but once he gets on a terrace at the match he becomes a raging fanatic." Ellis was naturally sore about the levels of criticism targeted at the "chap with the whistle", by enthusiasts who believed they knew the rules better than the referee. "I hate to say this," wrote Ellis, "but I think the vast majority of football spectators are very ignorant of the laws of the game."

Another vocal critic of the attitudes of some football fans

was Bobby Ancell, the manager of Berwick Rangers, the English team that was admitted into the Scottish League in 1951. Ancell said the "awful bias" of fans created an "atmosphere of viciousness". Instead, he said, "spectators should look on football as an art and a spectacle of beauty." Ancell was highlighting the aesthetic appeal of football, which was appreciated by many supporters. Football had evolved from a rough and tumble scuffle into a stylish and graceful contest. It had become "the beautiful game".

In 1952, writing in the *Sunday Times*, the author HE Bates explained his thinking that "football is the most beautiful game in the world". "I think we sometimes forget, or take for granted, the unique beauty of this game," he wrote. "It is the only game in the world played with the feet. In its simplicity it makes a mockery of all the complicated paraphernalia of golf, or even the sly and contradictory subtleties of cricket."

For many fans, the aesthetic qualities of a good football match could rival those of any work of art. Long passes, clean shots, leaping headers and acrobatic overhead kicks were visually pleasing, as was the shifting movement of the teams' formations across the chalk and limestone patterns of the green pitch. The grassy pitch itself, despite mud and bare patches, was a refreshingly verdant oasis in what was often a grey industrial town.

The author Barry Hines would later write about the aesthetic appeal of the markings on a football pitch. "It is as pleasing to the eye as the doubles in dominoes," wrote Hines. "I'm surprised no artist has painted a football pitch yet, just the white lines on a green background. Hanging in a gallery, nothing else would get a look in. There would be a crowd round it all day long waiting for the teams to come out."

The post-war golden age of vibrant football fandom was one of the beautiful game's most colourful periods. But declining attendances indicated that this era of rattles and rosettes would not last. It was effectively ended by an incident that reminded that football was only a game, albeit a game that mattered to very many people. On 6 February 1958, British European Airways flight 609, the Lord Burghley, crashed on take-off at Munich-Riem Airport. On board were six crew and 38 passengers, including the Manchester United team who were on their way home from Belgrade after beating Red Star in a European Cup tie.

The plane had landed in Munich to refuel, but struggled to take off in wintry conditions and, on the third attempt, skidded on the snowy runway, crashed, and caught fire. Twenty people died at the scene, and three more died in hospital. Among the dead were eight Manchester United players, three members of staff, eight journalists, one supporter and a travel agent. Manager Matt Busby survived, although he was not expected to, and had been read his last rites. Two other "Busby Babes" were so badly injured that they never played again.

Manchester United were so terribly damaged by the tragedy that it was speculated that the club might have to fold, but chairman Harold Harman dismissed such thoughts, saying the club would carry on, as it had "a duty to the public and a duty to football".

On the following Saturday, ahead of kick-off at League matches around the country, flags were at half-mast, players wore black armbands, reporters wore black ties, and fans and players stood and sang *Abide With Me*, then observed a two-minute silence – "a symbolic hush". In a report of the match between Tottenham Hotspur and Manchester City at a rain-lashed White Hart Lane, a *Times* staff reporter wrote that the crowd "stood in reflective silence, in a stillness broken only by the hum of newsreel cameras, and thought of those familiar figures who are now, suddenly and tragically, lost to the game".

This was not the first period of silence observed before football matches. A minute's silence was observed in Scotland and two minutes' were observed in England following the R101 disaster in October 1930, in which 48 people were killed when the British airship R101 crashed on its maiden voyage in France. And there were silences in January 1936 and February 1952 following the deaths of George V and George VI. But organised silences were not common. There had been no call for a silence to be observed following the Burnden Park disaster in 1946, for example, nor following the Superga disaster in 1949, when the entire Torino team were killed in a plane crash.

The Munich disaster, however, had a particular resonance with the British public, perhaps due to the unprecedented popularity of football, or due to the fact that so many football fans felt they knew the popular players of one of England's biggest clubs. Manchester United, and football itself, would recover, but Munich represented the end of an era, the end of the golden age.

12

Some people are on the pitch

"Welcome to *Match of the Day*, the first of a weekly series coming to you every Saturday on BBC2." Those were the opening words from Kenneth Wolstenholme on the first edition of TV's longest-running football show, broadcast at 6.30pm on 22 August 1964, the opening day of the 1964-65 season. Billed as "the best of league football", early editions provided highlights from one of the First Division's top games.

As commentator Wolstenholme delivered his introduction from Liverpool's Anfield ground, a pop song rang out in the background: "*She loves you, yeah, yeah, yeah...*" "As you can hear," said Wolstenholme, "we're in Beatleville for this Liverpool versus Arsenal match." Britain in the 1960s was experiencing something of a cultural revolution, with an explosion of interest in music, fashion and celebrity. This was the decade football went pop.

Match of the Day's original opening titles focused entirely on fans rather than players, and offered a glimpse into the changing makeup of the football crowd as the sixties began to swing. The flat-capped fan in his Saturday suit was still in attendance, but so too were an increasing number of fans with burgeoning Beatles-style mop-tops. Some wore shirts with skinny ties, under Harrington jackets or parkas. There were children in woollen hats with scarves wrapped around their necks, and women in headscarves and rollers – preparing their hair for a Saturday night out. Fans were seen queuing at turnstiles, smoking cigarettes and swigging from beer bottles, and waving and cheering in anticipation of the big match.

The game featured on the first *Match of the Day* was something of a classic. "I'd call it the Match of the Century, I don't know about Match of the Day," said Wolstenholme. Bill Shankly's Liverpool took a 2-0 lead, but Arsenal scored twice within a minute to draw level. A black cat caused great amusement among fans and viewers by running out of the stands and across the pitch. Then, in the 87th minute, Liverpool's Gordon Wallace hit a 25-yard deflected winner in front of a leaping and jubilant Kop end.

"The Kop's noise was as loud and ear-splitting as ever," wrote Jack Rowe in the *Liverpool Daily Post*, noting that the crowd was so noisy during the game that the players could not always hear the referee's whistle. The first *Match of the Day* was seen by only around 20,000 people on TV (compared to the 47,620 who saw the match at Anfield) as BBC2 was only available to viewers in London with relatively advanced "dual standard" TV sets. The show would soon move to BBC1, and become a football institution beloved of fans for generations.

Another iconic BBC TV show that debuted in 1964 was *Top of the Pops*. Broadcast from Manchester that January, the first edition featured the Rolling Stones, Dusty Springfield, the Hollies, the Dave Clark Five and – of course – the Beatles. The Fab Four performed *I Want to Hold Your Hand*. It was their fifth hit single, and their third UK number one. In 1964, the Beatles would release three more number one singles, plus two number one albums. They'd also appear on the *Ed Sullivan Show* and conquer the US, and star in *A Hard Day's Night* – a movie that neatly illustrated the all-screaming fan-frenzied phenomenon that was Beatlemania.

This type of hysterical music fandom was not entirely new – the Hungarian composer and pianist Franz Liszt had been the subject of "Lisztomania" more than a hundred years earlier, and more recently Frank Sinatra and Elvis Presley had attracted their fair share of rabid followers. But the mania that surrounded the Beatles, the Rolling Stones and other 60s groups did represent the arrival of a new fan culture. It was a consuming obsession that influenced how fans spent their free time and money, what they talked about, and how they dressed. Music fans became every bit as visible in society and in the media as football fans.

Being a music fan was not quite the same as being a football fan. It was entirely possible to be a fan of both the Beatles and the Rolling Stones, in a way that it wasn't possible to support both Liverpool and Manchester United. But it was possible to be a Rolling Stones fan and a Liverpool supporter, or a fan of the Beatles and Manchester United's "pop star footballer" George Best. In 1965, after Best scored two goals in a European Cup match against Benfica, Portuguese newspapers called him *"o quinto Beatle"*, "the fifth Beatle".

Best was featured as a pin-up in teenage magazines alongside Paul McCartney and Mick Jagger, and was chased by screaming girls in miniskirts, as his popular appeal spilled out of football grounds and into mainstream public consciousness. If not quite British football's first celebrity, Best was certainly its first superstar. Pop music was a major catalyst for change on the football terraces, affecting fans' attitudes, fashions and songs. And nowhere was the effect of this combination of music and football fandom more evident than on Liverpool's Kop, where pop music became part of the matchday experience.

Singing was already popular at football matches, as it was in the pub, at church and at other communal gatherings. Fans would sing patriotic songs, favourite hymns and other popular songs as a form of pre-match entertainment. Several clubs had specific fan anthems that were heartily sung before games. Portsmouth fans had been singing *The Pompey Chimes ("Play up Pompey, Pompey play up")* since the 1890s, and Norwich fans had been singing *On the Ball, City ("Kick it off,*

Throw it in, Have a little scrimmage...") since the early 1900s. West Ham's *I'm Forever Blowing Bubbles* had been adopted from the music halls during the 1920s, and Newcastle's *Blaydon Races* was another music hall number, dating back to the Victorian era.

After the pre-match singalongs, as games got underway, the songs were replaced by noisy choruses of cheers, boos and hoots. *"Play up!" "Lay him out!" "Foul!"* The more choreographed type of singing and chanting that modern football fans would recognise arrived via South America. During the 1962 World Cup, Brazil beat England 3-1 while the Brazilian fans sang and clapped: *"Bra-zil! Cha-cha-cha! Bra-zil! Cha-cha-cha!"* In the following season, Liverpool fans, who had most likely heard the Brazil song on television, began to chant: "*Liv-er-pool!* [Clap-clap-clap] *Liv-er-pool!* [Clap-clap-clap]".

Then the club installed a new tannoy system at Anfield, and appointed a DJ to play a countdown of the latest top ten hits, many of them by local Merseybeat groups, before every match. The fans sang along for an hour or so up until kick-off, and continued to sing their favourites during the match – sometimes with the lyrics altered for comic effect. In April 1964, ahead of a crucial end-of-season match – again versus Arsenal – BBC *Panorama* cameras captured iconic footage of the swaying Kop belting out *She Loves You* by the Beatles and *Anyone Who Had a Heart* by Cilla Black.

"I've never seen anything like this Liverpool crowd," said *Panorama* reporter John Morgan as he stood with his microphone in front of the Kop. "Their rhythmic swaying is an elaborate and organised ritual. They seem to know intuitively when to begin. Throughout the match they invent new words to express adulatory, cruel or bawdy comments about the players or the police, but even then they begin singing these new words with one immediate huge voice." Liverpool needed a victory against Arsenal to become league champions, and they did win – 5-0. The BBC cameras lingered on the packed terraces as the fans chanted "*We won the league, we won the league, ee-aye-addio, we won the league!*" (adapted not from a pop song but from the nursery rhyme *The Farmer's In His Den*).

"The Kop set this match to music, and sang their team to the championship with a wit and a warmth woven into the pattern of play so closely it became a part of the game itself," wrote Frank McGhee in the *Daily Mirror*. "Liverpool fans don't just watch a game. They take part. They live it. When they stride into Europe next season they'll never walk alone."

That last phrase was a reference to another Merseybeat hit that was popular on the terraces – Gerry and the Pacemakers' cover version of a Broadway show tune called *You'll Never Walk Alone*. Originally from the Rodgers and Hammerstein musical *Carousel*, Gerry Marsden and company's version first entered the top ten ahead of a home game against West Brom in October 1963, and that was the first occasion it was played at Anfield. The song spent four weeks at number one, and nine weeks in the top ten, but fans continued to sing it long after it dropped out of the charts. By 1965, Liverpool fans could be heard singing *You'll Never Walk Alone* at Wembley during the FA Cup final win over Leeds, with Kenneth Wolstenholme referring to the song as "Liverpool's signature tune". It would go on to become football's most recognisable fan anthem, gaining additional poignancy following the Hillsborough disaster in 1989.

Across Stanley Park, Everton fans were also gaining a reputation as noisy songsmiths. At the 1966 cup final, Everton fans altered "*God save our gracious Queen*" to "*God save our gracious team*". But Liverpool and Everton fans had also gained something of a reputation as troublemakers. In November 1963, these "Merseyside terrors" were branded "the roughest, rowdiest rabble who watch British soccer" by the *Daily Mirror* after Liverpool fans threw apple cores, orange peels, a piece of wood and "a chewed pork chop" at Leicester goalkeeper Gordon Banks, and Everton fans threw marbles, rice and – most seriously – a dart at Tottenham keeper Bill Brown.

Everton responded by erecting scaffolding barricades behind the goals at Goodison Park. This prompted Pat Collins in *Charles Buchan's Football Monthly* to suggest that it would not be long before moats and wire fences were installed at league grounds. "It is shocking," wrote Collins. "Handfuls of hooligans spattered around league club grounds are holding something like half a million ordinary fans to ransom. Here a few bottles, there a maniac with a dart. Lunatics who vent their spleen with brawls on the terraces, idiots who throw toilet rolls on the pitch, yobbos who wreck excursion trains. Put together it makes a savage, sad story. And put together like that it unfairly brands English soccer fans as an undisciplined mob, ripe for the cage – like zoo animals."

It was becoming increasingly common to see the term "hooligan" used in relation to football supporters. The term had been around since the Victorian era, and was first used to refer to a specific youth gang that caused violence in London in 1890s known as the "Hooligan gang". The gang leader was Irish criminal Patrick Hooligan (or Houligan). According to the original hooligan memoir, Clarence Rook's 1899 *The Hooligan Nights*, Patrick Hooligan "gave laws and a name to his followers". The term soon came to refer more generally to "young roughs", with Victorian newspapers explaining how they "hooliganised" and "hooliganed about" in "hooliganic" and "hooliganesque" ways.

Football hooliganism had existed since at least the 1880s, but through to the 1960s it was generally restricted to sporadic, uncoordinated incidents of bad behaviour. From the mid-1960s onwards, groups of fans began to become more organised and identifiable, wearing club colours, displaying their affiliations, and chanting in favour of their teams. They also became more mobile, travelling to away matches on coaches and trains in greater numbers and across further distances, and arriving at the grounds of rival groups of fans.

At the time, crowd segregation was relatively informal. Away supporters would usually be allocated a particular end of the ground, but few games were all-ticket, and there was little to stop fans passing through turnstiles at any end of their choosing. Inside the ground, there would rarely be fences or barriers between home and away fans, and it was often possible to move freely between ends and stands.

Much of the trouble was focused on football special trains. In the 1963-64 season, British Rail suspended its football specials for Liverpool and Everton away matches due to vandalism caused by what railway bosses labelled "Merseyside maniacs calling themselves football supporters". The trains were reinstated for the following season, but fans were warned they were "on trial".

Manchester United and Manchester City fans were also involved in train vandalism. Then in 1965, Manchester United banned eight youths from Old Trafford for the remainder of the season following "obscene chanting" from the Stretford End, although the ban was most likely a reaction to a pattern of more serious delinquent behaviour. The club was under pressure to clamp down on a "hooligan element" following fighting during a match at Burnley. "We cannot have a minority spoiling things for everyone else and damaging the reputation of the club and its supporters," said Matt Busby.

Football League secretary Alan Hardaker blamed the rise of football hooliganism on a minority of "dirty unwashed little thugs", who he said needed "a damned good hiding". "Hear! Hear!" responded a reader in *Football Monthly*. "If they behave like children, interfering with other people's enjoyment and wrecking trains, let them have a child's punishment. Tan their backsides – hard! Very few will want a second dose." Another *Football Monthly* reader suggested that placing fans' backsides on seats might be a better solution to the hooliganism problem. "Soccer rowdyism starts from the terraces," wrote the reader. "Seated people in the stands are well behaved. So the cure – no terraces. Seats everywhere. No standing."

What seemed to be agreed was that hooligan behaviour could spoil the World Cup, set to be hosted in England in the following year. "The present behaviour of football crowds is absolutely disgusting," wrote another correspondent. "Unless drastic action is taken, England as hosts of the 1966 World Cup will earn a poor reputation in world football. Please, let us have no more ugly incidents that mar so many of our games." The correspondent did not get his wish.

On one particular Saturday in November 1965, described as "the most shameful day in English football this season", there were several violent incidents, including a brawl at Liverpool's away match at Sheffield Wednesday, during which a policeman had his nose broken while trying to remove Liverpool "rowdies" from the terraces. Fourteen fans were due to appear before magistrates. At Old Trafford, Blackburn Rovers fans pelted Manchester United goalkeeper Harry Gregg with glass and stones. There were "tussles" in the crowd, and several fans were ejected. After the game, Manchester United fans stoned the Blackburn team bus, shattering a window while the visiting players dived for shelter.

In the Third Division, during a match between Brentford and Millwall at Griffin Park, Millwall goalkeeper Alex Stepney was attacked by a spectator, and the Brentford goalkeeper Chic Brodie was pelted with bottles – and a hand grenade. On discovering the grenade in his goalmouth, Brodie called for a policeman, who removed it in a bucket of sand. It was subsequently found that the grenade's firing mechanism had been removed, but the incident led to an explosion of outrage.

The headline in the *Sun* was: "SOCCER MARCHES TO WAR". It had been "the blackest day in British soccer," wrote the *Sun*'s reporter, "the day that showed that British supporters can rival anything the South Americans can do".

The mention of South America was most likely a reference to a terrible incident that had occurred during a football match in Peru in the previous year. The Lima football disaster, as it has become known, was blamed on the behaviour of fans, although the truth was somewhat more complicated and has been deliberately obscured. What is known is that it was the worst disaster in football history, taking the lives of more than 328 fans.

The date was 24 May 1964, and Peru were playing Argentina in a crucial qualifying match for the football tournament at the 1964 Tokyo Olympics. A capacity crowd of 53,000 were watching the match at Lima's Estadio Nacional. The trouble began after a fan ran onto the pitch to confront the referee. The fan was apprehended by police, and subjected to a brutal beating, in full view of the entire stadium. Angered by this shocking scene, more fans ran onto the pitch, and the referee suspended the game – which only further inflamed tensions. Police used horses and dogs to force fans back onto the terraces. Then, cruelly and fatefully, they fired scores of tear gas canisters into the crowd.

The panicked crowd began to flee, heading for the exits, or climbing the fences that surrounded the pitch. The vast majority were attempting to escape from the tear gas rather than to cause a riot. Nevertheless, the police charged fans with horses, released dogs on them, fired gunshots in the air, and fired more tear gas. "These tactics seemed to increase the panic," said the London *Times*, quoting reports from the *New York Times*. "Many of the exits to the stadium were locked, and bystanders were trampled or asphyxiated as people rushed toward open exit gates to avoid the tear gas and firing."

The official death toll of 328 is likely to be an underestimate – or a deliberate attempt to obscure the full extent of the tragedy. Some fans who attended the game were never accounted for. This is likely because they were killed not inside the stadium by the crushes, but outside the stadium by the police. Fans leaving the stadium, understandably angry at the brutality they had witnessed, were caught in a stand-off with armed police. "Then the shooting began," fan Jose Salas told the BBC. "Bullets were everywhere. I started to run and didn't look back."

The *Times* report said, "Most of those killed were trampled to death," but also stated that, "at least four of the dead were shot by police bullets". There were numerous eyewitness accounts of fans being killed by gunfire, although no bodies were found. Some accounts said the bodies were removed before judges investigating the incident could get to them. In his report into the disaster, the appointed judge, Benjamin Castaneda, wrote "there are well-founded suspicions of secret removals of those killed by bullets".

Even the likely-reduced official death toll figure remains difficult to comprehend in terms of its size. 328 people is roughly the capacity of a commercial 747 jet – and in fact there have only ever been five aviation disasters that have resulted in bigger death tolls. In a football context, the Lima disaster was the worst in the game's history, killing more fans than the Hillsborough, Heysel, Bradford, Burnden Park and two Ibrox disasters combined.

Another terrible disaster, at the Luzhniki Stadium in Moscow in 1982, is regarded by some sources as football's worst, but its details were obscured for years by Soviet-era secrecy. It was known at the time that there had been fatalities in a crush on an exit stairway at the end of a UEFA Cup match between Spartak Moscow and HFC Haarlem, but further details were not released to the public or the media.

Seven years later, following the Hillsborough disaster in 1989, *Soviet Sport* published an article headlined "Luzhniki's Dark Secret", which estimated the death toll at 340. That figure was quoted in media reports around the world. However, two weeks later the more-respected *Izvestia* newspaper revealed details of the official investigation, and stated that the real number of fatalities was 66 – less shocking but no less tragic.

Back in England, as the World Cup approached, league attendances were falling. During the opening weeks of the 1965-66 season, Football League officials reported the "absence" of some 300,000 fans. "Crowds everywhere are well down and if the slide continues figures could be half a million down on last season at the end of the first month," reported the *Daily Mirror*. Only eight clubs had average attendances of more than 30,000 in 1965-66, and only reigning champions Liverpool saw an increase in crowd numbers. The average First Division attendance was 26,903, down 10,000 since the "golden age" of the late 1940s and early 1950s.

Hooligans were blamed for keeping fans away, as was *Match of the Day*. But incidents of hooliganism were relatively rare, and matches screened on TV were relatively few. To prevent *Match of the Day*'s coverage from affecting attendances, viewers weren't told which match was being screened until 4pm on the Saturday afternoon, by which time fans were already at their games. More likely, fans were being kept away by poor play, shoddy facilities, and by all the exciting new entertainments that the so-called swinging sixties were presenting. Many fans seemed to be losing interest in football, and that was untimely news for Alf Ramsey and his England team.

Tony Pullein, secretary of the National Federation of Football Supporters' Clubs, called for more support for England ahead of the 1966 World Cup. He suggested that English fans only cared about England when they were playing

Scotland. "There are very few real supporters," he wrote in *Football Monthly*. "Not many, but they are genuine." Pullein praised the 5,000 members of the England Supporters' Association, which had been formed in 1963, and singled out the efforts of England cheerleader Ken Baily, who could be seen in Union Jack top hat and tails at many England games, but was banned from walking around the pitch before the team's World Cup matches because "that sort of thing is just not done at Wembley".

The apparent reticence of England fans was not matched by their compatriots from Brazil. The British media seemed astounded by the passion and fervour shown by the 12,000-strong "Brazilian invasion" that arrived in England ahead of their team's opening World Cup matches at Goodison Park. The *Times* said that, with their green and yellow flags, banners and tambourines, they were turning Liverpool into a "little Rio". "Brazilians will tell you proudly that *'o futebol'* is a truly national sport and that a football crowd is truly classless," wrote the paper's reporter. "But it is among the poorest people that enthusiasm has its deepest roots. The game is an escape from poverty and drudgery – often the only escape."

According to the *Times*, the Brazilian feeling for football "is more than passionate – it is religious". And, the paper said, "The god and the king of the whole thing is, of course, Edson Arantes do Nascimento – the incomparable Pelé." Pelé was the most famous footballer in the world, having first made his name ten years earlier at the 1956 World Cup. He was internationally famous for his footballing ability, which the *Times* said was "beyond the reach of any superlative", but he also had that indefinable X-factor that drew the public to him, even when he did not have a ball at his feet. Pelé was the player people wanted to see in the flesh, to wait outside his hotel, to reach out and touch. People all over the world had his posters, and crowded around TV sets to watch him play.

Unfortunately, Pelé was literally kicked out of the 1966 tournament, being injured in the opening game, missing the next one, then returning to be booted all over the pitch by a vicious Portugal team as Brazil were eliminated in the third group stage game. Brazil fans in England whistled and waved white handkerchiefs. Back in Rio, they strung a hangman's noose over a lamppost alongside a sign bearing the names of their team's officials and coaches.

When the Italy team flew home after being eliminated courtesy of a defeat to North Korea, the players were greeted at Genoa Airport with "screams, kicks, fists and flying tomatoes". Around 700 angry fans yelled, *"Assassins! You have dishonoured Italian sport!"* Police attempted to hold them back as they kicked the players' cars and beat on their windows. Public indignation led the Italian parliament to recommend a full inquiry into the team's failures.

Alf Ramsey's England team, meanwhile, improved as the tournament went on, inspired by flourishing support. The 1966 World Cup was the first to be broadcast live on television in the UK – on both BBC and ITV. So it was accessible even for those who couldn't get tickets for matches in London and the six other host towns and cities. And, although media coverage was hardly of the blanket variety that is familiar in the modern era, the World Cup was pretty hard to avoid. The fact that England looked strong, having been tipped by several pundits as possible winners, led to increased interest as expectation and excitement grew.

England supporters were able to make themselves as visible as club supporters, with all manner of favours and merchandise available as commercialisation took hold. Fans were able to buy 1966 World Cup T-shirts, caps, bags, mugs, tankards, towels, blankets, scrap books, stickers, footballs and more – many of which were emblazoned with an image of World Cup Willie, the tournament's popular lion mascot.

World Cup Willie soft toys were also available, and there was an official pop single, authorised by the English FA, called *World Cup Willie* by skiffle star Lonnie Donegan.

England supporters were also making themselves heard, bringing the increasingly popular chanting and singing from their clubs' league grounds to Wembley and the world stage. "Bravo fans," wrote Desmond Hackett in the *Daily Express* after England's opening draw with Uruguay. "I have never before heard such fervour and cheering that roared out to the last despairing seconds." And after the 2-0 win over Mexico, the *Daily Mirror* said England had a "growing, gladdening support". "The thundering chant of '*England! England!*' and the swinging chorus of '*When the whites go marching in!*' was evidence at Wembley that they now have support and sympathy," said the paper.

When England beat France to progress to the quarter-finals, a Wembley full house sang *Rule Britannia*. Argentina were beaten in the quarters, and then Portugal in the semis. England would play West Germany in the World Cup final, and they had the support of the country behind them. "Nothing has ever gripped the entire nation like this World Cup," said the *Mirror*, adding that it was "the greatest show ever staged in England".

Then came the final, on Saturday, 30 July 1966. It was watched by 96,924 fans inside Wembley Stadium, plus a TV audience of 38 million in the UK and up to 400 million in 75 countries around the world. England went behind to a goal from Helmut Haller, then equalised through Geoff Hurst. It was 1-1 at half time. Martin Peters scored for England, who looked to be heading for victory, only for Wolfgang Weber to score a 90th minute leveller. 2-2, and the game went into extra time. Then Hurst struck a shot that hit the crossbar and bounced onto the goal line – or possibly over it – and the Azerbaijani linesman awarded a goal.

Football's most famous piece of commentary focused on the fans rather than the players. It came right at the end of extra time, with England leading 3-2. Kenneth Wolstenholme looked to the referee: "It's all over, I think... No..." Then Bobby Moore's long ball sent Geoff Hurst clear in the German half. As Hurst raced towards goal, a handful of fans could be seen running onto the field. "And here comes Hurst," said Wolstenholme. "He's got... *[Wolstenholme is distracted]* Some people are on the pitch! They think it's all over! *[Hurst scores]* It is now! It's four!"

The final whistle was greeted by "the most triumphant and tumultuous din" - and caused there to be a lot more people on the pitch. Union Jacks were waved, people danced, hugged and wept, and there was a huge roar when Bobby Moore lifted the Jules Rimet trophy. During the lap of honour, the fans sang, again to the tune of *The Farmer's In His Den*, "*We won the cup, we won the cup, ee-ay-addio, we won the cup!*"

Afterwards it was "like coronation night" as the team bus was driven to a reception at the Royal Garden Hotel in Kensington past thousands of cheering fans who crowded pavements, windows and balconies waving banners and Union Jacks. The area around the hotel was packed with fans chanting "*England! England!*" There was a "tumultuous roar" as the bus carrying the England team arrived. The players headed up to the hotel balcony, where Bobby Moore held up the trophy to a great cheer. Elsewhere, there was dancing in a packed Trafalgar Square, where fans - inevitably - leapt into the fountains in celebration. Others made a "mighty din" with bugles, bells and horns, while one young man, holding a replica of the World Cup, "pranced through the throng".

England's victory, and the general success of the World Cup tournament, provided league football with a much-needed boost. The First Division's average attendance increased by 14% to 30,770 in 1966-67, and top-supported club

Manchester United's average attendance increased by 38% to 53,854. Average attendances went up again in 1967-68, to 33,036 in the First Division, and 55,552 at Manchester United. The aggregate Football League attendance for 1967-68 was more than 30.1m, up almost 1.25m on the previous season.

Crowds were up, and so, apparently, was entertainment value. There was much to be positive about, although the "hooligan element" had not gone away. "This is the slick soccer of the sixties," commented *Football Monthly*. "Big-time, brassy, exciting, intense and provocative. Crowds get bigger and more belligerent. Violence increases on and off the pitch. Yet today's game, despite its lunatic and moronic fringe, becomes even more socially acceptable. The big match night is a socialite occasion as once a big fight night used to be."

Singing was an increasingly important part of the entertaining matchday atmosphere, and the practices of adopting pop songs and rewriting traditional tunes were spreading. Fans would travel to away matches, hear a new song, and bring it home with them. In 1967, for example, it was reported that Arsenal fans were singing *You'll Never Walk Alone* "with a fair imitation of Merseyside confidence". Tottenham fans, meanwhile, were singing a rewritten version of American Civil War song *The Battle Hymn of the Republic*, having changed *"Glory, Glory, Hallelujah"* to *"Glory, Glory, Tottenham Hotspur"*. Leeds United and Manchester United fans would later adapt their own versions, but the original football rewrite of the song was most likely Hibernian's *"Glory, Glory to the Hibees"*.

By the late 1960s, the minimum admission fee to stand on the terraces was five shillings, but many paid it – plus an extra shilling for magazine-style match programmes, which *Football Monthly* said "make the old 2d teams sheets look like poverty-stricken relations". Arsenal were making a profit of £5,000 per season from their "most attractive" programme. Most big clubs had waiting lists for season tickets, "and only the mortality rate can hasten the queue". Manchester United sold £125,000-worth of season tickets. And many clubs installed executive boxes, as football began to move upmarket. Chelsea had six private boxes, which cost £500 per season. The boxes were fully carpeted, with six armchairs and a television set, and came with a buffet, wine, and waiter service.

At home, fans read footballer autobiographies and Sunday newspaper articles about the stars of the game, and bought breakfast cereals, hair products and – of course – football boots endorsed by their favourite players. And they watched football on TV. "Football", said *Football Monthly*, "can fasten a nation into one big easy chair beside its TV screens in the way that only the greatest Royal occasion can".

The huge TV audience for the World Cup final inevitably caused pound signs to appear in the eyes of football administrators, who began to consider the possibilities of having viewers pay to watch football. The UK already had a pay-per-view television company, Pay-TV, which launched in January 1966. Pay-TV promised live football, racing and boxing, accessed by pushing a few shillings into a coin slot on the side of television sets. "We see Pay-TV as the answer to live sport on television," said Football League secretary Alan Hardaker in the months following the World Cup. Pay-TV did show a handful of football matches, but the service could only be viewed on around 2,000 coin-slotted TV sets. Pay-TV's licence expired in 1968 and was not renewed.

At the end of the 1967-68 season, the British Market Research Bureau conducted a survey of football fans, asking what they wanted from the game, in an effort to determine why they went to matches – or why they had stopped going. Almost 50% of respondents wanted more comfort at matches, indicating that inadequate facilities at crumbling football grounds were a major concern. 40% wanted less crowd trouble, and 28% wanted lower admission charges. Of the fans who had stopped going to matches, 46% blamed crowd trouble, while 25% blamed a lack of comfort. The survey also found that football was "very much a young man's game", with relatively few fans over 45 due to "disillusion with the game after watching it for 20 years or so".

The survey could have acted as a warning to the football authorities that if it did not tackle the key issues of dilapidated grounds and crowd trouble then fans would drift away from the game. Post-World Cup, as England's feelgood factor dissipated, it became evident that both issues remained a problem. In the 1968-69 season, during a match between Nottingham Forest and Leeds United at the City Ground, the main stand caught fire and was completely gutted. Fortunately, due in part to swift action by the police, all spectators were safely evacuated from the front of the stand. This led the Fire Brigade to call for better safety at football grounds.

"Past history has indicated that remedial legislation has swiftly followed a disaster," said the chief fire officer, Mr Leese, "but the exception to this rule is the football industry, which appears to be in the realm of the untouchable." Among several recommendations, Mr Leese said it was important to "prevent cigarette ends falling through floor spaces and burning rubbish underneath". This recommendation would be ignored, with tragic consequences.

Meanwhile, hooliganism was becoming a regular subject of tabloid newspaper headlines due to several incidents of crowd trouble. One of the most high profile was a "soccer riot" that occurred when up to 22,000 Rangers fans travelled to Newcastle United's St James' Park for a Fairs Cup semi-final in May 1969. Many fans travelled without tickets, and some of them pulled down the ground's steel gates. Missiles were thrown onto the field and there were two pitch invasions, one of which resulted in a "battle" between Rangers fans and police. 89 fans were injured and 34 were arrested.

The incident prompted a huge reaction. Even the Queen was quoted as calling the hooligans "very stupid people", although she did add that she realised it was only a minority of fans who behaved in such a manner. And it *was* only a minority of fans, receiving disproportionate media coverage. But football violence was catnip for newspapers editors, who gleefully reported it, and in the process began to demonise all football fans. This represented something of a turnaround for editors who had once relied on football fans to boost sales, and had seen the newspaper industry grow alongside – and partly because of – the popularity of football.

In 1968, journalist Arthur Hopcraft published *The Football Man*, a book based on articles written for the *Observer* and the *Sunday Times*. In the book, Hopcraft profiled players and managers, but also drew a portrait of football fans. "Football matters, as poetry does to some people, and alcohol does to others," he wrote. "The football fan is not just a watcher. His sweat and nerves work on football, and his spirit can be made rich or destitute by it."

The Football Man is now regarded as one of the best football books ever written. Modern reissues have omitted the subtitle, which was *People and Passions in Soccer*. "The point about football in Britain is that it is not just a sport people take to," wrote Hopcraft. "It is inherent in the people." Hopcraft was concerned by incidents of crowd trouble, but said "soccer shame" headlines were "deliberately intended to shock rather than inform". Nevertheless, he wrote that football hooliganism "needs to be systematically removed if the game is not to be cripplingly disfigured in the future".

13

Villains of the piece

It was a Friday night in August 1971, and Manchester United fans were heading to a home game against Arsenal, chanting "*Uni-ted! Uni-ted!*" Many of them wore big sideburns and Beatles-esque mop-top hair, and carried red and white scarves. The swinging sixties had yet to properly morph into the groovy seventies, and terrace fashion remained relatively restrained. Some fans wore red hoop-necked football shirts under their jackets. They were drawn through the summer evening towards a floodlit football ground. But this was not Old Trafford. Manchester United were playing a home game at Anfield.

Old Trafford had been closed due to crowd trouble. There had been numerous incidents of violence during the previous season, most notably at a match against Newcastle when home fans threw various missiles, including a knife. As a result, it was decided the ground would be closed for the opening month of the season, and that Manchester United's two home games that month would be played at neutral venues – Liverpool's Anfield and Stoke City's Victoria Ground. To make matters even more unusual, the Anfield match would be played on a Friday night, under floodlights, to avoid affecting the attendance at Everton's Goodison Park on the following afternoon.

Some Manchester United fans reacted angrily to the ground closure punishment during a pre-season Watney Cup match at Halifax, where they "terrorised" the town, and caused £1,500-worth of damage. The *Daily Mirror*'s Bob Russell reported hearing "soccer hooligans boasting [about] showing the slobs who shut our ground". And, Russell wrote, "I heard these same morons boasting that they would do it again at Anfield."

Old Trafford wasn't the only First Division ground closed for the start of the 1971-72 season. Leeds United's Elland Road was also shut for the opening month, following an incident during a crucial end of season game against West Bromwich Albion. After the referee decided to allow Jeff Astle's winning goal for West Brom despite an offside flag, hundreds of Leeds fans invaded the pitch. The referee had to be protected by the players, and one of the linesmen was hit on the head with a bottle. Afterwards, fans smashed windows and "left a trail of wreckage" in surrounding streets. "They are usually very placid supporters," said Leeds manager Don Revie, "but you have to understand what that Astle goal meant." Leeds finished second in the league, losing out to Arsenal by a single point. "I do not condone the action of a few of our supporters," said Revie, "but I understand it."

As an attempt to reduce crowd trouble, the decision to play the Manchester United v Arsenal match at Anfield made little sense. Manchester United and Liverpool had battled for the First Division title during the 1960s, and, while the rivalry between the two clubs was not as intense as it would become in later decades, they were hardly the best of friends. Meanwhile, Arsenal were the 1970-71 league and cup double winners, and were the team everyone wanted to beat. It might have been difficult enough to control antagonism between Manchester United and Arsenal fans at the volatile Old Trafford. But the decision to move the match to Anfield created animosity between United and Liverpool fans, with many of the latter keen to protect their territory.

As Manchester United fans walked from Lime Street Station to Anfield on that Friday evening, 20 August, they were confronted by what the *Times* called “a mob of about 600 Liverpool skinheads, among whom were girls”. The mob was dispersed by police with dogs, but groups “rampaged” through the streets, smashing windows and damaging cars. Stones were thrown at police, and two officers had their helmets knocked off.

Inside the ground, as the teams warmed up, “thousands” of Manchester United fans charged out of the Kop and attempted to get into the opposite end, before retreating. Geoffrey Green wrote in the *Times* of the “stupid young United supporters” who swarmed across the pitch “like some migration of birds, sweeping officials and police out of their way in their mad passage”. A hundred fans were ejected from the ground, and there were several arrests inside and out. The Anfield pitch invasion was regrettable, but it wasn’t particularly violent, and almost certainly looked a lot worse than it was. Nevertheless, it was a high-profile example of fan disorder, and set something of a template for subsequent incidents that would occur throughout the 1970s and beyond.

The game, once it got underway, was perhaps unfairly overshadowed by what had preceded it. Manchester United – led by Charlton, Best and Law – came from a goal down to win a “fine entertaining match” 3-1, and went top of the league. But much of the media coverage concerned the fans. “Once again, certain sections of the crowd were the villains of the piece,” wrote Eric Todd in the *Guardian.* “Those psychiatrists, amateur or professional, who spend many hours trying to explore the minds – the word is used quite loosely here – of certain members of the footballing public would have enjoyed last night.”

The attendance was just 27,649 for the match at Anfield, compared to an average home attendance of around 45,000 at Old Trafford. Manchester United had to pay compensation to Arsenal for lost earnings (where takings would have been split between the two clubs), and also had to pay 15% of the takings to Liverpool for use of the ground. For Manchester United's next "home" match, at Stoke, the attendance was only 23,146. So it was an expensive punishment for the club. But it did nothing to reduce crowd trouble – now commonly labelled as football hooliganism.

The football authorities could hardly fail to recognise that hooliganism was becoming an increasing blight on the game, but they were unable to offer any solutions. "We have tried to find an answer to this problem," said Football Association chairman Dr Andrew Stephen, "and I must admit we are baffled to know what else we can do."

Hooliganism would generate the defining images of football in the 1970s, but the darkest incident of the decade involved not crowd trouble but a stadium disaster. It was Britain's worst stadium disaster up to that point, and it happened at the same venue as Britain's first stadium disaster, which had occurred 69 years earlier.

In 1902, 25 fans had been killed when part of a new stand collapsed at Ibrox Park. Following the disaster, Ibrox was remodelled and expanded, and there were no major safety issues for more than 50 years. But, by the 1960s, Ibrox was showing its age, and was suffering from the decay and disrepair familiar to many British football grounds from the Victorian and Edwardian eras. On 16 September 1961, after a 2-2 Old Firm draw with Celtic, two fans, George Nelson and Thomas Thomson, were killed in a crush after a barrier collapsed on the East Terrace's steep exit stairway – the ominously-named stairway 13.

Stairway 13 was a popular and crowded exit, and it was felt by some fans that the 1961 tragedy was an accident that had been waiting to happen. Safety improvements were made, at a cost of around £150,000, but the stairway remained dangerous. There were further serious crushes on stairway 13 in 1967 and 1969, in which there were more than 30 injuries but no fatalities. There were also fires at Ibrox, in 1968 and 1969. The 1968 fire damaged the main stand, and was thought to be caused by arsonists who had set fire to Hampden Park on the previous day. The ground was unoccupied during the fires, and there were no casualties, but the incidents did nothing to alter the opinion that Ibrox was dangerously unsafe.

What has become known as the second Ibrox disaster (although, taking into account the deaths in 1961, it should perhaps be referred to as the third), occurred at the end of an Old Firm match on a damp and misty day, 2 January 1971. The match was played in front of an all-ticket 80,000-strong crowd. It was goalless right up until the final minute, when Jimmy Johnstone scored for Celtic, then Colin Stein swiftly equalised for Rangers. The match was filmed, but the disaster unfolded out of view of the cameras, over the lip of the stadium bowl, on the exit steps of stairway 13.

Initial reports suggested that many Rangers fans had gone to leave the ground when Johnstone scored, then turned back when Stein scored, leading to a deadly crush. This theory directed a level of blame for the disaster at those fans, but it was proven by an official inquiry to be false. A more likely explanation, offered by witnesses, said that a young boy had fallen from his father's shoulders onto the stairs, where the descending crowd tumbled over him, precipitating a lethal domino-like chain reaction as fans toppled on top of each other down the stairs. Steel railings bucked and collapsed under the weight of the crowd, exacerbating the crush.

News of the disaster was first broken by a BBC Radio commentator on the *Sports Parade* programme. "Now this has been very serious indeed," announced the commentator. "From where I'm sitting high up here in the press box, through the darkness and the fog, the ambulances are still there... They're still taking away the spectators who have been injured, [voice cracks] and from where I'm sitting here I can see, oh, what looks to me like bodies, I'm afraid... Beneath me here everything is in turmoil, the kiss of life is being given, all available ambulances and police have been hurried here. It is, and has been, a very serious accident indeed."

Sixty-six fans died in the disaster, most of them from asphyxiation. More than 200 were injured. Many of the dead were children. The youngest was just eight years old. Five of the children came from the single small town of Markinch, Fife. It was estimated that around a quarter of the 80,000 crowd had used stairway 13, later referred to in a newspaper headline as "The Death Steps". The majority of those who had exited via other stairways had no idea the disaster had occurred, having been prevented from witnessing it by the banking of the east terrace.

"It was only from the top of the terracing that the full enormity of the situation could be seen," wrote the Glasgow correspondent of the *Times*. "A wedge of emptiness had been created part of the way down the long flight of stairs. In it was the twisted remains of the heavy steel division barriers. They had been mangled and pressed to the ground by the weight of bodies. Lying on the steps were scores of shoes that had been ripped off in the crush. Beyond, the steps were covered with dead and injured. There was a numb silence, broken only by shouts for stretcher bearers."

Among those stretcher bearers was the Celtic manager Jock Stein. Afterwards, still visibly shocked, Stein was asked by reporters to discuss the match. He angrily refused, instead conveying this sympathies to the relatives of those who had died, and praising the emergency workers and volunteers who had helped the injured. "This was a black, black day in the history of Scottish football," he said.

Stein also called for an end to sectarianism. The Old Firm rivalry had long been blighted by sectarian bigotry between traditionally Catholic Celtic and Protestant Rangers. During the Victorian and Edwardian eras the rivalry was a relatively friendly one, but the partition of Ireland in the 1920s aggravated religious and political divisions in Scotland, and particularly in Glasgow, where there were many Irish immigrants. These divisions were carried onto the football terraces, fostering increasing tension, hatred and violence.

From the late 1960s, Old Firm sectarianism became exacerbated by the Troubles in Northern Ireland, with some fans aligning themselves with, and singing and chanting for, republican and loyalist groups and paramilitaries. Jock Stein, as the protestant manager of catholic Celtic, was particularly frustrated with sectarianism. "Surely this terrible tragedy must help to curb the bigotry and bitterness of Old Firm matches," he said. "When human life is at stake, then bigotry and bitterness seem sordid little things. Fans of both sides will never forget this disaster."

A sheriff's judgement in a claim for damages regarding the death of Rangers fan Charles Dougan found that the disaster had occurred due to the "fault and negligence" of Ibrox Park's owners, Rangers FC. Rangers did not dispute the finding, and paid damages to the families of Dougan and around 60 other victims. Prompted by manager Willie Waddell, Rangers subsequently embarked on a major reconstruction project that saw the old ground almost completely replaced and rebuilt, and renamed – from Ibrox Park to Ibrox Stadium.

In the aftermath of the latest Ibrox disaster, there were calls for legislation to be introduced to ensure football grounds met adequate safety requirements. But Sir John Lang, who had chaired a government working party on crowd behaviour at football matches, told the *Times*, "I am not a believer that you will get over problems of this sort by having a law about them."

Legislation was supposed to have been introduced following the Burnden Park disaster in 1946, when it was recommended that all grounds should be licensed for public safety, with licenses issued following inspections from the police and local authorities. 25 years later, after the 1971 Ibrox disaster, FA Secretary Denis Follows admitted, "Unfortunately at present no British standard is laid down for the safety of crush barriers, terraces, stands and so on. No doubt this will come in time."

"It is high time," responded Geoffrey Green in the *Times*. The government had been slow to act, and emphasis had wrongly been placed on crowd behaviour and overcrowding rather than on the decrepit and unsuitable state of football grounds. "Too many of our grounds grew up in the late 19th century, hemmed in by tight little mean streets," wrote Green. "Approaches to entrances and exits have become bottlenecks for disaster, like [stairway] 13 at Ibrox, which, in a few appalling minutes, became a funnel of death."

The working party led by Sir John Lang published a report that examined a wide range of problems associated with "crowd behaviour", including the improvement of ground safety and the reduction of football hooliganism. But the introduction to the report stated that the working party had "not found a single solution". The report was undoubtedly flawed. The working party considered anything that happened away from football grounds to be "outside our terms of reference", and ignored social issues and other external factors that affected crowd behaviour. Crucially, the report broadly overlooked the failings of government, football authorities, clubs, and police, and focused almost exclusively on the bad behaviour of fans – and on hooliganism.

The most eye-catching instances of football hooliganism during the early 1970s were mass pitch invasions, such as the one at Anfield in 1971. That and subsequent invasions were examples of "taking ends" (or "seeing off"), essentially a boisterous game that involved groups of fans charging across the pitch or through the stands at their rivals, with the aim of driving them from their respective ends, and perhaps stealing their scarves or flags as trophies. Psychiatrist Dr JA Harrington, following an investigation into crowd behaviour and hooliganism, called taking ends "the football fan game". "This is a game played with its own techniques," said Harrington. "It symbolises the game seen on the field, except there are no rules, and no referee apart from the police."

Taking ends was largely a symbolic display of aggression, and, although kicks and punches were often thrown, it was primarily about territorial dominance rather than violence. Nevertheless, it was a highly-visible spectacle, often broadcast on television, and photographed and written about in newspapers. It made for good copy, particularly for the sensationalist tabloids. Inevitably, the media coverage was often out of proportion and inflammatory. By the 1970s, it became common to see front page photographs of groups of fans swarming across pitches, printed underneath headlines such as "SOCCER SHAME" and "SATURDAY AFTERNOON THUGS".

Such inflammatory coverage helped create something of a moral panic among the public. Dr Harrington, based on his investigation, suggested that the football hooligan might be a scapegoat for more widespread discontent, particularly among the middle aged and middle class. "They want to make the hooligan both literally and metaphorically the whipping-boy for their anger about the present state of the game," he said. "I have to ask myself if the football hooligan is the latest focus in the battle between the generations."

The high-profile coverage also served to promote hooligan behaviour, and to provoke hostilities between fans. When fans of one club saw fans of another taking ends or seeing off on television or on tabloid front pages, they were inclined to do the same. An atmosphere of one-upmanship was fostered, and it became a competition. Groups of fans began to look upon taking ends in the way their teams might look at winning matches. The *Daily Mirror* introduced a "League of Violence", ranking hooliganism by club, and the *Daily Mail* launched a "Thug's League". If the aim was to shame hooligans, the result was only to encourage them.

Inevitably, increased competitiveness between groups of fans also amplified the violence. In 1975, after Chelsea fans ran on to the pitch at Luton, the *Mirror* printed a front page photo labelled "INVASION", under the exclamatory headline "MADMEN!" According to the accompanying report, the match was halted for several minutes. "Players traded punches with hooligans," said the report. "Two stewards, a policemen and a bystander were attacked." The paper said 350 "young fans" were ejected from the ground, and violence continued outside of the ground, and on the train back to London. There was no mention of any arrests.

There had certainly been serious disorder at the Luton v Chelsea match, and also at other matches on the same day, that merited coverage. The *Times* covered it in a column on the football pages, where Geoffrey Green gave those fans involved deserved short shrift. "Whatever pleasure there is to be had from football these days is rapidly being eroded by the violent behaviour of some of its so-called supporters," he wrote. Football hooliganism was a growing problem, but it needed to be viewed in a wider context than much of the media's coverage allowed. In particular, violence was not restricted to football, and was representative of a much wider problem across society.

In 1971, the *Mirror* published a special report into what it called "the new age of violence", headlined "The Wild Ones". The report covered violence on football terraces, which it said was "providing many people with a regular weekly war game". But more prominent coverage was given to "the rising tide of violence" in school classrooms and on public transport. The report said violent crime had "soared", with more than a hundred reported cases of assaults and beatings reported every day.

A year later, a similar report was published in the *Mirror*'s special "Shock Issue". The section on football deplored "senseless violence among 'supporters'", and spoke of "women and children terrified, windows smashed, police attacked, boys stabbed". However, the report said, magistrates were getting tough. Two girls, aged 17 and 18, had been put on probation after punching an opposition fan. "Now the soccer bovver birds join the bovver boys in stirring up club hatred," said the paper.

According to the *Mirror*, a key factors behind the increase in youth violence was the "breakdown of family and religious disciplines". There were also wider issues. The 1970s saw a decline in the British economy, and a rise in unemployment. By 1977, the unemployment rate had risen to 6.2%, its highest level since the 1930s. A lack of jobs meant a lack of prospects. The decade that gave us colour television, decimal currency, digital watches, Concorde and Raleigh Choppers also brought rising oil prices, mass industrial action, the three-day week and the winter of discontent. For many young people, Britain in the 1970s was a pretty unpleasant place to be.

It was during the mid-1970s that the first hooligan crews or firms began to emerge. In some ways, these firms represented a natural progression from other existing anti-establishment and counter-culture youth movements, from teddy boys, to mods and rockers, and skinheads. It was primarily about disenfranchised and marginalised youths coming together with like-minded individuals to seek a sense of belonging.

Among the earliest hooligan firms was Manchester United's Red Army, a hardcore minority that really came to prominence around the time of the club's relegation to the Second Division in 1974. Hundreds of United fans invaded the pitch during their last match in the First Division, in a futile attempt to have the match abandoned, and avoid relegation. Then, in the Second Division, the Red Army emerged as a large travelling body that followed the club around the country, often outnumbering the home support, and regularly causing trouble. They also caused trouble at Old Trafford. For their first home game of 1974-75, against Millwall, Manchester United fans found themselves caged behind newly-installed steel fences that surrounded the terraces, "for all the world resembling some zoo".

On the same day, at another Second Division match between Blackpool and Bolton Wanderers at Bloomfield Road, 17-year-old Blackpool fan Kevin Olsson was stabbed to death. A 14-year-old boy was charged with his murder. This tragic incident shocked football into action. While violence was becoming increasingly common, fatalities were extremely rare, and Kevin Olsson may have been the first football fan ever killed as a result of violence at a British ground.

In October 1975, before the Red Army travelled to watch Manchester United play West Ham at Upton Park, the tabloid build-up placed more emphasis on the expected clash between fans than the actual match. Despite a huge security operation involving up to 500 police, the Red Army did invade the pitch, only to be forced back by West Ham fans. This "defeat" for the Red Army delighted the tabloids, with the *Sun* celebrating "the day the terrace terrors were hunted like animals and HAMMERED!"

West Ham's own hooligan crew would come to be known as the ICF (Inter City Firm). Other prominent firms that emerged in subsequent years include Leeds United's Service

Crew, the Chelsea Headhunters, and Portsmouth's 6.57 Crew. But perhaps the most high-profile and notorious hooligan firm of the 1970s was Millwall's F-Troop (later known as the Millwall Bushwhackers).

Millwall had a long history of trouble on the terraces, dating back to at least 1906, when Millwall and West Ham fans fought during a Western League match. According to Simon Inglis, author of *Football Ground of Britain*, the Den "held the dubious honour of being closed by the FA on more occasions than any other ground". Located on the seemingly aptly-named Cold Blow Lane, the Den had been closed in 1920, 1934, 1947 and 1950. More recently, there had been the 1965 "Soccer Marches to War" hand grenade incident, and several high-profile pitch invasions through the late 1960s and early 1970s. In 1975, a linesman was beaten up after officiating in a match between Millwall and Colchester. In 1976, Millwall fan Ian Pratt was killed when he fell under a train during a fight between Millwall and West Ham fans at New Cross Station. And in March 1977, Millwall fans attacked Cardiff defender Phil Dwyer on the pitch, and threw bricks at the Cardiff supporters' coaches.

In December 1977, after trouble at a match between Millwall and Tottenham, local residents sought legal advice to try to have the Den closed once again. But Millwall's general manager Graham Hostop said closing the ground was not the way to deal with hooliganism. "If we are closed down, then most of the other clubs in the country will have to close, too," he said. "This is a problem for society in general and not for football alone. It is highlighted in soccer because it is always in the public eye. If the hooligan minority that every club has did not cause trouble on grounds, then they would cause it somewhere else."

Millwall's F-Troop became known for carrying weapons, or being "tooled-up". Police began to search fans, and displayed for the media various arrays of confiscated weapons, including studded belts, chains, coshes, darts, scissors, razors, flick-knives, machetes, axes and more. In the absence of confiscated weapons, F-Troop devised the "Millwall brick", a cosh that was formed by tightly rolling and folding an innocent-looking newspaper. It was also possible to modify the "brick" into a makeshift knuckleduster by wrapping coins inside the newspaper.

In March 1978, a front page headline in the *Mirror* called on authorities to once again "CLOSE THE LIONS [sic] DEN!" This followed a pitch invasion during an FA Cup tie with Ipswich that halted the match for 18 minutes, and led to 11 policemen being injured, three of them seriously. One Ipswich fan quoted by the *Mirror* described the scene. "Hundreds of us were penned in on all sides with bottles, tins, and blocks of wood flying at us," he said. "Children whimpered and women fainted."

Millwall fans were perhaps reacting to the poor performance of their team – they lost the match 6-1. Twenty-three Millwall fans and eight Ipswich fans were arrested. The match was broadcast on *Match of the Day*, and the *Mirror* reported that BBC riggers working on the show were refusing to work at the Den ever again.

After the match, Ipswich manager Bobby Robson issued an uncharacteristically brutal reaction to the Millwall hooligans. His team had required a police escort to the outskirts of London, and Robson himself had been subjected to what the *Mirror*'s reporter described as "some of the sickest personal abuse I have ever heard". Robson's reaction was: "Get the flamethrowers out and burn the bastards."

On the following day, Robson gave a more measured response: "When people go to games with the sole intention of inflicting damage on human bodies, the only answer is not to play football in that part of the world." The *Mirror*'s Harry

Miller agreed. "The emotional reaction of any sane fan at the game is to say the Den should be closed down for good," he wrote. "Football would not miss Millwall, or their hooligan followers."

F-Troop's notoriety grew after it was featured in a 1977 edition of the BBC's *Panorama*. The TV programme would also become notorious, with the perception being that it glorified football violence. It would have a lasting negative effect on the reputation of Millwall, who must have regretted being the only football club to agree to participate. However, when viewed with hindsight, the programme's apparently sympathetic treatment can be seen as a rare attempt to understand hooliganism by speaking to the hooligans themselves – something few other media outlets had bothered to do.

Preceded by a warning that it would feature "language you don't usually hear on television", the programme saw reporter David Taylor interview members of F-Troop and the firm's junior divisions, Treatment and the Halfway Line. F-Troop were the "real nutters" and "self-confessed loonies", who went looking for trouble, and often found it. Fans were seen arguing over F-Troop's desire for a punch-up. "That's not what football's about, is it?" said one fan. "It is these days," responded another.

The most revealing part of the programme was an interview with a young Millwall fan named Billy Plummer. Plummer lived with his mother, and spoke of a violent father, and a step-father who was in prison. He had left school at 13, worked odd jobs, and was well aware of his "limited horizons". "I've never had a chance to fulfil my ambitions," he said. "If I have any ambitions, I don't know what they are."

The contrast between this football fan, in his jeans and V-neck sweater, and the BBC reporter, in his suit and tie, was pronounced. "I've had a hard life, as it happens, compared to some guys, like you," Plummer told David Taylor. "Whereas you've been brought up with university, I've been brought up with street fighting."

That violence had migrated from the streets to the terraces, aggravated by a tribal and confrontational atmosphere. "You get a lot of geezers taking the piss out of you at football," Plummer said. "They start shouting at you, chanting at you. And you just lose your temper." And it wasn't possible to ignore the provocation: "You don't want to be called a coward."

It wasn't just about violence. For a lad from a tough background with few prospects, football – and the camaraderie that accompanied it – was a welcome release. It provided companionship, and a sense of belonging. "Just as long as I've got enough money to go and see Millwall that does me," said Plummer. "They're a shitty team. They've never been in the First Division or nothing like that. But it's the fans really. It's your mates down there. Your mates you rely on. They've never had nothing except their reputation. They've always got their reputation."

Plummer had been arrested and fined for his part in hooliganism, although he claimed not to have paid his fines. In any case, he considered fines to be a waste of time. "How are they a deterrent?" he asked. "They're not a deterrent at all, really."

Another issue highlighted by the *Panorama* programme was the increasing influence of the National Front (NF), the far-right organisation with links to racism, fascism and neo-Nazism. The NF was growing in popularity, largely based on an anti-immigration stance during a period of high unemployment. At the same time, racism was becoming an increasing problem in football. There were a relatively small number of black players in the British game, perhaps fewer than 50 in the late 1970s. Among the most highest-profile were West Bromwich Albion's Laurie Cunningham, Brendon Batson and Cyrille Regis. The trio, labelled "The Three Degrees" by West Brom boss Ron Atkinson, were regularly subjected to racist abuse, and became targets for the NF.

"What shocked me when I joined West Brom was the volume," Brendon Batson later recalled. "The noise and level of abuse was incredible." On arriving at away grounds, the black players would be confronted by the NF, and would have to run a violent gauntlet between their coach and the players' entrance. They were spat at and booed, and had fruit thrown at them during matches. At home, they received hate mail. On one occasion, Laurie Cunningham had a petrol bomb pushed through his door.

The NF became an increasingly visible presence outside football grounds, whether handing out recruitment leaflets or holding demonstrations. It also began to infiltrate the terraces. A growing number of fans – particularly the hardcore hooligan minority – appeared to identify with the NF, whose initials began to appear on some fans' club flags. Disturbingly, in the *Panorama* programme, David Taylor concluded that the NF "seem more prepared to understand the soccer hooligan's psychology that our football's official bodies".

Taylor spoke to NF leader Martin Webster, who gave his assessment on why fans were turning to hooliganism, and to the NF. "I think people resort to mindless violence and vandalism because they have not been given by society a point and a meaning to their lives," said Webster. "People do like to identify, they do like to associate themselves with something that is big and glorious... and feel proud that they somehow belong."

The majority of football fans shunned the NF, just as the majority avoided any involvement in hooliganism. But there were still high-profile incidents of mass disorder. After

Scotland beat England 2-1 at Wembley in 1977, around 10,000 Scottish fans invaded the pitch, tearing up pieces of turf and pulling down the goal posts. More than 2,000 police, many on horses, were unable to hold the fans back. FA secretary Ted Croker called it "the worst invasion I have ever seen". Afterwards, it was announced that Wembley authorities would erect an eight-foot fence around the pitch.

The *Mirror*'s headline was "Shame of the Scots", and its leader article was titled "Clod off, Mac!" But, while more than 300 Scottish fans were charged with offences including criminal damage and being drunk and disorderly, police said there was no serious violence at the ground. "The Scots arrived here in a boisterous but peaceable mood," commented Scotland Yard, "and remained in that state until they left." Sports Minister Denis Howell agreed that the fans had not been "vindictive", but "rather in a mood of euphoria".

Images taken of Scottish fans at Wembley in 1977 showed how terrace fashion had evolved since the beginning of the decade. Shaggy hair and untucked shirts indicated that things were getting less formal. There were no suits in evidence, and almost every fan wore blue jeans. Many wore tartan scarves and bonnets, and some were draped in yellow Lion Rampant flags. And several showed their allegiance for their country and their team by wearing a brand new type of fan uniform – replica shirts.

For the 1977 match, the Scotland kit was manufactured by Umbro, and the England kit by Admiral. It was Admiral – an underwear manufacturer – that had introduced the replica shirt to football during the 1973–74 season, via a branded Leeds United kit that fans could buy from club shops and via mail order. Prior to that, fans wanting to emulate their idols had to make do with generic football tops – which, to be fair, were pretty much exactly the same as the ones that the players wore.

Replica shirts really took off in the following season, when Admiral began producing the England kit. Admiral quickly snapped up the rights to produce kits for Manchester United, Tottenham, West Ham and other major clubs, and expanded beyond Britain, making kits for the emerging North American Soccer League (NASL). Inevitably, rival manufacturers such as Umbro, Patrick and Bukta entered the market, and soon fans of almost every club could buy replica shirts. According to a mid-1970s mail order advertisement, Admiral's England shirts cost £8.40 for kids and £9.70 for adults.

Admiral's bold and often gaudy design choices – with deep V-neck inserts and wide collars, and all manner of stripes, sashes and yokes – reflected the adventurous fashions of the times. A classic example from the era is the Coventry City away kit introduced for the 1978-79 season, which was chocolate brown with huge white collars, and with curved white tramlines running down the shirt and shorts from shoulders to thighs. Although reviled as "the worst strip in English football history", it's now much sought-after among modern collectors.

Not all fans chose to wear replica shirts. The crews and firms preferred to be more anonymous, and chose not to wear any kind of colours that could identify them to opposition fans – or the police. But the crews did care about what they wore, and developed their own distinct styles. Initially, this meant straight-leg jeans instead of flares, sportswear V-necks instead of mohair jumpers, and Adidas trainers instead of Doc Marten boots. Gradually, the look became focused very much on expensive sportswear and designer fashions. From this trend was born the subculture of the casuals.

Post-mod, post-skinhead, and almost post-punk, casual culture began in the north-west of England, initially among Liverpool fans, and particularly the Anfield Road, or "Annie Road", crew. The team was enjoying great success in Europe

(Liverpool won the UEFA Cup in 1973 and 1976, and the European Cup in 1977, 1978, 1981 and 1984) and the fans were being exposed to previously-unseen continental fashions. They saw opposition fans wearing sportswear brands such as Sergio Tacchini and Fila, and they began to visit European fashion boutiques. By their own accounts, some fans found that these boutiques were less security conscious than the shops back home, and many of them were cleared out by shoplifters, with their stock exported back to Merseyside.

According to Manchester United fan Phil Thornton, author of *Casuals: The Story of a Terrace Cult*, casual culture "has always been a lifestyle that operated on the margins of criminality and gangsterism". In his book, Thornton was frank about the connection between the culture and hooliganism. He wrote that casual culture "brimmed with vibrant self-confidence and optimism, and yet was all too often disfigured by needless, internecine violence".

Casual culture has evolved and survived into the present era. Trends have changed, with brands such as Stone Island, Aquascutum and CP Company finding favour with different sets of casuals. Inevitably, as football violence has declined, the connection between casual culture and hooliganism has diminished. Many modern casuals completely reject violence. (One popular casual brand is called Peaceful Hooligan.) But the culture does remain linked with hooliganism, and has been appropriated by far-right groups. (One football-related far-right group affiliated with the English Defence League is called Casuals United.) Nevertheless, it remains an important subculture that has played a significant part in the history of football fan from 1970s to the present day.

Writing in *Soccer and Society*, author and academic Steve Redhead called the history of casuals "the missing key to the sociology of British soccer hooligan culture over the last 30 years". "Casual designer fashion has been intertwined with the history of football fan culture and soccer hooliganism in Britain since the late 1970s and early 1980s, and remains intertwined today," wrote Redhead. "The shape and contours of the events of hooliganism at and around football matches over a quarter of a century connect with the rise and fall and rise (again) of soccer casuals."

Football hooliganism continued beyond the 1970s, into the 1980s and beyond. It remains a problem, although it can no longer be said to define the game, as it did in the 1970s and early 1980s. While only a minority of fans were involved in hooliganism, and the majority of violent incidents involved only those fans who went looking for trouble, it did affect football fans as a whole. The widespread media perception was that all fans were thugs and louts.

Figures suggest hooliganism did have a negative effect on football attendances. By 1977-78, the average First Division attendance was 28,692, having fallen by almost 5,000 in the ten years since 1967-68, and by 10,000 since the unparalleled golden age season of 1948-49. By 1979-80, the First Division average had fallen to 26,327. In subsequent seasons it would continue to fall by around 2,000 a year, until, by 1984-85, it was just 18,834, down almost 10,000 in the seven years since the 1977-78 season (and down almost 20,000 since 1948-49).

The period from 1977 to 1985 was British football's most violent in terms of hooliganism, and it seems unlikely to be a coincidence that the biggest fall in attendances coincided with the worst excesses of football hooliganism. But there were other factors at play, too. Decrepit facilities, lackadaisical safety, inept policing and negligent governance were also driving fans away from the game. Going to football was becoming less enjoyable, and it was also becoming more dangerous. Such widespread disregard for football fans would have tragic consequences.

14

Victims of contempt

It was a bright spring day, and more than 50,000 football fans were descending on Sheffield. They turned off the M1 in packed supporters' coaches full of songs and cheer, and trundled along the A61 in Ford Cortinas and Austin Allegros, with scarves flapping from hand-cranked windows. Others arrived by train, and took buses from the city centre up through Owlerton towards the football ground. There, they strolled through the surrounding streets, buying programmes, cups of tea and bags of chips, as the atmosphere built to a heady buzz ahead of the big match. It was an FA Cup semi-final, and the venue was the Sheffield Wednesday stadium, Hillsborough. The teams involved were Tottenham Hotspur and Wolverhampton Wanderers. The date was 11 April 1981 – eight years before the Hillsborough disaster.

Like many British football grounds, Hillsborough was a relic of the Victorian and Edwardian eras. It was built in 1899, and was originally known as the Owlerton Stadium. It was renamed Hillsborough before the first world war, following a series of ground improvements. Those improvements included the building of a new retaining wall at the Penistone Road end of the ground. In February 1914, just a few weeks after it had been built, the new wall collapsed during an FA Cup tie, injuring more than 70 spectators. "There was a sudden crash and we were thrown to the ground with a terrific weight of bricks on top of us," recalled one of the injured. "It is remarkable no one was killed." Further alterations were made in the 1960s, when the north stand was demolished and replaced, and the West Stand was built at the Leppings Lane end. Then, in 1977, blue perimeter fences were erected around the playing area.

The 1981 semi-final was due to kick-off at 3pm, but travel delays caused the late arrival of many fans, and the decision was made to delay kick-off until 3.15. Spurs fans with tickets for the West Stand were to enter the ground via turnstiles at the narrow Leppings Lane entrance. By 2.10, more than an hour ahead of kick-off, the Leppings Lane entrance was severely congested, and police made the decision to open an exit gate, gate C, in order to admit fans and relieve pressure. On entering the ground, fans were presented with a central tunnel signposted "standing". There were other access points to the left and right, but these weren't as visible, and most fans proceeded straight down the central tunnel onto an already-packed Leppings Lane terrace.

By 2.30pm it was clear that the terrace was dangerously overcrowded. Fans were yelling for help, and others had fainted. Some were attempting to scale the perimeter fence in order to escape the crush. The decision was made to open the gates in the perimeter fence, and allow fans to spill out from the terrace and sit around the touchline. Police also closed the entry gates to the central access tunnel, and directed fans to the left and right access points. When the match kicked off, fans were sitting three and four deep around the pitch with their backs against the perimeter fence. They could be seen in TV footage, and in a photograph printed alongside a match report in the *Times*, although there was no mention in the newspaper of the congestion problems. Several fans were injured in the crush. 38 were treated by St John Ambulance volunteers, and some required hospital treatment.

In a post-match meeting, the police faced criticism from Sheffield Wednesday chairman Bert McGee, who said the actions they had taken were "completely unnecessary and made the ground look untidy". But even without the benefit of hindsight it was clear that a disaster had been averted. Assistant Chief Constable Robert Goslin, who gave the order to open the gates in the perimeter fence, said the decision was taken because "serious injuries or even fatalities were a real possibility". Bert McGee's response was: "Bollocks – no one would have been killed."

McGee's comment was indicative of the contempt in which football fans were held by those in authority, and even by those involved in the game who were happy to take their money. Fans were herded and corralled by baton-waving police, rammed and squashed into decrepit and unsafe grounds, caged like wild animals behind perimeter fences, and provided with disgraceful and disgusting facilities – such as the ubiquitous brick wall urinal, a fetid open-air piss-trough that was emblematic of the shockingly unacceptable state of 1980s grounds. This dehumanising treatment was what football fans deserved, the authorities seemed to believe, after a decade of hooliganism and disorder.

Football violence was back on the front pages. England fans were involved in battles with riot police during the 1980 European Championships in Italy. Bobby Charlton, working as a TV commentator, described the fans as "England's shame", and England manager Ron Greenwood said they should all be "put on a boat and dropped in the ocean".

Jack Charlton, the Sheffield Wednesday manager, was reduced to tears after Wednesday fans rioted at Oldham in September 1980. He called the rioters "the scum of society" and said people who caused trouble at football matches were "the dregs who just turn up anywhere there might be trouble".

Wednesday's Bert McGee, of "bollocks" fame, was not content to blame a minority of troublemakers. "It is no good blaming the hooligan element," he said. "There must have been 300 supporters involved. It appeared to be mass hysteria."

There were 13 arrests at Oldham. On the same day ("Soccer's Day of Shame", according to the *Daily Mirror*), 42 people were arrested at a match between Chelsea and West Ham. All of this was a boon for tabloid newspaper editors, who gleefully published violent reports and photographs in the knowledge that their readership would be both appalled and titillated. The tabloids put football hooliganism on page one, and topless women on page three. Violence, like sex, sold newspapers. Football violence was sporadic and involved only a minority of fans, but the remaining majority were tarred by association. Football fans were being demonised rather than protected.

In many ways, football fans became scapegoats during a period of intense civil unrest. Violence was by no means restricted to football, and was symptomatic of much more widespread problems. In 1981 there were major riots in Brixton, Toxteth, Moss Side and elsewhere, ignited by inner city deprivation, racial tensions, and disillusionment with the government and the police. Britain in the 1980s was not all yuppies and Lady Diana and Duran Duran. The fact was that for many people it was a grim place to be. The economy was in recession, and the unemployment rate reached an all-time high of 12%. And this was against a background of the bleak brutality of the Falklands War and the IRA bombing campaign.

Under the Thatcher government, the rich were getting richer, and the poor were being trampled underfoot. The working class – from which football drew the majority of its support – were becoming disenfranchised and ostracised. Nowhere was this more clearly demonstrated than during the miners' strike, which began in March 1984, and was characterised by violent clashes, with the police effectively given free rein to quash the dispute. The most notable of these clashes was the so-called "Battle of Orgreave", in South Yorkshire, where 5,000 truncheon-wielding police officers cavalry-charged unarmed striking miners in "a brutal example of legalised state violence". South Yorkshire Police were subsequently ordered to pay compensation to 39 arrested miners for assault, false imprisonment and malicious prosecution.

Inevitably, though, emphasis continued to be placed on football violence, with little thought given to underlying and surrounding social and political issues. In March 1985, Millwall fans rioted during a live televised FA Cup tie at Luton, ripping up seats, throwing bottles, and fighting with police. 47 people were injured, and 31 fans were arrested. This incident seemed to be the final straw for the authorities.

Margaret Thatcher arranged an urgent meeting with the FA and Football League, and backed home secretary Leon Brittan's suggestion that football hooligans should be jailed for lengthy terms – including life. When Thatcher was asked in the House of Commons for her thoughts on the causes of hooliganism, and what she intended to do about it, she replied that the causes "vary from lack of parental discipline to lack of teacher discipline, background and everything". "When one has said that, it is not exactly easy to cure it," said Thatcher, "and we have to tackle it by increased number of police."

It was the prime minister's intention to deal with football fans as she had with striking miners. Also on her mind was the suggestion from Luton Town chairman David Evans (who would later become a Tory MP) that the hooliganism problem could be solved by the introduction of an identity card scheme. Evans introduced an ID card scheme at Luton that prevented non-members from attending matches, and also banned all away supporters from Kenilworth Road, following the rioting at the Millwall match. Despite protests from fans and the Football League, the government set into motion plans to roll out an ID card scheme across football.

Another wrong-headed suggestion came from Thatcher's press secretary, Bernard Ingham, who in 1985 proposed an anti-hooligan campaign, "Goalies Against Hoolies", which would utilise "the more articulate goalkeepers" in an effort to "implant in the public mind" the message that "enough is enough". Ingham's letter to Thatcher, released to the public 20 years later, revealed that the idea had originally been suggested by Watford chairman Elton John. "We are proposing you should give an interview to Gary Bailey, Manchester United and England goalkeeper, from Piccadilly Radio, Manchester, an interview which we should get networked," wrote Ingham. "Bailey is an articulate graduate." What exactly Gary Bailey and his fellow keepers were supposed to say to hooligans was unclear, and the idea only confirmed opinions that the authorities were entirely out of touch with regard to football fan issues.

Then football suffered a terrible disaster that had nothing to do with hooliganism and everything to do with failures of authority. It was the final day of the football season, 11 May 1985, and Third Division champions Bradford City were playing Lincoln City. A crowd of 11,076 fans – almost twice as many as usual – were at Valley Parade to celebrate Bradford's promotion. Built in 1886, the 99-year-old Valley Parade was one of the most antiquated grounds in football. Its main stand had barely been altered since it had been erected in 1911. There were 3,000 fans in the stand when the match kicked off. Bradford City had been warned that the stand was dangerous, particularly with regard to decades-worth of litter that had fallen through gaps in the floorboards. "There is a build-up of combustible materials in the voids beneath the seats," wrote a council inspector in a letter to the club. "A carelessly discarded cigarette could give rise to a fire risk."

The fire was first spotted at 3.40pm, five minutes before half time. Initially there was a plume of smoke, and glowing embers. Then fans could see rubbish burning beneath their seats. The police were informed and the fire brigade were called. Within a couple of minutes, the blaze had taken hold, and the stand was filling with smoke. Some fans spilled onto the pitch (Valley Parade did not have perimeter fences). Others moved to the back of the stand, where the exits were located. Flames began to lick the seating area, and the match was stopped. Those who had headed to the back of the stand found themselves in congested, smoke-filled corridors. They made their way to the exits only to find, tragically, and in many cases fatally, that the exits had been locked.

The fire brigade arrived within four minutes of being called, but found the stand well ablaze, engulfed with intense flames and billowing black smoke. Fans were pulled from the seats, some of them on fire, with rescuers using their coats to extinguish the flames. "It was sheer hell," recalled Patsy Hollinger of the Bradford City supporters' club. "We just picked up kids and people and threw them onto the pitch to get them away from the flames. There just seemed to be this ball of fire everywhere." At the back of the ground, fans smashed open the locked exit gates. For many, it was too late. Fifty-six people died in the fire, and 265 were injured.

A brief inquest determined that the fire had been caused by a discarded cigarette and a condemnable stand, and delivered a verdict of misadventure. Bradford City chairman Stafford Heginbotham denied that he or his board had ever received safety warnings suggesting that the stand was a hazard. "I don't share the view that it was a fire trap," he said.

Thirty years later, author Martin Fletcher, who survived the disaster but tragically lost his brother, father, grandfather and uncle, revealed in his book *56: The Story of the Bradford Fire* that it was one of at least nine different fires at businesses owned by or associated with Stafford Heginbotham. "Could any man really be as unlucky as Heginbotham had been?"

asked Fletcher. Heginbotham received more than £2.7m in insurance payments from the nine fires.

The Bradford City fire has come to be regarded as football's forgotten disaster, and some of the coverage in the aftermath was needlessly insensitive and flippant. The *News of the World* printed a horrifying front page photo of a desperate fan fully ablaze alongside the exclamatory headline "Human Fireball!" But there was genuine anger from some commentators at the institutional failures that had allowed the tragedy to happen.

Writing in the *Times*, Brian Glanville said a similar disaster could happen again at any of Britain's neglected grounds. Football had always been poorly led, he said, and clubs run by the "nouveau riche" would rather spend money on players than on facilities. Fans were crammed onto terraces "like beasts at a market", in stadiums where toilet facilities and refreshment provision were "atrocious" and "inept". "The government has said it wants football again to become a family game," wrote Glanville. "It has never been a family game; rather it has been a proletarian game run by a jumped-up middle class, in which the true interests of the fan have been ignored."

Any widespread sympathy for football fans was, however, short-lived. On 29 May 1985, 18 days after the Bradford fire, 39 fans were killed and around 600 injured ahead of the European Cup final between Liverpool and Juventus at the Heysel Stadium in Brussels. Heysel was Belgium's national stadium, but it was dilapidated and decaying, and every bit as neglected as Britain's worst grounds. Both Liverpool and Juventus had requested that the final be played at a more suitable venue, but UEFA refused.

58,000 packed into the cinderblock stadium, with Liverpool fans behind one goal, and Juventus fans behind the other. The Liverpool fans were placed in two standing sections, separated from a neutral section by a chain-link fence. However, tickets for the neutral section had ended up on the black market, where they were mainly sold to Juventus fans.

The trouble began an hour before kick-off, with missiles – including pieces of concrete from the crumbling stadium – being thrown over the fence between opposition fans. Then, groups of Liverpool fans broke through the fence, pushed past a thin line of police, and charged the Juventus fans in the neutral section. The Juventus fans fled, and the resulting surge caused severe crushing and trampling, and led to the collapse of part of the perimeter wall. "The wall collapsed and people were trapped by rubble and dead bodies," said Liverpool fan John Welsh. "It was terrible, and nobody seemed to be doing anything." Another witness said emergency services were prevented from getting onto the terraces because the gates were locked.

Meanwhile, violence escalated around the ground, including at the Juventus end, where fans spilled onto the pitch. The chaos continued for almost an hour, with supporters and red-helmeted emergency workers carrying injured bodies from the stadium on makeshift stretchers, while other fans fought with riot police. Eventually, after an 83 minute delay, the match kicked off, with authorities worried that abandoning it would only have led to more violence. The BBC broadcast the match in full, leading to hundreds of complaints. It was clear by that point that many people had died.

Liverpool fans were blamed for the disaster. "Only the English fans were responsible," said UEFA observer Gunter Schneider. "Of that there is no doubt." "There could be little doubt that Liverpool supporters were primarily responsible, and it must be expected that British clubs will be banned from European football," wrote David Miller in the *Times*, adding, "but it has to be said that the security arrangements were woefully inadequate."

English clubs were banned from European competitions by UEFA for an indeterminate period that would eventually last for five years (plus an extra year for Liverpool). But a Belgian inquiry found that Liverpool fans were not solely to blame, and that responsibility should be shared with the police and football authorities. Fourteen Liverpool fans were convicted of involuntary manslaughter. Police captain Johan Mahieu, the officer in charge of the terrace where the disaster occurred, and Belgian Football Union secretary-general Albert Roosens, who was responsible for the ticket sales shambles, were also convicted.

Heysel was one of football's blackest days, yet it would come to be relatively overlooked or ignored, certainly in Britain, perhaps because it was overshadowed by other events, or perhaps because of a kind of embarrassment that the national game could have led to such a terrible tragedy. Jingoistic newspaper coverage looked to shift the blame – onto gun-toting Juventus fans, incompetent Inspector Clouseau-type Belgian cops, and anti-British European football bosses – then swiftly moved on. The worldwide press, meanwhile, condemned England's "obscene fans", and mourned the death of the beautiful game. France's *L'Equipe* said, "If this is what football has become, let it die."

Rapidly-falling attendances suggested that football might be dying, and hooliganism was certainly driving some fans away from the game. But the majority of fans never experienced football violence. By contrast, the majority of fans – certainly those who stood on the terraces – did experience dangerous crushes. It seemed common to become caught in surges, with arms trapped, chest squeezed, and feet lifted from the floor. This while caged behind fences, encircled by police, and stuck in decrepit grounds, while the authorities turned a blind eye. It was, as every football fan knew, an accident waiting to happen.

Hillsborough was not used as an FA Cup semi-final venue for six years following the 1981 crush. Changes were made to the ground, including the introduction of radial fences that divided the Leppings Lane end into separate pens, preventing fans from moving sideways across the terrace. The ground's safety certificate was not updated following these changes. In 1987, the FA chose Hillsborough to host the semi-final between Coventry City and Leeds United, and then, in 1988, the semi between Liverpool and Nottingham Forest. On both occasions there were crushes at the Leppings Lane end that led fans to fear for their safety.

In 1988, several fans were injured, and collapsed or fainted. In the aftermath of the match, one Liverpool fan wrote a letter to the FA to "protest in the strongest possible terms at the disgraceful overcrowding that was allowed to occur (in an all-ticket match) in the Leppings Lane terrace area". According to the fan, the terrace was "packed solid to the point where it was impossible to move", and he and others around him "felt considerable concern for personal safety". "I would emphasise that the concern over safety related to the sheer numbers admitted," the fan added, "and not to crowd behaviour, which was good." In a separate letter, another fan wrote, "As far as I am concerned, when there is a large crowd entering this part of the ground, it will always be a death trap."

Saturday 15 April 1989 was another sunny spring day, and another 50,000-plus football fans - again supporters of Liverpool and Nottingham Forest - arrived in Sheffield to watch another FA Cup semi-final at Hillsborough. Nottingham Forest fans were to enter the ground via 60 turnstiles on two sides of the ground. Liverpool fans were to enter via 23 turnstiles at the Leppings Lane end. Of those turnstiles, only seven provided access to the standing terrace, for which there were 10,100 ticket holders - more than 1,400 per turnstile.

Although the tickets advised fans to take their places just 15 minutes before the 3pm kick-off, many fans arrived much earlier. The mood was described as "one of carnival, good humour and expectation".

The match commander was Chief Superintendent David Duckenfield, who had recently been promoted to his post, and had very little knowledge of football or experience of controlling matches. He was positioned in a control box overlooking the Leppings Lane terrace, with a bank of CCTV screens that provided clear views of the situation inside and outside the ground.

By 2.15pm the Lepping Lane central pens were visibly crowded. Outside, a large crowd was building at the Leppings Lane turnstiles. By 2.40, there were around 5,000 fans packed into the turnstiles area, and the crush was becoming dangerous. At 2.52, Duckenfield gave the order to open exit gate C. He made no attempt to close the central "standing" tunnel to prevent fans entering the central pens on the Leppings Lane terrace, nor to open the gates in the perimeter fence to allow fans to escape onto the pitch.

Over the next five minutes, around 2,000 fans entered through gate C, and the majority of them headed straight through the central tunnel and into the already overcrowded central pens. Here there was an overwhelming crush. This intensified as the match kicked off at 3pm. Fans attempted to climb the perimeter fences, or to tear holes in them through which to escape. Some were pulled up to safety by fans in the seats above the terrace. Others were immovably trapped, and were dying – or were already dead.

"I was vaguely aware that the game had kicked off, and that people were dead on their feet," wrote Liverpool fan Adrian Tempany in his book *And the Sun Shines Now*. "I had no control or feeling in my body from the neck down. I was exhausted, and stiff with shock. Unable to move, too exhausted now to shout, I began to take in the final minutes of my life." Tempany gave last thoughts to his girlfriend and family as he counted down the seconds to his death. Then, the police finally opened the perimeter gates. Fans spilled onto the pitch, many of them injured and dazed. Others keeled over where they had stood. Tempany described "a heap of tangled corpses piled up off the ground, three feet high".

At 3.06, the match was stopped. BBC television pictures, broadcast live on *Grandstand*, indicated the magnitude of the disaster. There were horrendous scenes of motionless bodies being laid on the grass, and desperate attempts to save their lives. Forty-four ambulances arrived at the stadium, but only one was allowed to enter the pitch. Ninety-four people died on the day. Another, Lee Nicol, died four days later in hospital, and another, Tony Bland, died almost four years later, having been on a life support machine. Of the 96 victims, 38 were children or teenagers.

The cover-up began while fans were still dying on the pitch. At 3.15pm, Chief Superintendent Duckenfield told FA Chief Executive Graham Kelly that the tragedy had been caused by Liverpool fans forcing open gate C. Police officers were told not to write anything in their official pocket books – representing a major breach of protocol. Officers' statements written on plain paper were subsequently altered in an attempt to remove blame from South Yorkshire Police and shift it onto Liverpool fans. The coroner, Dr Stefan Popper, requested that blood alcohol levels be taken from all of the victims, including the children, with the implication being that they might have caused the disaster by being drunk.

And this was a cover-up that went all the way to the top. On the following day, Margaret Thatcher visited Hillsborough, and, according to Bernard Ingham, was told by police that the disaster had been caused by "tanked-up yobs". Ingham subsequently wrote, in a remarkable letter to a Liverpool fan and campaigner, "Who if not the tanked-up yobs who turned up late determined to get into the ground caused the disaster?" To blame the police, Ingham wrote in the letter, was "contemptible".

These lies were cemented into the public consciousness on 19 April 1989, four days after the disaster, when the *Sun* published a notorious front page story headlined "THE TRUTH", claiming that Liverpool fans had picked the pockets of victims, urinated on police officers, and beat up an officer who was giving the kiss of life. The story was provided to the *Sun* by Sheffield news agency White's. *Sun* editor Kelvin MacKenzie did not check its veracity, and was personally responsible for the headline.

An investigation by the Press Council, prompted by thousands of complaints, found the article to be "unbalanced and misleading", and the headline "insensitive, provocative and unwarranted". "The Press Council condemns its publication," concluded the investigation's report. The *Sun*'s regional circulation fell by around 40%, representing around 200,000 readers, in the days after the article was published. Kelvin MacKenzie was forced to apologise by the newspaper's owner, Rupert Murdoch. But in subsequent years MacKenzie, still employed by the *Sun* as a columnist, continued to insist he had been right. Football fans in Liverpool and further afield have refused to buy the *Sun* since April 1989.

The *Sun* was not the only publication to print the lie that fans were to blame for the disaster. The Press Council received complaints concerning 35 newspapers. But much of the subsequent coverage did highlight the reality – of police incompetence, of a decrepit ground, and of a broken system that had utterly failed football fans. "The people who died are victims of contempt," wrote Simon Barnes in the *Times*. "Football supporters have long been held in total contempt by the government, by the police, by the football authorities, and by the clubs that these people support." Barnes wrote that greed was also to blame, saying that English football was happy to take fans' money, but less inclined to spend it on ground safety or comfort.

Such disregard for public safety was not restricted to football, and the football-related disasters should be considered in a broader context. Between Bradford and Heysel in 1985 and Hillsborough in 1989, Britain was blighted by a string of major disasters. In March 1987, the British-owned ferry *Herald of Free Enterprise* capsized after leaving Zeebrugge for Dover, killing 193 passengers and crew. The disaster was caused by negligence fostered by what an inquest called a "disease of sloppiness". In November 1987, the King's Cross fire, caused by rubbish that had been allowed to build-up beneath an escalator, killed 31 people. In July 1988, 167 oil workers died in the Piper Alpha disaster. An inquest found operator Occidental had inadequate maintenance and safety procedures.

In December 1988, 35 people were killed and almost 500 injured in the Clapham rail crash, caused by a signal failure. Nine days later, 270 people died when Pan Am Flight 103 was blown up over Lockerbie. In January 1989, 47 died when a Boeing 737 crashed on the M1 motorway embankment near Kegworth. Also within this four-year period, 55 people were killed when a holiday flight crashed on take-off at Manchester Airport, and 43 died in a Chinook helicopter crash near Sumburgh Airport in the Shetland Islands – caused by inadequate testing and inspection procedures. Four months after Hillsborough, in August 1989, 51 died in the Marchioness pleasure boat disaster on the Thames. An inquest found that the victims had been unlawfully killed.

The inquest into the Hillsborough disaster was conducted by Lord Justice Taylor. Peter Taylor, from Newcastle, was primarily a rugby fan, but he also supported Newcastle

United, and had experienced what it was like to be part of a big football crowd. In August 1989, Lord Taylor produced his interim report, which concluded that the disaster had occurred due to overcrowding caused by a failure of police control.

The report was presented to Margaret Thatcher by her home secretary Douglas Hurd, who said in a memo that he welcomed "the broad thrust of the report", and suggested that the chief constable of South Yorkshire Police would have to resign given "the enormity of the disaster and the extent to which the inquiry blames the police". Thatcher replied: "The broad thrust is devastating criticism of the police. Is that for us to welcome?" The chief constable would not be forced to resign, and South Yorkshire Police would not have to accept responsibility for the disaster.

The final Taylor Report was published in January 1990. It concluded that there was "a general malaise or blight over the game" due to factors including crumbling grounds, inadequate facilities and poor leadership. "The years of patching up grounds, of having periodic disasters and narrowly avoiding many others by muddling through on a wing and a prayer must be over," wrote Lord Taylor. "A totally new approach across the whole field of football requires higher standards both in bricks and mortar and in human relationships."

The report made 76 recommendations, including the removal of "prison-type" perimeter fencing, the creation of a Football Licensing Authority for ground inspection, and a review of police operations at grounds. Although the report found that standing at football matches was not intrinsically unsafe, its headline recommendation was a switch to all-seater accommodation. The government quickly announced that all major football grounds would be converted to all-seater, and that First and Second Division grounds would be converted by the start of the 1994-95 season.

The recommendations of the Taylor Report would have major implications for the future of football safety and the future of football itself. Perimeter fences were already being torn down, and the government's plan to introduce ID cards was abandoned. The all-seater recommendation would be rapidly implemented, forcing clubs to build new stands – and new grounds. But the report's specific findings on the causes of the Hillsborough disaster were effectively buried. A flawed inquest into Hillsborough in 1991 returned a verdict of accidental death, to the dismay of the families and others who had been campaigning for "Justice for the 96".

It took 27 years for that justice to be delivered. In April 2016, a new inquest – the longest in English legal history, involving more than 500 witnesses and 4,000 documents – finally concluded. The jury was asked to consider 14 questions regarding the Hillsborough disaster. Question six was: "Are you satisfied, so that you are sure, that those who died in the disaster were unlawfully killed?" The jury answered: "Yes." Question seven was: "Was there any behaviour on the part of the football supporters which caused or contributed to the dangerous situation at the Leppings Lane turnstiles?" The jury answered: "No."

Afterwards, the victims' families gathered outside the courtroom and sang the Liverpool anthem *You'll Never Walk Alone*. The victims had been unlawfully killed, and Liverpool fans were entirely blameless. This really was The Truth.

15

Enhanced patriotism

One night in Turin a helicopter buzzed over an illuminated bowl that was filled with sound and life. This was the Stadio delle Alpi, the Stadium of the Alps. Europe's highest mountain range could be seen to the west, looming out of the evening dusk. The brand new stadium had been purpose built for the 1990 World Cup finals – Italia 90. Like some futuristic update of an ancient Roman amphitheatre, its sleek oval design seemed more reminiscent of a downed flying saucer than a traditional football ground. In the streets around the stadium, streams of football fans and convoys of supporters' coaches filed closer as kick-off approached. The date was 4 July 1990, and the occasion was England v West Germany in the World Cup semi-finals.

Inside the stadium, England fans were heavily outnumbered. The Football Association had been given an official allocation of just 3,000 tickets, in a stadium that held more than 70,000. But the English were highly visible, sunburnt and merry after a month in Italy. Many wore Umbro England shirts with a shiny diamond-embossed fabric and logo-trimmed collars and sleeves. Some were shirtless, with British bulldog tattoos, Union Jack shorts and Three Lions caps.

The advertising hoardings, concrete barriers and perimeter fences were draped with Union Jack and Cross of St George flags bearing the names of teams and towns from up and down the football pyramid and all across England, from Wolves to Workington. Among the flags was a large white sheet bearing the message "Pay No Poll Tax", a protest against the recently-introduced community charge, which had provoked mass riots across the UK, and would lead to the downfall of Margaret Thatcher. One England fan was photographed standing on the terrace reading the *Sun*, with the tabloid's front page on the day of the match reporting a knighthood for the disc jockey Jimmy Savile, who would later be revealed as a serial paedophile. These were indications that, even with the 1980s consigned to history, not all was rosy in England's green and pleasant land.

Facing the England fans, beyond the perimeter fences on the running track that circled the pitch, stood a line of Italian carabinieri, caps on their heads, sashes over their shoulders, pistols on their hips, and German shepherds at their sides. The atmosphere ahead of England's biggest football match since 1966 was equal parts excitement and tension. This World Cup semi-final, and Italia 90 as a whole, would help shape the future of football, and change what it meant to be a football fan.

Italia 90 was the World Cup of Toto Schillaci's goals, Roger Milla's shimmies, and, ultimately for England fans, Gazza's tears. It wasn't necessarily a classic tournament, with negative tactics and a lack of goals contributing to some pretty dour matches. But the lasting influence of Italia 90 has more to do with what happened off the pitch than on it. Football had been the popular game for more than a hundred years, yet football fans remained, to some extent, outsiders. Society in general tended to look down on football fans, particularly following the troubles of the 1970s and 1980s. Outside of the working class, it wasn't socially acceptable to be a football fan. Italia 90 helped begin to change that.

On the night of the semi-final, while England played at the Stadio delle Alpi, the Rolling Stones played at Wembley Stadium. Across London, 75-year-old Frank Sinatra played a Fourth of July concert at the former Docklands Arena.

Ordinarily, Stones and Sinatra fans with expensive gig tickets might have entirely ignored the football. But on this night concert-goers followed the semi-final on pocket radios and mini televisions, and, when their team did well, chanted, *"Eng-er-land, Eng-er-land."*

Meanwhile, in homes and pubs around the country, 26.2 million people – half the population – watched the match on television. "England's roads and places of entertainment were virtually deserted," reported the *Times*, adding that an evening debate in the House of Commons was interrupted so MPs could watch TV. BBC viewers were greeted by the network's now-iconic Italia 90 theme tune, the *Nessun Dorma* aria from Puccini's *Turandot*, sung by Pavarotti. (ITV viewers had to make do with Peter Van Hooke's *Tutti Al Mondo.*) The popularity of *Nessun Dorma*, which reached number two in the UK singles charts during the World Cup, united opera and football fans, and helped create a bridge between two supposed high-brow and low-brow cultures.

The tournament also had another soundtrack (actually England's official World Cup theme), *World in Motion* by New Order, fresh from the success of their Ibiza-infused *Technique* album. The genius of *World in Motion* was, as John Barnes' now-famous rap admitted, *"this ain't a football song"*. There was talk in the lyrics of creating space and beating your man, but it was really a song about peace and love – a celebration of togetherness. *"Love's got the world in motion,"* the chorus proclaimed before, only at the end, throwing in *"We're playing for England, En-ger-land!"*

World in Motion seemed to reflect a change that was occurring on Britain's football terraces, propelled by the emergent new youth movement – rave culture. The rise of rave was undeniably linked to the growing popularity of MDMA, popularly known as Ecstasy or E. The recreational drug became widely available in Britain from around 1988, fuelling all-night underground dance parties, or raves, in clubs and warehouses. Underground raves were an enticing proposition for Britain's working-class youths, and inevitably attracted football fans from the same demographic. But the psychedelic effects of E created a very different atmosphere than could be found at matches.

"Almost overnight, the box cutter-wielding troublemaker metamorphosed into the 'love thug'," wrote Simon Reynolds in his book *Generation Ecstasy*. Rival football firms were going to the same clubs and raves, but there was no trouble because they were "so loved up on E" and "too busy dancing and bonding with their mates". It would be easy to overstate the influence of E on football. Not all fans were loved up on artificial stimulants. But the rise in popularity of rave culture was representative of a change in attitude and atmosphere that did filter onto the terraces.

World in Motion tapped into the connection between football and rave culture, and promoted a tolerant and peaceful approach to football fandom. It also promoted positive belief in an England team that arrived at Italia 90 with pundits giving them little to no chance. New Order's Peter Hook said the song "enhanced patriotism". This was an era before every other vehicle on English roads flew a Cross of St George during an international football tournament. Before 1990, just about the most commitment the casual fan gave to showing their support for England was to collect World Cup coins or Panini stickers. *World in Motion*, and the atmosphere that inspired it, encouraged fans to go out in replica shirts, have a couple of beers, throw their arms around their mates and holler, *"En-ger-land!"* It encouraged England fans to love the game again.

But England might not have participated in the 1990 World Cup had the government, in the aftermath of Hillsborough, agreed to a suggestion to withdraw from the tournament. Although Margaret Thatcher was advised that the forthcoming Taylor Report would be "very damning" of the police and would attach "little or no blame" to the fans, the government's focus remained on crowd trouble. A government committee suggested the World Cup would provide a "natural focus" for hooliganism, and the national team should be withdrawn. However, writing to Thatcher in late 1989, her then-deputy Geoffrey Howe advised that withdrawal would not be useful as "determined hooligans will make their way to Italy anyway and find a different cause to champion".

In fact, crowd trouble at football was declining, and the media's lust for violence had seen its focus shift in the first half of 1990 to the Poll Tax riots, the Strangeways prison riot, and the continuing series of IRA bombings. Arrests at football matches in England and Wales fell by nine percent in the 1989-90 season. There had been no discernible drop-off in match attendances following Hillsborough, although crowd numbers remained in a plateau, with a First Division average of 20,757 in 1989-90. So football violence was down, but football itself remained in the doldrums.

With English clubs still banned from European competition, the England national team was effectively exiled to the island of Sardinia for its three group-stage World Cup matches. Around 5,000 England fans stayed in Sardinia for the duration of the group stage, with several thousand travelling to the mainland after the team qualified for the knock-out stages. Fan-led efforts to support travelling fans included the creation by the recently-formed Football Supporters' Association (FSA) of football embassies, which provided advice and information, and aimed to act as a form of "damage-limiter" to keep fans away from trouble.

In a further effort to prevent trouble, the Football Association and the Home Office had compiled a list of a thousand banned supporters. Football fans had been subject to banning orders since the implementation of the 1986 Public Order Act, originally introduced by the Thatcher government to tackle striking miners (referred to by the prime minister as "the enemy within"). Then fans were singled out in the 1989 Football Supporters Act, which was supposed to restrict foreign travel, but was wrongly drafted and could only be applied to domestic football. As a result, several of England's most "notorious" hooligans were able to travel to Italy.

The worst trouble involving English fans during Italia 90 was the so-called "Battle of Rimini", in which around 60 troublemakers in England shirts clash with police in riot gear, exchanging plastic chairs and tear gas. Groups of local youths, some thought to be ultras, were blamed for igniting the violence. The ultras were fanatical groups associated with Italian clubs that emerged during the late 1960s and early 1970s, at the same time as British hooligan firms. But England fans survived the Battle of Rimini, and England won the round-of-16 match against Belgium, then beat Cameroon in the quarter-finals to set up the semi-final against West Germany.

For England fans heading to Turin, there was as much trepidation as excitement. Fears of heavy-handed police and Italian ultras were as much of a concern as the potential actions of a minority of English troublemakers. On arrival at Turin railway station, English fans were separated from other travellers, and violently shoved and corralled by baton-wielding police. "Turin had hooligan psychosis like no one else," wrote Pete Davies in his acclaimed Italia 90 account *All Played Out*. Davies despaired of the "drunkenness, stupidity and violence" of some England fans, but he also criticised the aggressive policing, which he said was a "paranoid over-reaction to media and ministerial prophecies of doom". English football fans, Davies said, had effectively been criminalised for the duration of the tournament.

Then came the match, the England v West Germany semi-final in the Stadio delle Alpi, with only a few thousand English fans in attendance, and half the population of England watching on TV. The key moments of the match would remain familiar to all who saw them. Andreas Brehme's shot was deflected into the England net off Paul Parker, then Gary Lineker scored an equaliser. It was 1-1 after 90 minutes, and still 1-1 after extra time. Then came the penalty shoot-out. Stuart Pearce and Chris Waddle both missed, and England lost. (West Germany would go on to beat Argentina in the final.) England fans in the Stadio delle Alpi held their heads in their hands. Those at home did what the English seem to do in times of adversity – they made a cup of tea.

Half the population switched on their kettles after Waddle's miss, creating a huge surge in demand for electricity rated at 2,200 megawatts ("equivalent to that used by four Liverpools"). But, after such a devastating result, some England fans needed something a little stronger than a cuppa. At the end of the BBC's match coverage, presenter Des Lynam addressed viewers and said, "If you are having a drink tonight, have a drink with pride, not aggression."

Some fans did go out and vent their frustrations, smashing windows and "damaging German makes of cars", but the majority were able to swallow their pride and accept the defeat with dignity. England fans had suffered together, and there was something comforting about that fact that it had been such a large-scale communal experience. As long-standing fans already knew, and newcomers were just finding out, winning isn't everything in football.

The semi-final defeat was a unifying experience, bringing together people from different backgrounds and walks of life, all united by their support of a football team. Italia 90 seemed to push football towards the forefront of British popular culture, making it more widely acceptable to be a football fan.

"Lots of different kinds of people got interested in football, all different classes of people," reflected England's Gary Lineker. "I think it had a significant effect on the growth of football."

The England team did not win the World Cup, but they did win the Italia 90 FIFA Fair Play trophy. And the behaviour of the vast majority of England fans was equally creditable. According to the *Guardian*, far from retaining their position as the world's number one football hooligans, England fans had behaved "rather better" than either the West Germans or Italians. Two days after the World Cup final, UEFA agreed to re-admit English clubs into European competition (with the exception of Liverpool, who would be readmitted in the following season). It felt like the beginning of a fresh start for English football, with the slate wiped clean. "1990 may come to be seen as a turning point in the course of football," said the *Times*.

But there was still a way to go before the game could properly move on from the failings of the 1970s and 1980s. Clubs were busy upgrading their grounds ahead of the government's 1994-95 season deadline, in line with the recommendations of the Taylor Report. The removal of perimeter fences, many cut away within days of the Hillsborough disaster, was the most visible sign of change. However, progress was slow. An independent inspection of league grounds carried out within two years of Hillsborough found a litany of inadequacies, including blocked emergency exits, missing fire extinguishers, untrained stewards, and, in one case, a stand roof that was held up with a car jack.

These failures were largely due to continued negligence and apathy on behalf of clubs, but there were also financial reasons. Upgrading grounds was expensive, and not all clubs could easily afford to do it. Several clubs introduced debenture bond schemes to pay for their ground redevelopments, and required fans to purchase bonds in order to be allowed to buy season tickets. West Ham launched the Hammers Bond, which cost between £500 and £975. Only around 500 bonds were sold before fan protests saw the club remove the requirement to be a bond holder in order to buy a season ticket. A similar bond scheme was defeated by fan protests at Arsenal.

Whether out of necessity or greed, clubs continued to chase money. And it was money that prompted what was arguably the biggest change in British football since the formation of the Football League back in 1888. The big change – some say the revolution – came in 1992, with the formation of the Premier League.

The popular narrative says that the Premier League, along with BSkyB (British Sky Broadcasting) and a £304m TV rights deal, saved English football and turned it into a more respectable, more fashionable and more desirable game. But, while the Premier League was the high-profile, glossy representation of this football revolution, the game and its image had already begun to be revived and redefined. And it was football's fan base, not the Premier League or BSkyB, that grabbed the dying game by the scruff of the neck and shook it back to life.

This revival – the revolution before the revolution – began in the mid-1980s, post-Bradford and Heysel, among fans disillusioned with the state of the game, the way it was governed, and the way it was reported in the media. This was a reaction to the disasters and their wholly avoidable causes, to the hooligan problem and the associated perception of fans, and to the general malaise that hung over the game and made being a football fan much less enjoyable than it should be. After decades of neglect and apathy on behalf of clubs and authorities, football could not be relied upon to save itself. It was up to the fans to take back the game.

The first clear indication of a fan-led movement for

change was the formation in a Liverpool pub in 1985 of the Football Supporters' Association, the first national organisation to give a democratic voice to football fans. The nearest equivalent organisation had been the National Federation of Football Supporters' Clubs, which formed in 1926. But the Federation was an organisation for supporters' clubs, not individual supporters, and its members were chiefly occupied with running supporters' shops and organising away match travel. They were often closely affiliated with football clubs, and so acted primarily for the benefit of clubs rather than supporters. The FSA, meanwhile, was independent and politicised. It represented fans during the Hillsborough inquiry, opposed the government's ID card scheme, and operated the influential football embassies at Italia 90.

Writing in the *Observer* in September 1985, FSA chairman Rogan Taylor said disregarded fans were "the great untapped resource of football", and had never been consulted at any level when decisions were made regarding the running of the game. "Such gross neglect of the ordinary supporter... can no longer be tolerated," wrote Taylor. "The FSA is uniting fans on a nationwide basis, demanding representation of their interests on the bodies which govern football."

Also providing fans with an increasingly powerful voice was the emergent fanzine movement. The first football fanzine was *Foul*, published between 1972 and 1976 by Cambridge University students, and intended as a football version of satirical magazine *Private Eye*. But the most influential fanzine was *When Saturday Comes*, first published in March 1986 and still going more than 30 years later. *WSC* was born out of disenchantment with a beleaguered game, and it tackled some very serious fan issues, but it managed to do so in a passionate, articulate and humorous manner.

"This paper isn't going to be any sort of crusade," wrote founder Mike Ticher in the first issue. "Of course the game's in a bad way, but if everyone's just going to be miserable about it and go around wringing their hands all day, then there's not much point trying to save it at all." Initial issues were sold to a small number of enthusiasts via mail order (priced 34p, including postage and packing), but by 1991 *WSC* had a circulation of 35,000 copies – more than many mainstream magazines.

Alongside *WSC* were scores of club-specific fanzines, lovingly produced using Letraset, Tipp-Ex and photocopiers. Many of the most influential are still around today, such as Bradford City's *The City Gent* (first published in 1984, and regarded as the oldest-surviving football fanzine), Arsenal's *The Gooner* (1987), Charlton Athletic's *Voice of the Valley* (1988), Middlesbrough's *Fly Me to the Moon* (1988), Stoke City's *The Oatcake* (1988), Manchester United's *United We Stand* (1989) and Sunderland's *A Love Supreme* (1989).

Humour was a vital part of the football fanzine movement, and many fanzines had suitably irreverent and unusual names. Some of the most memorable include Queens Park Rangers' *A Kick Up The Rs*, Barnsley's *West Stand Bogs*, Watford's *Blind, Stupid and Desperate*, Gillingham's *Brian Moore's Head Looks Uncannily Like London Planetarium* (from a Half Man Half Biscuit lyric), and Sheffield Wednesday's *War of the Monster Trucks* (named for the TV show that Yorkshire Television broadcast rather than staying with Wednesday's post-match celebrations, to the chagrin of Wednesday fans, following their 1991 League Cup final win over Manchester United).

Fanzines provided a refreshing alternative to the often-anodyne match programme, and to an undesirable publication that had become increasingly conspicuous outside football grounds – the National Front newspaper. In an era in which football fans were marginalised, oppressed and disparaged, the fanzine movement sought to articulate fans' views, influence authorities, and change perceptions. And it was in changing perceptions, following two decades of high-profile football hooliganism, that the movement had most success. Fanzines helped redefine the image of football fans, from knuckle-dragging yobs to intelligent, articulate, peaceful members of society.

The irreverent sensibilities of fanzine culture would filter into the mainstream media – partly because many fanzine writers became mainstream journalists. And the influence of fanzines wasn't restricted to print media. For the 1991-92 season, BBC Radio 5 launched the football fans' phone-in *6.06* (named for its Saturday evening timeslot). *6.06* was presented by Danny Baker, a Millwall supporter who began his career writing in punk fanzines. His show provided fans with a platform to voice their unfiltered opinions, challenge the football authorities, and explore the often-absurd minutiae of the game. Humorous reminiscences about fans wearing giant wooden bow-ties or being struck in the face by wayward shots were interspersed with rants against the FA and club directors (and, inevitably, referees).

After Baker moved on to Radio 1, Radio 5's *6.06* format was watered down to focus on hot-takes from fans returning from away matches and, latterly, from those who had watched matches on TV. (Baker did revive his irreverent fanzine-style phone-in, alongside Danny Kelly, on Radio 5 and Talk Radio through the 1990s.) In 1992-93, the first Premier League season, *6.06* was presented by David Mellor, the Conservative MP. Mellor had been outed as a Chelsea fan when his affair with actress Antonia de Sancha was revealed by the *Sun* under the front page headline: "Mellor Made Love in Chelsea Strip".

New Prime Minister John Major was also a football fan, and a Chelsea season ticket-holder. While Thatcher had vilified football fans, Major aligned himself with them, which was surely an indication of changing times. Major, who had spoken of creating a "classless society", might have been seeking *Nessun Dorma*-style crossover appeal when he stated a love of opera as well as football. "We went to opera and football before I was in politics and I intend to keep doing so," Major said in 1992. "It beats reading white papers."

It has been said that football post-Italia 90 became more middle class, and that may be true. Football had primarily been a working-class game, although the middle classes had certainly not been immune to its charms. But if it was acceptable for a Conservative prime minister to talk about football, then it was surely acceptable to talk about football at dinner parties. The game certainly became more accessible, more comfortable and more attractive in the wake of the post-Hillsborough changes to grounds, governance and attitudes. Then Italia 90, with *Nessun Dorma* and Gazza's tears, pushed football to the forefront of public consciousness, and to the forefront of popular culture.

Italia 90 had already seen football intersect with opera, and then it crossed over into theatre. The 1991 stage play *An Evening with Gary Lineker*, written by Arthur Smith and Chris England, was nominated for an Olivier Award. Set during a family holiday in Ibiza, the play followed husband Bill as he attempted to avoid family duties in order to watch a football match. The match was, of course, the England v West Germany semi-final.

Football also began to infiltrate literature. Pete Davies' Italia 90 memoir *All Played Out* pushed open the door for intelligent, fan-focused football books. The most notable, and the most successful, was *Fever Pitch* by Nick Hornby, published in 1992. *Fever Pitch* followed the match-going life of an Arsenal supporter from 1968. "I have measured out my life in Arsenal fixtures," wrote Hornby, "and any event of any significance has a footballing shadow." In detailing how football can pervade all aspects of an obsessive's existence, Hornby managed to capture the endless joys and pains of being a fan.

"I fell in love with football as I was later to fall in love with women," he wrote, "suddenly, inexplicably, uncritically, giving no thought to the pain or disruption it would bring."

Fever Pitch sold over a million copies. It won the William Hill Sports Book of the Year award in 1992, and was adapted into a movie starring Colin Firth in 1997. It is regularly included in lists of the best-ever sports books. Hornby went on to become one of Britain's bestselling authors. In 2012 he was presented with the Outstanding Contribution to Sports Writing accolade at the British Sports Book Awards.

Before *Fever Pitch*, the most high-profile football fan book had been 1990's *Among the Thugs* by Bill Buford. This was one of the first of many "football hooligan memoirs". Buford, an American journalist, embedded himself with the Inter City Jibbers, a branch of Manchester United's Red Army firm, and spent eight years travelling with them to matches, often witnessing and participating in violence – including in Italy during the 1990 World Cup. Buford made few apologies for the violence, but provided some insight into the thinking of football hooligans. "I was surprised by what I found," he wrote. "I had not expected the violence to be so pleasurable."

Fever Pitch was different. In his introduction to the book, Nick Hornby didn't explicitly mention *Among the Thugs*, but did reference books like it. "I have read books written, for want of a better word, by hooligans," wrote Hornby, "but at least 95% of the millions who watch games every year have never hit anyone in their lives. So this is for the rest of us."

"I've read no better account of what being a fan really means," wrote Pete Davies in his review of *Fever Pitch*. "The book performs two invaluable services. First, it's a sound corrective to Bill Buford's inaccurate and morally repellent *Among the Thugs*. Second, it explains one of the great mysteries of life in our time – namely, why does anyone become an Arsenal fan?"

The climax of *Fever Pitch* concerned not the 1990 World Cup semi-final but the 1988-89 Football League decider. This was Liverpool v Arsenal, at Anfield on 26 May 1989, six weeks after the Hillsborough disaster. Liverpool were three points ahead of Arsenal at the top of the First Division, and Arsenal needed to win by two goals to beat Liverpool to the title. After 90 minutes, Arsenal were leading by only one goal, and Liverpool were on course to win the league. In the 92nd minute, Michael Thomas scored a famous breakaway goal to make it 2-0, and Arsenal were champions. Hornby called it "the greatest moment ever".

Hornby watched the match at home on TV – another indication of the changing nature of football. It was broadcast live, on a Friday evening, by ITV. The programme, which began at 8pm – a full five minutes before kick-off – was presented by Elton Welsby, with guest pundit Bobby Robson, and commentator Brian Moore. "It's up for grabs now!" exclaimed Moore as Michael Thomas raced clear. "Thomas! Right at the end! An unbelievable climax to the league season!" According to ITV, the match was watched by 10.3 million viewers – the biggest audience there had ever been for a league match.

The Liverpool v Arsenal match, a classic for all but Liverpool fans, remains one of the most memorable games in recent history. But its significance went beyond its entertainment value. Post-Hillsborough, as a communal experience for football fans around the country, the match seemed cathartic. Even Liverpool fans, who needed respite more than most, seemed to find some form of relief at the end of what had been the most devastating of seasons. At Anfield, the Liverpool fans applauded as Arsenal were presented with the championship trophy. It was a wonderful display of sportsmanship, which seemed to indicate that, despite the horrors that had occurred six weeks earlier, football would go on.

But football would not go on as it had before. It would survive, then thrive, and become bigger and more popular than ever. Improvements were made across the board, but whether football became "better", certainly in terms of the fan experience, would remain open to debate. Many new and existing fans would fully embrace this new and modernised version of the game, but others would develop a love-hate relationship with "modern football". The fans had kick-started a revolution, but the revolution they got was very different from the one they had expected.

16

Armchair supporters

Here we go, weekends will never be the same," said television presenter Richard Keys, wearing a dayglo yellow sports jacket that threatened to cause permanent screen burn to the viewing audience's cathode ray tubes. The date was 16 August 1992, a Sunday – or a "Super Sunday" according to BSkyB. The match was Nottingham Forest v Liverpool, the first Premier League fixture to be broadcast on Sky Sports. "It's a whole new ball game," Keys told viewers. "And remember this is the only place you'll see live Premier League football."

Heavily trailed in glossy TV ads, soundtracked by the Simple Minds song *Alive and Kicking*, this "whole new ball game" kicked off at the City Ground with a 1-0 win for Forest, courtesy of an excellent goal from Teddy Sheringham. Stuart Pearce, who had missed a penalty in front of the TV cameras in England's 1990 World Cup semi-final, was in the Forest team. Michael Thomas, who had scored the injury time goal in Arsenal's televised 1989 League decider, was now playing for Liverpool. Martin Tyler and Andy Gray were the commentators. "A new league," noted Tyler ahead of kick-off, "even a new button to press on your television sets."

Fans settled into their armchairs and perched on barstools in homes and pubs around the country. Sky Sports' five-hour *Super Sunday* programme (or *Ford Super Sunday*, given its prominent corporate branding) began at 2pm, with two hours of pre-match build-up – complete with fireworks and cheerleaders – before the 4pm kick-off, plus more than an hour of post-match analysis, interviews and phone-ins. ITV's Football League coverage had generally started five minutes before kick-off and ended five minutes after the final whistle. Nothing like this had ever been seen on British television.

The first televised Football League match had been Blackpool v Bolton, played at Bloomfield Road on 10 September 1960. To be accurate, it was the first part-televised Football League match, as not much more than half of it was shown live. The match kicked off on the Saturday evening at 6.50, but ITV's live coverage didn't start until 7.30. ITV had agreed a £150,000 deal with the League to show 26 live games over the course of the 1960-61 season. But a dispute over how much of the £150,000 would find its way from the League to the clubs saw the deal scrapped before a second match could be screened. Bolton's "drab" 1-0 win over Blackpool remained a rare TV curiosity for almost a quarter of a century.

Football didn't entirely disappear from TV screens, as FA Cup matches and internationals were still screened live, and the launch of *Match of the Day* in 1964 brought regular televised highlights into the homes of "armchair supporters". The armchair supporter wasn't a new phenomenon. Newspaper coverage had allowed fans to follow football from their armchairs for more than a century, and radio had transmitted matches into living rooms since the 1920s. But it was television that was regarded from its earliest days as the biggest threat to traditional match-going. By the 1980s, with attendances dwindling and gate money falling, the growing prospect of fans being able to watch regular games on their colour TV sets rather than clicking through the turnstiles caused many in football to panic.

Nevertheless, after protracted on-off negotiations, league matches began to be regularly televised during the 1983-84 season, with rights shared between the BBC and ITV. The first league match shown live and in full on television was

Tottenham v Nottingham Forest, on ITV on 2 October 1983. Spurs came from behind to win 2-1 with a late goal. *Times* TV reviewer Peter Ball said the live broadcast was "a reasonable advertisement for the game", but said the additions of close-ups and action replays could not compensate for not being on the terraces. "It did nothing to persuade this live fan that it was anything but a second-hand version of the real thing," wrote Ball. As ITV pundit Ian St John remarked during the match, "It's better being here than sitting at home shouting at the television set."

Despite fears that TV would keep fans away, Spurs' biggest crowd of the season, 30,596, turned up at White Hart Lane. They were treated to a four-hour "gala" involving musicians, celebrities, skydivers, and the stilt-walking world record holder. Spurs manager Keith Burkinshaw noted that, on the poster advertising the event, "the game was a little item down at the bottom of the bill". It seemed quite possible that the actual game might get lost amid the hubbub, but it was felt that, if clubs were to continue to attract fans to their grounds in this new era of television, there would need to be more such razzmatazz surrounding televised matches.

The arrival of regular TV coverage had a pronounced effect on the tribal nature of football support. Traditionally, football fans had supported their local teams. This was partly due to the connection fans had with their place of birth or residence. But it was also due to convenience. Fans supported their local team because it was the only one they could conveniently watch. Television changed this, allowing fans to regularly watch teams from outside of their local areas. Grown-up fans who had already established their loyalties were unlikely to change affiliations. But younger fans, watching football on TV during their formative years, might be more inclined to support a faraway team they saw regularly on television than a local team they never saw at all.

Children growing up during the mid-1980s, at the advent of regular TV coverage, might support Liverpool or Everton due to the Merseyside teams' dominance of the league, regardless of where they lived, at the expense of their local sides. This echoed the phenomenon of kids supporting the club that won the first FA Cup final they could remember watching on television. Young fans whose first memorable TV final was 1985's Manchester United v Everton might end up supporting Manchester United due to Norman Whiteside's extra-time winner. Schoolkids in playgrounds around the country might wear Manchester United scarves rather than those of their local teams. These "foreign" football scarves would be in a minority, but they were indicative of a new trend that would grow quickly over the coming decades.

During this new era of football on television, armchair fans embraced another way to follow the game via their TV sets. Ceefax was a teletext service developed by BBC engineers, originally as a way of providing subtitles for the deaf and hard of hearing. It evolved to provide pages of news and sport coverage, presented in white text on a black background, with coloured headlines and occasional pixelated graphics. Launched in 1974, Ceefax only really became accessible to most football fans during the early 1980s, when teletext-enabled TV sets became affordable. By 1985, more than two million UK homes had access to BBC Ceefax, and to ITV's Oracle counterpart.

Although it appeared simplistic, Ceefax was a comprehensive and innovative service. Pages were called up by keying numbers into the TV remote control – another technological advance introduced in the 1980s. It was Ceefax page 302 that became the go-to destination for a generation of fans, providing football news, league tables, transfer rumours, plus a live score service. The latter was a real game-changer for football fans, and created the new pastime of "watching" games via teletext. Live scores were presented over a rotating series of pages, with scores and scorers updated in (almost) real time. Fans endured anxious waits for pages to rotate and refresh before revealing their teams' latest scores.

One of the many remarkable things about Ceefax was that every headline on page 302 (and across the service) was written to exactly 35 characters. But Ceefax was most notable for the way it brought "instant" football coverage into homes. The service was a clear predecessor of the internet, but its football coverage also preceded the Sky Sports News tickertape, Twitter feeds, smartphone alerts and other real-time football updates.

ITV's version of Ceefax, Oracle (later renamed Teletext), presented its football coverage on page 140. Oracle relied on advertising revenue, and featured banner ads at the bottom of most pages. The football pages often featured ads promoting another type of service to fans – ClubCall. This was a premium-rate telephone line providing club-specific football news, interviews and live commentaries. ClubCall, initially operated by British Telecom, launched in 1986 with services for top First Division sides, and quickly expanded to cover all 72 league teams.

Calls cost 38p per minute at peak times and 25p at evenings and weekends (and double those prices from public call boxes), so listening to the regularly-updated six or seven-minute loops of reports and interviews, never mind 90-minute commentaries, looked prohibitively expensive. Nevertheless, ClubCall was hugely successful, receiving 12m calls within its first two years of operation, and generating up to £4.5m in revenue. ClubCall lines for top clubs received up to 2,500 calls per day, and the clubs themselves took a 50% share of the revenue. By 1989, it was estimated that ClubCall was putting as much money into football as Barclay's were for their sponsorship of the Football League.

Much of ClubCall's success stemmed from the enticing Teletext banner ads, which teased exciting news and/or rumours in the manner of "Arsenal linked with international star". Fans eager to find out just which international star their club was linked with, in the absence of other sources, would be compelled to pay 38p per minute. In the internet era, ClubCall's Teletext ads might be considered "clickbait". Much has changed, but ClubCall has survived – albeit in an online form with hundreds of competitors. Ceefax didn't survive the internet revolution. It was closed in 2012, three years after Teletext, ahead of the switchover from analogue to digital TV.

Back in the analogue world, while Tim Berners-Lee was still spinning the World Wide Web, the experience of being a TV-watching, Ceefax-reading, ClubCall-ringing armchair football fan was slowly evolving. But fans were only just getting used to watching regular televised football when the evolution stalled. After just two seasons of regular coverage, the 1985-86 season began with a TV blackout when the Football League failed to agree a deal with the BBC and ITV. Regular coverage did eventually resume, and in 1988 ITV secured exclusive rights to televise the Football League, showing around 20 matches per season, generally on Sunday afternoons. With the addition of regular FA Cup matches on the BBC, plus occasional internationals, fans could expect to watch a live match almost every week from their armchairs.

ITV had paid the not-inconsiderable sum of £44m for a four-year deal. But by 1991, with the ITV deal set to expire, it became clear that it was unlikely to be renewed at anything like the same price. A dispute had escalated between the Football League and leading clubs over control of commercial activities – primarily TV rights. Five of those clubs (the so-called "big five" of Arsenal, Everton, Liverpool, Manchester United and Tottenham Hotspur) led a breakaway from the Football League to form the Premier League.

The breakaway prompted a bidding war for TV rights between ITV and BSkyB. ITV bid £262m for a five-year deal. BSkyB bid £304m. Premier League clubs voted for their preferred bid, with a two-thirds majority required. BSkyB won by 14 votes to six. Four of the "big five" voted for the ITV bid. The fifth – Tottenham Hotspur – voted for BSkyB. According to his own reckoning, the deciding vote was cast by Tottenham owner Alan Sugar, who also owned Amstrad, which manufactured set-top boxes for BSkyB.

The Premier League breakaway was clearly going to be beneficial for the top clubs, with the £304m TV windfall being almost seven times the value of the previous deal. And it promised to be good for fans – or at least for those who supported top-flight clubs, and could afford a satellite dish and a subscription to BSkyB's Sky Sports channel. In 1992, a satellite dish and receiver cost £179.99 plus £79.99 installation, and a subscription to the encrypted Sky Sports and Sky Movies channels cost £19.98 per month.

BSkyB would show 60 live games per season, and the BBC would revive *Match of the Day* after winning the rights to show Premier League highlights. Meanwhile, ITV signed a new deal to show live Football League matches, and Channel 4 launched live coverage of Serie A games with *Football Italia* (featuring England's Italia 90 stars Paul Gascoigne, David Platt and Paul Ince). Add Scottish football, the FA and League Cups, European competitions and international games, and British viewers now had access to around 200 televised matches per season.

But was that necessarily a good thing? Writing in the *Guardian* ahead of the opening Premier League matches, David Lacey wondered if football might be moving towards a saturation point that could see fans, "spurned by some, ripped off by others", walk away. "The game is entering a risky period," wrote Lacey, "when it stands to freeze out the hard core of its support on the terraces without raising the theoretical new breed of spectators from their armchairs."

At this time, despite the improvements that had been made to the game in the late 1980s, and the profile-raising shot in the arm that was Italia 90, relatively few fans were watching domestic football. The average attendance across the First Division for the 1991-92 season was just 21,622. The attendance at Nottingham Forest's City Ground for the first Sky Premier League match in August 1992 was lower than that average, at 20,038. Empty seats and sections could be seen in the TV coverage, in between the banks of replica kit-wearing fans who would become so familiar during this new era.

TV viewing figures had been pretty healthy prior to the formation of the Premier League – hence the frenzy for TV rights. During the 1991-92 season, Football League matches shown on ITV attracted an average audience of 1.4m. But ITV was available to almost all of the UK's 20m-plus households, and it was clear BSkyB would struggle to match that figure.

When the Premier League kicked off in August 1992, around 2.5m UK households had satellite dishes, and around 700,000 of them subscribed to Sky Sports. By December 1992, there were a million Sky Sports subscribers, and televised Premier League matches attracted average audiences of around 600,000. ITV's second tier Football League matches were attracting around 800,000, while Channel 4's rival Sunday afternoon offering, *Football Italia*, also had a healthy audience. More viewers were watching First Division and Serie A football than were watching the new Premier League.

Meanwhile, those fans who preferred to watch football in person were also seeing changes. Not only were the traditional Saturday 3pm games being shifted to Sunday afternoons or Monday evenings for the TV cameras, but ticket prices were rising. In the 1989-90 season, the cheapest First Division tickets cost £3.50. In the 1992-93 season, the cheapest Premier League tickets (on the soon-to-disappear standing terraces) cost £8, more than double the price. The most expensive 1992-93 Premier League tickets, at Chelsea, cost £30.

Inevitably, as ticket prices increased, some fans were priced out. The shift to all-seater grounds squeezed capacities, and football gradually became less accessible. This change was perhaps most clearly visible at Arsenal's Highbury. Not only had the lowest ticket prices increased from £6.25 in the 1989-90 season to £10.50 in 1992-93, but, due to ground improvement work during the first Premier League season, the under-demolition North Bank was hidden by a huge painted mural depicting a packed new stand full of supporters in replica shirts. Real fans had been replaced, albeit temporarily, with fake ones.

The Highbury mural was controversial, and something of an embarrassment for Arsenal fans, with an absence of black faces failing to reflect the make-up of the club's real fanbase, and painted-in advertising hoardings promoting the contentious Arsenal bond scheme. It was a ham-fisted attempt to hide construction work, but it was also emblematic of a major change that was occurring in English football. Longstanding fans felt they were being forced out of the game – that they were literally being replaced.

A survey of football fans published in December 1992 found that supporters felt disenfranchised, exploited and expendable. Even dedicated fans were attending fewer games because of increased prices, and there was widespread dissatisfaction with the move to all-seater stadiums, and the breakaway of the Premier League to the "satellite ghetto" of BSkyB. According to the *TV Football* report, the Premier League was viewed as "the same old product in new packaging", and the shift to satellite TV had "weakened supporters' sense of involvement" with the live game. Overall, fans felt football was "moving away from them". There was a sense that the game's traditional fanbase was being lost.

A major implication of the BSkyB Premier League deal was that the financial wellbeing of top-flight clubs was no longer so wholly linked to gate revenue. For the Premier League, TV audiences were now as important – if not more so – than ground attendances. Football was increasingly catering for the armchair supporter, and this shift towards a more passive, less engaged spectator filtered into football grounds. Fans were turning up at their new all-seater stadiums expecting a sedentary TV-type experience. "Football is fast becoming just another sitting-room sport," wrote Mark Jolly in the *Times* during the first Premier League season. "Attendances are slipping, and the crowd chanting is getting quieter. The passion has gone."

Grounds were changing rapidly, with other popular terraces following Arsenal's North Bank into the history books. In 1994, Liverpool's Spion Kop and Aston Villa's Holte End terraces were both demolished. Then, in 1995, Middlesbrough left Ayresome Park, their town-centre home for 92 years, and moved to the £16m out-of-town Riverside Stadium. Ayresome Park's location, amid Victorian red-brick terraced streets, had limited the club from carrying out necessary improvements. The all-seater, 30,000 capacity Riverside was bigger and shinier, but was not necessarily better. "The stadium has the look of an airport hangar on a bombsite," said the *Times*. "There is neither the atmosphere nor aroma of Ayresome." Over the next couple of years, Derby, Sunderland, Bolton and Stoke would all follow Middlesbrough in moving to new out-of-town stadiums.

Simon Inglis, author of *Football Grounds of Britain* and a member of the Football Stadia Advisory Design Council and the Football Licensing Authority (both set up following recommendations of the Taylor Report), wrote in the *Observer* about calls for the intimate atmosphere of traditional "tightly-enclosed, inner-city" football grounds to be preserved in new stadiums, many of which were "soulless, steel and concrete sheds". Inglis quoted then-Leeds United striker Eric Cantona on his appreciation of traditional grounds. "You are close to the public," said Cantona. "It is warmer. There is room for love."

That quote might have come back to haunt Cantona a couple of seasons later when he got rather too close to the public in a football ground, with little apparent warmth or love. It was January 1995, and Cantona was playing for Manchester United at Crystal Palace's Selhurst Park. Just after half time in a bad-tempered match, Cantona lashed out at Palace's Richard Shaw and was sent off. As Cantona walked towards the tunnel past the family stand, he was confronted by a 20-year-old Palace fan.

The snarling fan, Matthew Simmons, ran from his 11th-row seat to the front of the stand and shouted, by his own recollection, "It's an early bath for you, Mr Cantona!" (Witnesses suggested Simmons actually yelled, "Fuck off back to France, you French bastard!"). In response, Cantona, "the nitro-glycerine in human form" according to the *Guardian*'s David Lacey, "briefly went berserk". He leapt into the air, over the advertising hoardings, and aimed an infamous "kung-fu kick" at Simmons' chest, then threw a couple of punches for good measure.

Newspaper front pages were emblazoned with headlines such as "Cantona on Rampage", "The Shame of Cantona", and "You Thug!" The *Sun* managed to drag the story out across 12 pages (and subsequently paid Simmons for his side of the story). There were numerous calls for the Frenchman to be kicked out of the English game. "If professional football is to retain any lingering pretensions to be a part of sport, as opposed to a product guided by market forces," wrote David Lacey, "then Eric Cantona has surely played his last game for Manchester United."

Fan-orientated outlets were much more forgiving. Danny Baker, on his *6.06* radio phone-in, asked, "Why the moral outrage? Most fans just found it incredibly funny." *When Saturday Comes* pointed out that, despite the media furore, football had not been thrown into crisis. "For all the fuss," said the fanzine, "it really doesn't signify much – players get sent off, spectators have a go at them. Cantona is a one-off. Matthew Simmons sadly isn't. We know which we'd prefer to see in English football."

Cantona was suspended by Manchester United for the remainder of the season, and for another couple of months by the FA. He was also found guilty of assault and sentenced to two weeks in jail, although this was later reduced to 120 hours' community service. Simmons, who had a previous conviction for violence, was found guilty of using threatening behaviour. Upon hearing the verdict, Simmons jumped over a bench and attacked the lead prosecutor, before being dragged away by six policemen.

The furore surrounding the Cantona kung-fu kick was no doubt fuelled by the media attention given to the Premier League and the related television coverage afforded by Sky Sports. It was plastered all over the newspapers, debated from every angle on radio programmes, and placed front and centre on TV news bulletins. But it was also one of the first big football stories to be discussed via a new medium that would, even more than the Premier League and BSkyB, completely revolutionise the way fans consumed the game. As the *Times* reported in April 1995: "Football fanatics are going online as the information superhighway offers a new avenue for their obsession... the internet."

Dial-up internct access (and what would become known as the World Wide Web) had arrived in the UK in 1992, the same year as the Premier League. At the time, few football fans would have recognised that the former would be even more revolutionary than the latter. But a small band of fans were ahead of the curve, and had already created experimental football websites on the early internet's proto-web.

One of football's very first internet pioneers was Ipswich Town supporter and British Telecom employee Phil Clarke, who set up an experimental Ipswich fans' website in 1990. Both Sheffield United and Sheffield Wednesday had early fan-run websites. Wednesday's was launched by a Nottingham University student in 1993. The longest-running football fan website is likely Reading's biscuit-inspired Hob Nob Anyone?, which was founded by Graham Loader in November 1994, and is still going strong in the superfast broadband era.

By 1995, fans of more than 40 clubs had set up "computer fanzines" on the web. "Supporters are harnessing the network that links computer users across the globe to trade jokes, terrace anthems, match reports, photographs, and reams of statistics about their favourite teams," reported the *Times*. Almost every Premier League club had a fan website, as did half of all First Division clubs, plus non-league clubs including Halifax Town and Barrow. It was noted that Third Division Colchester United's website had attracted a full 127 surfers in just ten days.

The first major tournament to be properly covered on the internet was Euro 96, via websites such as the *Guardian*'s Eurosoccer (the newspaper's very first website of any description), and the influential Soccernet (which would later become ESPNFC). But, with internet usage still a niche activity, few fans had access to football websites, and those who did were restricted to torturously slow (by modern standards) "narrowband" dial-up connections. Only 4% of the UK population had access to the internet in 1996. And there was only so much Euro 96 content that could be enjoyably consumed at 56 kilobits per second. So the majority of fans followed the tournament on their televisions.

The prospect of England hosting Euro 96 had filled many with dread. Following the 1990 World Cup, English hooligans had been involved in violence at the 1992 European Championships in Sweden, with 250 England fans arrested for violence and disorder. England had failed to qualify for the 1994 World Cup in the US, to the relief of the organisers. "There were three countries in the world whose presence would have created logistical problems, so we're very pleased they won't be coming," said USA 94 organising committee chairman Alan Rothenberg, naming the three countries as, "Iraq, Iran and England."

At Euro 96, fears were highest ahead of the England v Scotland group stage match at Wembley on 15 June, due to the rivalry between the home nations, and the large number of Scots who were likely to attend. But Scotland fans had no reputation for violence, and they treated their trip to Wembley like a day-long party. Unlike in 1977, there was no pitch invasion. "The supporters' behaviour, boisterous but good-humoured, was all the more remarkable," said the *Times*, "considering the vast amount of alcohol consumed before the kick-off."

England fans, too, were placid. The mid-1990s were, after all, the era of Cool Britannia – the heyday of Oasis and Britpop, Kate Moss and *Loaded*, Tony Blair and New Labour. On the surface at least, things seemed a lot brighter than they had during the 1980s. As Labour's campaign theme suggested: *Things Can Only Get Better*. That wasn't necessarily true, but it was nice to believe it for a while. It was nice to believe that Euro 96, the Cool Britannia tournament, might represent a bright new start for football fans.

England won the match against Scotland, thanks to a penalty save from David Seaman and a classic goal from Paul Gascoigne. There were 76,864 fans inside Wembley. Euro 96 was a last hurrah for the great Empire Stadium. It would be closed at the end of the decade, its twin towers demolished to make way for a new Wembley that would be entirely unrecognisable from the original. This was another reminder that Euro 96 represented the end of an old era and the beginning of a new one.

After the match, as the England players took the acclaim of the fans, the stadium DJ played a pop song called *Three Lions.* Every England fan knew the words and, in scenes reminiscent of those from Anfield during the Merseybeat era, the entire home crowd sang along. In replica England shirts, they held aloft red, white and blue scarves, waved Cross of St George flags, and sang the song's chorus: *"It's coming home, it's coming home, it's coming, football's coming home."*

Three Lions was written and performed by comedians David Baddiel and Frank Skinner with Lightning Seeds musician Ian Broudie. A remarkably bittersweet song (given it was the FA-approved official England record), the lyrics reflected on the national team's *"30 years of hurt"* since the glory of 1966. Repeated failures at major tournaments had, Skinner and Baddiel sang, *"never stopped me dreaming"*. It was likely that the England team would continue to let their fans down, but there was hope, always hope. If nothing else, the song represented a refreshing change in attitude.

England lost to Germany in the semi-finals of Euro 96 – on penalties, of course – just as *Three Lions* had suggested they might. There was rioting afterwards in Trafalgar Square, proving that not everything had changed. But, after the pain of defeat had been washed away, a newfound hope seemed to linger. As at Italia 90, the England team's performance at Euro 96 united the country. And, with the pains of the 1980s receding in the rear-view mirror, a new feel-good factor emerged among fans. Here was optimism – something English football fans had been without for decades. Perhaps football really had come home.

23.8 million viewers watched the England v Germany semi-final on BBC and ITV. It was the biggest UK TV football audience since the 1990 semi-final, between the same teams and with the same outcome. The *Guardian*'s Eurosoccer website received a million hits per week during the tournament, suggesting that football could perhaps be as big a draw on the internet as it was on TV. By 1997, Sky Sports, the Premier League and several leading clubs had all launched official sites, and the *Guardian* had launched its general football website, Football.co.uk (later renamed Football Unlimited). By the end of that year, there were an estimated 300 football sites on the web.

From the earliest days of the internet it was recognised that this new media represented a threat to the old media. Football coverage had been a key driver of newspaper sales for more than a hundred years. But when fans could read match reports on the internet within minutes of the final whistle, why would they bother to buy a newspaper? Newspapers responded by improving their offerings to retain football readers, with colour photos, weekly pull-outs, and initiatives such as fantasy football. The *Telegraph*'s weekly fantasy football results page drew an extra 50,000 readers every Wednesday.

More printed football coverage could be found in football magazines, which had evolved substantially since the days of *Charles Buchan's Football Monthly*. There were some survivors from the latter years of *Football Monthly*, with *World Soccer* and *Shoot* both still around in the Premier League era. *Shoot* and rival *Match* would increasingly target younger readers. Older fans could enjoy *90 Minutes*, a glossy attempt at a fanzine, which ran from 1990 until 1997. During the early years of the Premier League, new big-budget glossies appeared. *FourFourTwo* first hit the shelves in 1994, and *Total Football* and *Goal* arrived in the following year.

Match programmes were also evolving. In colour, with pull-out posters, interviews and features, they had advanced from simple team sheets to glossy magazines. This was a sign that clubs were recognising the need to provide fans, and customers, with a better product. Obviously this better product would come at a price. Manchester United's programme cost £1.50 in 1996-97, Chelsea's cost £1.80 and Arsenal's cost £2.00, all having increased in price by around 50% since the launch of the Premier League.

Meanwhile, Premier League ticket prices – and fan dissatisfaction – were continuing to rise. Top-priced tickets for the 1996-97 season at Chelsea were £40, up 25% since the launch of the Premier League. In addition to gate revenue and TV money, top-flight clubs were raking in cash from sponsorship deals, corporate hospitality and replica kit sales. That the Premier League itself was now known as the FA Carling Premiership was clear evidence of the game's growing commercialisation.

"A working-class game has become a textbook example of rampant free market capitalism," wrote Richard Williams in the *Guardian*, "and is currently enjoying a boom which, like all booms, appears irreversible." Some aspects of this boom were positive. Attendances were rising, and an increasing number of women and children were attending games, creating a more family-friendly atmosphere. "In this sense, the game has begun to purge itself of some unhelpful traditions," wrote Williams.

But, as Williams noted, there were cracks in the Premier League's glossy façade. Longstanding fans were being priced out, while blocks of expensive seats were left unsold. Noise levels had fallen, and the atmosphere had been dampened. Clubs were marketing £60 replica kits to children, complete with beer and betting company sponsor logos. And televised matches remained hidden behind the BSkyB paywall. Even one of football's most high-profile fans seemed to be falling out of love with the game.

"I used to watch absolutely everything, even the schoolboy internationals," said *Fever Pitch* author Nick Hornby. "Now I just don't bother half the time." There was too much football on TV, Hornby reckoned, and the shift to all-seater stadiums and rising ticket prices had alienated many fans. "The atmosphere was better before," said Hornby. "It's important to remember that the reason television has been interested in football is because of the atmosphere. It's not going to be much good to them if it's just zombies sitting there."

At many grounds, working-class match-goers were being replaced by more affluent fans who were willing to pay extra for their (padded) seats, often in prime areas of the grounds. It was no real surprise that the redevelopment of Premier League grounds involved the expansion of lucrative corporate hospitality areas, with longstanding fans – and their traditions – being squeezed out. The match pie was being replaced by the prawn sandwich, and the new breed of "zombie" fans, many of whom seemed to attend matches to enjoy the hospitality rather than the actual football, became known as the "prawn sandwich brigade".

That phrase was invented by the media following a remarkable post-match rant from Roy Keane in which the then-Manchester United captain criticised sections of the Old Trafford crowd. "Away from home our fans are fantastic, I'd call them the hardcore fans," said Keane. "But at home they have a few drinks and probably the prawn sandwiches, and they don't realise what's going on out on the pitch. I don't think some of the people who come to Old Trafford can spell football, never mind understand it."

Despite the perceived poor atmosphere, the ground redevelopments, the threat from television, and the loss of many traditional fans, Premier League attendances began to rise. The average attendance in the opening Premier League season of 1992-93 had been 21,125. By 1996-97, the season following Euro 96, the average was 28,434. By 1999-2000, it was more than 30,000, and by 2002-03 it would exceed 35,000 – reaching a ceiling that would remain comparable to average attendances well into the following decade.

2002-03 was the season in which the old Wembley Stadium was demolished and work began on its replacement. The stadium had been empty for a couple of years, having been stripped of any and all saleable assets. 73 lots of items, ranging from signs and seats to fixtures and fittings, were sold in an online auction. Several of the lots, including the Wembley goalposts and nets, were bought by FC Barcelona for the Nou Camp museum. It seemed fitting that an auction representing the end of a footballing era was conducted on the internet.

As old Wembley was replaced by new Wembley, dial-up internet was replaced by broadband. New faster connections meant football websites could run more advanced and interactive content. This included audio commentaries, then video footage, beginning with highlights, and moving on to live matches. Where dial-up internet had threatened newspapers, broadband now threatened radio and television, as fans found new ways to follow football.

And this was just a taste of how the internet and related new technologies would transform the football fan experience. Over the next decade, the rise of social media would change the way fans communicated with each other, and with players, clubs and journalists. Smartphones would give fans access to instant football scores, news and videos at the swipe of a thumb. Streaming would allow fans to watch matches on trains, in cafes and in parks. Laptops, tablets and phones would allow armchair supporters to leave their living rooms and take the game with them via wherever they went. The armchair fan was going mobile.

Many fans embraced this new super-connected era, but others yearned for a return to the more traditional pre-internet and pre-Premier League fan experience. Much had improved since the dark days of the 1970s and 1980s. Football grounds were certainly safer, more comfortable and more family-friendly. But some aspects of the game had worsened, with increasing prices, growing commercialism and dwindling atmospheres causing disaffection and alienation. Some fans were happy to be swept along by the modern football revolution, but others began to dig their heels in. There was about to be a revolution against the revolution.

17

Against modern football

AFC Wimbledon started at the bottom – specifically at Bottom Meadow, the home ground of Sandhurst Town. Crowds in the Combined Counties League, in the ninth tier of the English football pyramid, rarely exceeded double figures. Yet, as fans began to stream through the sunshine towards Bottom Meadow's hastily-erected beer tent and improvised hay bale terracing, it became clear that this crowd would be significantly bigger than usual.

The date was 17 August 2002, and this was the first fixture of a club that had technically only existed for six weeks – although its fans would argue that it was a direct continuation of a club with 113 years of history. AFC Wimbledon had been formed by supporters of Wimbledon FC, following the extraordinary decision of the Football Association to allow the First Division club to be moved 70-plus miles up the M1 to Milton Keynes. But the club's fanbase could not be so easily moved. "AFC" did not, on this occasion, stand for "Association Football Club". It stood for "A Fans' Club".

By the time the hastily-assembled team kicked off their opening game, there were almost 2,500 fans crowded around the pitch, many of them already in possession of AFC Wimbledon scarves and flags. The atmosphere was jubilant even before AFC scored through Kevin Cooper, then doubled their lead through Keith Ward. Sandhurst pulled a goal back in the second half, but the final score was 2-1 to AFC. The official attendance was 2,449. This had been a triumph on and off the pitch for a pioneering fan-owned club.

Meanwhile, on the same afternoon, the club still officially known as Wimbledon FC were playing at Watford in the First Division. The crowd of 10,292 included fewer than 200 Wimbledon fans, even taking into account a trio of cardboard cut-outs that had been drolly placed in the away section. Wimbledon FC scored an equaliser in the 86th minute, then conceded in the 87th minute, and lost to Watford 3-2. They had already lost the majority of their supporters. The club still officially known as Wimbledon FC were known to their former fans as Franchise FC.

The lock-and-stock relocation of clubs was virtually unheard of in British football, and is more commonly associated with US sports franchises. There are scores of examples from baseball, American football, basketball and hockey. Particularly controversial relocations have included the Brooklyn Dodgers swapping east coast for west to become the Los Angeles Dodgers in 1958, and the Cleveland Browns becoming the Baltimore Ravens in 1996. The US franchise system has allowed club owners to up sticks virtually on a whim, regardless of their fan bases.

In the UK there was no franchise system, although various football clubs had made relatively major moves. Arsenal relocated from Woolwich in South London to Highbury in North London, and Manchester United relocated from Newton Heath to Stretford, with both clubs changing their names accordingly. The then-Football League club South Shields moved a similar distance – around ten miles – in 1930 to become Gateshead FC. But no club in the modern era had relocated so significantly, leaving their fan base so far behind, as Wimbledon FC.

Founded in 1889, Wimbledon's glory years came a century later, when a rapid rise to the First Division was followed by the famous 1988 FA Cup final win over Liverpool, courtesy of the "Crazy Gang" team, featuring Vinnie Jones, Dennis Wise and John Fashanu. Wimbledon didn't have a huge fan base, and the club's average attendance was the lowest in the First Division at around 7,000 before the launch of the Premier League. But the club was holding its own in the top flight, certainly until 1991 when it left Plough Lane, its home of more than 80 years.

Claiming it would be too difficult and expensive to redevelop Plough Lane to meet the requirements of the Taylor Report, owner Sam Hammam agreed a groundshare with Crystal Palace at Selhurst Park. The club left Wimbledon, never to return. A plan was mooted to move Wimbledon FC even further afield, to Dublin. Then Hammam sold the club to a pair of Norwegian millionaires, who brought in South African Charles Koppel, a former speedboat racing team manager who had apparently never been to a football match in his life, to run the club.

Koppel was convinced the club had to relocate to survive. Then he met Pete Winkelman, a former 1980s pop music executive who was now head of the Milton Keynes Stadium Consortium. Milton Keynes was the biggest city in Europe without a football team, it was claimed. Winkelman had already been turned down by Barnet and Queens Park Rangers, and now wanted Wimbledon. Koppel saw this as a golden opportunity. Wimbledon would get a share in the new stadium, and financial security would surely follow. So Koppel announced his intention to move Wimbledon to Milton Keynes.

In fact, Milton Keynes was not the only city in Europe (nor in England) without a professional football club, and was not actually a city – it was designated a new town in 1967. Most professional clubs were founded during the Victorian and Edwardian eras, when Milton Keynes, then a tiny village, was barely on the map. The nearest professional club, Luton Town, was founded more than 80 years before Milton Keynes became a new town. It seemed logical that Milton Keynes would not have a professional football club. But Milton Keynes did have a non-professional football club, the incongruously-named Milton Keynes City FC. Unfortunately, that club was effectively killed off by the Wimbledon move, folding due to "a lack of significant interest" and "the confused situation with the relocation of Wimbledon to Milton Keynes".

Immediately following Koppel's announcement, the Wimbledon Independent Supporter's Association (WISA) launched the biggest fan protest British football had ever seen. Fans from other clubs united behind WISA's campaign, and the Dons Trust, a one-fan one-vote co-operative, was set up to raise funds. But Koppel ignored fans' protests, apparently convinced he could fill the Milton Keynes stadium with that town's locals, and didn't need Wimbledon's existing fans. WISA pressed the football authorities for assistance but an FA commission eventually sanctioned the move.

Within hours of the FA's decision, plans were made to form a new club. AFC Wimbledon's founders tapped into the wide-ranging skills and contacts of the existing fanbase. A £100,000 sponsorship deal was secured, and a deal was arranged to groundshare with Kingstonian FC at Kingsmeadow, around four miles from Wimbledon, but significantly nearer than Milton Keynes. An open trial on Wimbledon Common attracted 230 potential players, and a new team was assembled under the management of former Wimbledon player Terry Eames. "For the last two years supporters have been going to games and protesting," said Eames after the opening match win. "Now they've got their own football club, they've all got a share of it, it's just fantastic."

4,215 fans turned up to AFC Wimbledon's first home match at Kingsmeadow. The club had sold 1,150 season tickets. They would eventually buy Kingsmeadow, later selling it to Chelsea to fund a proposed move back to Plough Lane.

Meanwhile, only 628 Wimbledon FC supporters turned up for that club's home game against Brighton, and were outnumbered three to one by away fans. When just 21 Wimbledon FC fans travelled to Grimsby, the *Daily Mirror* named every one of them, revealing that several were players' family members. Then, for a home match against Rotherham in October, the official attendance at the 26,000-capacity Selhurst Park was just 879 – including 227 Rotherham fans – a First Division record low. After several delays, Wimbledon FC finally moved to Milton Keynes in September 2003. In the following year, with AFC Wimbledon disputing Wimbledon FC's continued use of the name, the relocated club were renamed MK Dons.

The goal of AFC Wimbledon's fans and founders was to reclaim the club's rightful place in the Football League. This was achieved after just nine seasons, with AFC winning promotion to League Two via the play-offs in 2011. Even the club's founding chairman, Kris Stewart, was shocked by the club's rapid rise. "I thought it was possible," he said, "but it did not seem likely or even probable." In 2016, AFC Wimbledon were promoted to League One, where they would face MK Dons. And, that October, AFC went above MK in the table, a historic achievement for A Fans' Club.

AFC Wimbledon were one of the first fan-owned clubs in British football's modern era, although their existence harked back to the game's earliest years, when clubs were formed by and for their members and communities. Following in the footsteps of AFC, scores of fan-owned clubs emerged, including supporter takeovers Exeter City, Newport County and Wrexham, and phoenix clubs Chester FC, Darlington 1883 and AFC Rushden and Diamonds.

Another prominent fan-owned club was FC United of Manchester, formed in 2005 by disaffected Manchester United fans following the takeover of the Premier League club by US businessman Malcom Glazer and his family. Formed as a community benefit society, FC United published a founding manifesto that set out the club's core principles of democracy, inclusivity and affordability. The manifesto stated that the club would work closely with the local community, keep admission prices low, and aim, wherever possible, to avoid commercialism.

This last principle was particularly important, as it wasn't just the Glazer takeover that FC United's founders were protesting, it was the way football in the Premier League era was increasingly chasing profit at the expense of its supporters. Ticket prices were rising, terraces were being replaced by corporate areas, and traditional fans were being forced out. TV games were hidden behind paywalls, players were routinely paid more in a week than their fans earnt in a year, and every aspect of the game was being plastered with sponsor logos. Protesters wanted a return to the traditional fan experience. They were against modern football.

For many fans, the world of FC United represented a kind of football utopia, far removed from the excesses of the Premier League. The democratic one-member, one-vote system put the running of the club firmly into the hands of its fans. (By the 2016-17 season, FC United had 3,944 member-owners.) Shares and grants enabled the club to build the impressive £6.3m Broadhurst Park stadium, providing sport and education facilities for the wider community. And the FC United fanbase built a reputation as a boisterous and noisy following. One early FC United fan banner read, with a reference to the famous Roy Keane quote: "Pies not prawns." And a popular terrace song, aimed at the man who had driven them from their previous club, was: *"Glazer, wherever you may be, you bought Old Trafford but you can't buy me."*

But for others, the club was a rebellious annoyance. Some Manchester United fans regarded FC United fans as deserters and traitors. (Manchester United manager Sir Alex Ferguson described FC United, during a press conference, as "sad".) There was also some disharmony among FC United fans – and owners – as the club attempted to adjust to the financial realities associated with their new stadium. Was it possible for a successful football club to avoid commercialism? And, given the many improvements made to the game over the previous couple of decades, was modern football really so bad?

On the surface, football did not appear to be suffering as a result of fan dissatisfaction. Premier League attendances had increased, from an average of 31,180 in 1999-2000 to 33,899 in 2004-05. Stadiums were pretty much packed, filled to 94% of capacity on average for every Premier League game. And, while TV audience figures had remained fairly constant at around 900,000 per match, total viewing had increased, with more live televised games and a bigger audience reach. Many fans, it seemed, were willing to accept the various shortcomings of the modern game.

"Football fans are idiots," wrote Sean Ingle in the *Guardian* in 2005. "Or, to rephrase that sentence using less incendiary language: when it comes to football, intelligent people act stupid. And yes, that probably includes you." Football was getting increasingly expensive, more predictable, and less atmospheric. And yet fans were still buying season tickets, still travelling to away matches, and still subscribing to Sky Sports. But in football, perhaps uniquely, price did not seem to affect demand. The majority of fans – if they could afford to – would willingly pay increased prices, out of loyalty if not enjoyment. And those who wouldn't or couldn't pay would be replaced by others who would and could.

An Arsenal season ticket for 2005-06 (the Gunners' last season at Highbury before moving to the new Emirates Stadium) cost an unprecedented £1,825. A single match ticket in the East Lower stand cost £39, up from £19 in 1999-2000, and up from £10 in the pre-Premier League 1991-92 season. This was more than two or three times the price of comparable tickets in Italy or Germany. Sean Ingle noted that match tickets at Roma could be purchased for £15, and at Borussia Dortmund for £10. "Fans stand up for themselves more in mainland Europe," he wrote. "In England they just roll over."

The "Against Modern Football" movement began on the continent, initially among the politically-active ultras in Italy and Germany. The main complaints of Italian and German fans were similar to those of their British counterparts: increasing prices, dwindling atmospheres and growing commercialisation. The Italian game was riddled with corruption, culminating in the 2006 Calciopoli match-fixing scandal that saw Serie A champions Juventus, plus Fiorentina and Lazio, relegated to Serie B. And the German game was becoming overly-sanitised, with the mostly-peaceful ultras feeling ostracised and victimised by efforts to drive out an aggressive minority. Protest banners began to appear on the Serie A and Bundesliga terraces: *Contro il Calcio Moderno* and *Gegen den Modernen Fussball.*

It was Germany in particular that led the way in setting out the values and ideals that fan movements elsewhere could aspire to. The Bundesliga was the best-attended football league in the world. The average Bundesliga attendance in 2005-06 was 40,799, compared to the Premier League average of 33,864. Borussia Dortmund's average attendance in the same season was 72,808, compared to Manchester United's 68,765. Dortmund's Westfalenstadion was famous for the *Gelbe Wand*, the Yellow Wall, a fervent mass of 25,000 fans with yellow shirts, scarves and flags that filled the south stand in a riot of colour and noise.

The Yellow Wall was known for its tifos – choreographed fan displays involving flags and banners. Tifo culture originated in Italy (in a football context, the Italian word *tifo* means support), and spread across Europe, into South America, and then, after the revitalisation of Major League Soccer, into North America. But the often-spectacular displays were not replicated in the UK, perhaps because tifo culture was closely associated with the ultras movement, which didn't have a foothold in Britain. British football fans were generally more spontaneous and less organised, which was simultaneously to their credit and to their detriment.

For many British fans, it looked like their German contemporaries had little to complain about. German football was cheaper, less predictable and more atmospheric than English football. The Germans had safe standing areas, could drink alcohol on the terraces, and orchestrated those fantastic tifo displays. And yet many German fans were still against modern football. Bundesliga matches were increasingly corporate affairs, with growing numbers of executive seats, and more and more visible sponsorship deals. And the ultras in particular felt they were being persecuted as part of a crackdown on a minority of troublemakers, with the peaceful majority also subject to over-zealous policing and regulations.

But German fans were better-placed to do something about the problems of modern football than their British contemporaries. Bundesliga regulations included the "50+1 rule", which required members to own at least 50% plus one share of their club, meaning no external investor could own more than 49%. In theory, the rule gave members – or fans – a controlling influence over the running of their clubs. In practice, however, it wasn't a perfect solution. Exceptions were granted for investors that had substantially funded clubs for several years, such as pharmaceuticals company Bayer at Bayer Leverkusen. And some membership schemes were so expensive as to exclude general fans, such as at RB Leipzig, where many members were associated with energy drink manufacturer Red Bull.

So German fans continued to push for change, under their *Gegen den Modernen Fussball* banners. The ultras-led fans behind the Against Modern Football movement were written off by some as radicals or anarchists, although their calls for a return to traditional ideals and a better fan experience didn't seem particularly unreasonable. Perhaps the most prominent group of German football "radicals" were the fans of FC St Pauli, the Hamburg-based club, whose skull-and-crossbones flags indicated the self-styled pirates' alternative sensibilities. Many St Pauli fans were politically and socially active, with a strong anti-violence, anti-racist, anti-fascist, anti-homophobic and anti-sexist stance. Regarded as a "Kult" club, St Pauli, based near Hamburg's Reeperbahn red-light district, became a worldwide symbol of the alternative fan movement.

It was fan influence that helped the German Bundesliga challenge the assertion that the English Premier League was the best league in the world. The TV-led expansion of the Premier League had given the English league a bigger profile (and deeper pockets), but the German league seemed to offer a better fan experience. "Few can seriously question the rise of the Premier League over the past 15 years," wrote Jeremy Wilson in the *Telegraph* in 2008, "yet it is doubtful whether any country has succeeded quite like Germany in transporting the soul of football from yesteryear into a safe and modern environment."

One feature of German football that was envied by many British fans was safe standing. Many German grounds had railed safe standing areas, with each fan allocated a ticketed space. A long-running supporters' campaign suggested that 90% of British fans wanted the option to stand. As well as benefitting those who wanted to stand, safe standing was likely to benefit those who preferred to sit, but did not want their view to be blocked by people standing in the seated sections. It was also thought that safe standing could improve football's flagging atmospheres. Safe standing was debated in parliament in 2008, but lingering opposition to any form of standing at football matches meant it would take several years to be approved. (Bristol City installed a safe standing area in 2014, and Celtic became the first top-flight club in the UK to install safe standing in 2016.)

British football was clearly lagging behind the German game, and the Against Modern Football movement would take a while to take off in the UK. The efforts of the Wimbledon fans who had formed AFC Wimbledon and the Manchester United fans who had formed FC United of Manchester proved there was an appetite for a shift away from the negative aspects of modern football. But could such a shift be made without physically walking away from the Premier League? Could fan influence work in English football?

Following the sales of Chelsea to Russian billionaire Roman Abramovich in 2003, Manchester United to the Glazers in 2005, and Aston Villa to Cleveland Browns owner Randy Lerner in 2006, Liverpool were sold to US investors Tom Hicks and George Gillett in 2007. (Manchester City would subsequently be sold to Sheikh Mansour bin Zayed Al Nahyan's Abu Dhabi United Group in 2008.) Liverpool fans quickly turned against Hicks and Gillett after promised investments in a new stadium and players failed to materialise. Within a year, fans were protesting at matches, and the newly-formed Spirit of Shankly group had mobilised. Fan pressure led Gillett to announce he would sell his shares, but Hicks blocked the deal. It wasn't until 2010 that Hicks and Gillett sold the club – certainly as a result of fan protests – to Boston Red Sox and *Boston Globe* owner John W Henry's Fenway Sports Group.

John Henry cited the actions of Spirit of Shankly in particular as one of the reasons he had decided to buy the club. But the Spirit of Shankly group had not finished its work. The Liverpool supporters' union's stated long-term aim was to bring about supporter representation at board room level, while its ultimate aim was supporter ownership of Liverpool FC. The group placed a quotation from Bill Shankly at the top of its website: "The socialism I believe in is everyone working for each other, everyone having a share of the rewards. It's the way I see football, the way I see life."

Efforts to increase fan influence and ownership in football led to the creation of Supporters Direct, an umbrella organisation for supporters' trusts and community owned clubs. The organisation's first managing director was Brian Lomax, one of the founders of the Northampton Town Supporters' Trust, which was English football's first supporters' trust, founded in 1992. By 2014, according to Supporters Direct, there were 185 supporters' trusts or community-owned clubs in the UK, with 355,450 members.

Also mobilising to represent fans was the Football Supporters' Federation (FSF), formed in 2002 after the amalgamation of the Football Supporters' Association and the National Federation of Supporters' Clubs. The FSF campaigned against high ticket prices and for the introduction of safe standing, and took over the operation of overseas fan embassies. The FSF also campaigned for fan rights with regard to over-zealous policing and stewarding under the banner: Watching Football is Not a Crime.

Of particular concern was a new piece of legislation, Section 27 of the Violent Crime Reduction Act 2006, which allowed police to remove from an area for a period of 48 hours any individual they believed might contribute to an alcohol-related disorder. Any individual refusing to comply with a Section 27 request could be arrested. Police began to use the legislation to control football fans, regardless of whether they had actually contributed to any alcohol-related disorder – or even drunk any alcohol. Fans were detained, moved, and prevented from attending matches.

In one case, in November 2008, 80 Stoke City fans were detained by police in a pub in Manchester ahead of a match against Manchester United. The fans were loaded onto coaches and escorted to Stoke, regardless of where they had travelled from. Witnesses, including the pub landlord, said there was no disorder, nor even any chanting or singing. Fans were ordered to sign a Section 27 form, and were threatened with arrest if they refused. All were unable to watch their match. Following FSF representation, the fans received compensation and an apology from Greater Manchester Police.

Fans were routinely herded, kettled and detained by police – often with dogs – and regularly filmed, harassed, and even struck with batons, for nothing more than attempting to go to watch a football match. It was accepted that police needed to take action against hooligans and other troublemakers, but all football fans seemed to be subject to treatment that would not be acceptable in wider society. "Fans are discriminated against," said Sarah Ricca, a lawyer who had represented fans. "The unspoken prejudice is that everyone going to a match might cause trouble. The more power you give to the police the more dangerous they become."

"I have come to be horrified at some of the treatment that law-abiding fans have experienced," said Shami Chakrabarti, director of Liberty, the campaign group for civil liberties and human rights. "We are in danger of demonising anyone who goes to football matches. They have grown used to being herded en masse. If you want people to behave well, treat them with respect."

Since the relatively peaceful Euro 96 on home turf, England fans had rebuilt their reputation for hooliganism. At the World Cup in France in 1998, England fans rioted in Marseille, and 274 were arrested. At the European Championships in Belgium and the Netherlands in 2000, there was rioting in Charleroi. Almost 1,000 England fans were arrested for violence and disorder, and UEFA were ready to expel the England team from the tournament. (That might have happened, had the team not been knocked out at the group stage.)

But Euro 2004 in Portugal was relatively trouble-free, with only around 50 England fans arrested, mostly in holiday resorts away from the matches. Then at the 2006 World Cup in Germany, with around 100,000 England fans in attendance, there were 200 "preventative" arrests, but only three fans were charged with criminal offences. It seemed that English football might finally be shaking off the blight of hooliganism.

Then, in August 2009, an incident occurred that harked back to the darkest days of the 1970s and 1980s. A League Cup match between West Ham and Millwall provided the opportunity for a pre-arranged clash between rival firms. It was the first time the clubs had met for several years, as they had been in different divisions. The violence, beginning outside Upton Park tube station on Green Street and continuing inside the stadium, involved several thousand fans and more than 700 riot police, and lasted more than six hours. A 43-year-old bystander was knifed in the chest, another man was hit in the head with a dart, and others were struck with bricks and concrete bollards. Thirteen people were arrested.

The shock that greeted the incident seemed indicative of the fact that incidents of hooliganism were no longer commonplace. Most level-headed football fans were appalled, although one Millwall supporter, named as Jonny, told the *Independent* he was pleased the hatred between the two clubs had been reignited. "I'm delighted," he said. "Shame it can't be like that every week."

Thankfully, it wasn't like that every week. While the modern football revolution might have robbed fans of some of the game's traditional pleasures, football was safer and more accessible than it had been for a long time. Home Office figures for 2008-09 showed that football-related arrests during that season were down by a third compared to 1988-89. The total number of people arrested represented just 0.01% of all spectators, with more than two thirds of matches being completely arrest-free. According to the Home Office, the five years up to 2009 saw the lowest number of football-related arrests since records began.

Figures for the same season released by the Premier League showed football crowds were becoming increasingly diverse. Of the 13.6 million fans who attended matches in the 2008-09 season, 19% were women, while 8% were black and minority ethnic. Of new attendees, who had started going to matches in the previous five years, 33% were women, and 16% were black and minority ethnic. The fact that 13% of Premier League season ticket holders were children suggested that football was becoming increasingly family-friendly. The survey showed that nine out of ten fans who attended matches with children felt comfortable doing so.

However, such progress had come at a price, and there was no getting away from the fact that the cost of football was becoming prohibitively expensive. According to Virgin Money's Football Fans' Index, the average cost of watching a match in the 2008-09 season, including ticket, transport and food and drink, was £106.21, with a quarter of fans saying they would attend fewer matches due to price rises. By 2010, the average matchday cost had fallen slightly, to £97.50, with the average ticket price £24.84 across all divisions and £36 in the Premier League. But, while matchday costs had fallen, merchandise costs had risen. The average price of an adult-sized Premier League replica shirt was £40.89, with personalised number and name printing costing an additional £10 to £15. This time, almost half of fans surveyed said they would spend less on football due to the high cost.

And it was the continuing price rises and perceived exploitation of football fans that drove British fans towards the

Against Modern Football movement – alongside more trivial fan issues, such as a dislike of fireworks, cheerleaders, and the playing of "goal music" when teams scored. "Against Modern Football" became a shorthand response to virtually any non-traditional occurrence or innovation, from players wearing multi-coloured boots to stadium food kiosks selling halloumi burgers. At its heart, though, the AMF movement was pushing back against the commercialisation, corporatisation and gentrification of football.

When the fanzine STAND launched in 2012, it featured the words "Against Modern Football" on its cover. The fanzine's editors stated that, while they identified with "AMF", they were not the voice of the Against Modern Football movement. "We do not want the return of a game blighted by hooliganism, racism and death-trap stadiums," said the STAND website. "The game had to change but the scale of change has [taken] the game away from the many who so enjoy it." The fanzine explored issues such as ticket prices, fan ownership, safe standing, and the mistreatment of football fans. And STAND was "absolutely and totally against anything to do with a certain club from Milton Keynes". For many fans, MK Dons had come to represent the unacceptable face of modern football.

But there was still a lot to love about the modern game. It was difficult to argue that football wasn't better off without some of its rough edges. Watching football was a safer and more comfortable experience, and the game was now more inclusive. The various ills associated with the Premier League did not all extend down the football pyramid. A more traditional, and for many more rewarding, experience could be found at lower league and non-league football. Here there was no pandering to TV cameras. Matches might still kick-off on a Saturday at 3pm, and it was still possible to stand on the terraces with a pie and a Bovril.

One fan-led initiative aimed at encouraging supporters of higher-level clubs to sample grassroots football was Non-League Day, which launched in 2010. The annual event, held during international break weekends, boosted attendances and coffers at non-league clubs, and raised awareness of the grassroots alternative to modern football. There was little commercialisation, corporatisation or gentrification apparent in the Bedfordshire County Football League, the Spartan South Midlands League or the West Riding County Amateur League.

Some Premier League fans, whether forced out by high prices or fatigued by modernisation, swapped the top flight for lower league or non-league football. Others, enjoying new-found comforts and those halloumi burgers, remained to pack out Premier League grounds. But, whatever level of football they preferred, the experience of being a fan was irrevocably changing. Much of this had to do with the internet. The success of campaigns such as Against Modern Football and initiatives such as Non-League Day had been built via blogs and social media. The game was going digital, and that would change what it meant to be a football fan.

18

Akin to religion

The big match kicked off at 8pm in Liverpool, 9pm in Paris, 11pm in Dubai, 3am in Beijing, 6am in Sydney, 12 noon in Los Angeles, and 3pm in New York. It was Monday 17 October 2016, "Red Monday", and the match was the much-anticipated clash between the Reds of Liverpool and the Red Devils of Manchester United. There were 52,769 fans inside Anfield, wrapped in scarves and huddled on plastic seats, their breath condensing in the air under the stadium's floodlights. And there were three million watching on UK TV, splayed out on sofas and perched on barstools, cradling cuppas and pints in the warmth of homes and pubs. The match was also broadcast around the world, to a global TV audience of three billion.

Away from TV sets, as many as several million fans were watching the match on smartphones, tablets and laptops via live streams. And hundreds of millions more were following the match on Facebook, Twitter and other social media. In back bedrooms, in coffee shops and on public transport, fans' faces were bathed in the blue glow of electronic screens, their network of supposedly solitary personal devices providing access to an extraordinarily communal event. Much of the world, it seemed, had come together, via satellite, cable and the internet, to follow Liverpool v Manchester United. This was football on a new super-connected digital global stage. Could the match live up to such huge expectations? No, of course it could not.

The match was billed as Red Monday by Sky Sports, who screened it in their Monday Night Football slot. "It is a blockbuster, a rivalry which runs very deep indeed," said Martin Tyler in Sky's heavily-rotated trailers. The *Telegraph* called the Red Monday branding "preposterous". "One of the most eagerly savoured matches of the season needs no such hype, even if it were played at teatime on Thursday," said the paper, adding: "Nonetheless the 'sell' will be contagious."

And it was. An average of 2.8 million viewers, and a peak of 3.1 million, watched the match on Sky Sports, representing the network's biggest audience in three years, around three times the size of their average Premier League match audience. Outside of the UK, the match was broadcast across 225 territories to 730 million homes and that total potential TV audience of 3 billion fans. The Red Monday match was also available via hundreds of internet streams, most of them illegal, some watched by up to a million viewers each. Millions more were following the match – often without actually watching it – via Facebook and Twitter.

At 6.59pm on Red Monday, just over an hour before kick-off, the official Manchester United Twitter account, @ManUtd, posted the team news in a line-up graphic, along with obligatory hashtags: "Here's how we'll line up at Anfield tonight... #MUFC #LIVMUN." The big story from the team announcement was that Manchester United manager Jose Mourinho had left United and England captain Wayne Rooney on the bench, and instead selected Marouane Fellaini. This news was posted on Twitter before TV, radio or newspapers got hold of it. The club had effectively bypassed the media, and delivered the news directly to fans. And this type of direct engagement between club and fans worked both ways, with fans able to offer their instant reactions.

"Oh thank God, no Rooney," responded one fan in a tweeted reply. "Mou! Where is @WayneRooney??!!" asked another fan. "How does Fellaini keep getting games? HOW?" tweeted another. Some Twitter users reacted using emojis.

One fan posted the word "Fellaini" followed by three "loudly crying face" emojis. It seemed unlikely that the club would have either the time or the inclination to reply to the hundreds of responses to each of its tweets, but Twitter did allow fans to air their opinions in a public forum, and interact with each other as they might if they were in a pub before the match, or in the ground awaiting kick-off.

At 7.01pm, the Liverpool Twitter account, @LFC, posted their team line-up graphic. "Why no Lallana?!?!" asked one Liverpool fan. "Easy three points," said another. "This is Anfield! #WeAreLiverpool," posted someone else. Another fan posted, "Come on @LFC #letsdothis," followed by four emojis – "eyeglasses", "large red circle", "OK hand sign" and "face with stuck-out tongue and tightly-closed eyes". It was fair to say that pre-match chat had evolved considerably over the course of football fan history. It was also fair to say that social media had become an important part of football, and that football had become an important part of social media. A large proportion of football fans were active on social media, and a large proportion of social media users were football fans. On any given day, much of the content read, posted and shared on social media could be football related.

According to Facebook executive Glenn Miller, in 2014, out of the platform's 1.3bn active users, 500m were "hardcore football fans". By October 2016, Facebook had 1.86bn active users, and, based on the 2014 ratio, more than 700m would be football fans. At the time of the Red Monday match, Manchester United had more than 71m likes on Facebook, and Liverpool had more than 29m. The @ManUtd and @LFC Twitter accounts had more than nine million and six million followers respectively, with each club drawing followers from more than 200 countries.

As kick-off approached, the social media chatter continued. "You can feel the buzz around #CapeTown today, it's almost game time @LFC vs @ManUtd," tweeted a Manchester United fan from South Africa. "There's no noise like the Anfield noise #LFC #comeonliverpool #YNWA," said a Liverpool fan from Menen, Belgium. "Just look at the atmosphere as the Liverpool anthem echoes round Anfield," tweeted another fan, from Lagos, Nigeria.

With 15 minutes to kick-off, the @ManUtd account posted a short video of a black cat wandering past the warming-up players on the Anfield pitch. "Pre-match pitch invasion at Anfield..." read the accompanying message, with a "smiling cat face" emoji and the #LIVMUN hashtag. The post was quickly liked and retweeted thousands of times, and "Anfield Cat" briefly became a Twitter trending topic. (None of this had happened when a black cat had similarly invaded the Anfield pitch during the first ever *Match of the Day* game back in 1964.)

Also appearing across social media were links, and requests for links, to live streams. Illegal streams were a major problem for the Premier League, and for football rights holders. Football, perhaps unsurprisingly, had been slow to react to the threats posed by broadband internet access. Live streaming of matches provided a particular threat, when it should perhaps have represented a wonderful opportunity. As technology advanced and internet access got faster, fans became increasingly keen to watch live streams, and there was particular demand for matches that weren't shown on UK TV, including Saturday 3pm kick-offs, which were covered by a "blackout" rule, designed to protect attendances at grounds across the football pyramid.

Here, the Premier League became a victim of its own popularity. From 2007 a huge overseas rights deal, then worth £625m, had taken the brand global. Premier League matches were being broadcast worldwide, from the US to China, across Europe, the Middle East, Africa and Asia. Many of these territories showed every game live, with multiple matches broadcast simultaneously on different channels. So fans in the United Arab Emirates or Hong Kong or New Zealand could watch every 3pm kick-off, while fans in the UK could not watch any of them – at least not legally.

Inevitably, illegal streams of foreign TV broadcasts of Premier League matches appeared online, and could be accessed by fans in the UK and around the world. Stream quality was variable, and pictures often cut out or were obscured by pop-up advertising, but that seemed to be accepted when the cost was free. Links were swapped in fan forums and on social media, and on an increasing number of streaming portal websites. Soon, illegal streaming became an epidemic. In a related problem, pubs were showing foreign broadcasts rather than subscribing to Sky Sports, and in order to get access to the 3pm kick-offs. The Premier League and Sky took legal action against publicans, and against sites and individuals broadcasting matches via streams, in order to protect their TV cash cow.

In 2015, the Premier League sold its domestic TV rights for the three seasons from 2016-17 for £5.136bn. Global deals, including more than £500m each from China and the US, brought the overall value of its TV rights to £8.3bn. The domestic deal had been shaken up by the arrival of Setanta Sports and ESPN, and then BT Sport, which ended Sky's monopoly on showing Premier League matches. BT would show 42 Premier League games from 2016-17 in addition to Sky's 126. (BT also won exclusive rights to show Champions League and Europa League matches.) This split deal meant fans would need to subscribe to both Sky Sports and BT Sport in order to watch the full range of matches. The increased cost, and the failure to make all matches legally available, led more fans to turn to illegal streams – or to switch off altogether. During the 2016-17 season, audience figures for Premier League matches on Sky Sports were down by 19%.

The Red Monday match was available to stream legally in the UK, to fans with Sky Sports subscriptions, and to those with paid access to Sky's NOW TV service. However, the vast majority of fans streaming the match in the UK and abroad were doing so illegally. The Premier League estimated that around a million fans were watching illegal match streams every week. But, with one online copyright protection agency stating that it was identifying more than 500 streams every week, and that some single streams were being viewed by more than a million people each, the Premier League's estimate seemed fairly conservative.

As the Liverpool v Manchester United match got underway, fans around the world turned to their televisions and their live streams. But they did not necessarily turn away from their social media accounts. A growing phenomenon linked with "event TV", and particularly live sport, was second screening. This involved watching the event on one screen, usually a television, while also following it on a second – a smartphone, tablet or laptop. Second screening seemed ideal for football fans, who could watch a match on one screen, and follow social media on another. Research carried out during the Euro 2016 tournament found that more than three quarters of all TV viewers also used a second screen device to browse social media, visit football websites, place bets, check other scores, and send and receive messages.

However it was watched, followed or otherwise consumed, the Red Monday match turned out to be a dull affair. Manchester United "parked the bus", and Liverpool were unable to get around it. There were few chances or talking points, and this was reflected on social media. "I'm currently pairing my socks," tweeted one fan. "I was watching #LIVMUN but this has been infinitely more entertaining." "This game's so boring I've started on the washing-up," posted another. "We have a dishwasher." Live streamers were also dissatisfied.

One streamer tweeted: "The #LIVMUN match is so dull I'm not even bothered I can't find a stream that works," with the "see-no-evil monkey" emoji. Another tweeted two "turtle" emojis with: "Only thing worse than the #LIVMUN game was the speed and quality of the stream, freezing every few mins!"

The match ended 0-0, with even purveyors of good defending regarding it as a bore draw. "That was a wretched game of football and don't let anyone tell you otherwise," wrote Jacob Steinberg on the *Guardian* website's liveblog. "It was pure filth."

The Red Monday match would soon be forgotten, even if the stench of the hype that surrounded it lingered. Much more important than the result was the way the match had been consumed. Only a tiny proportion of the fans who had followed Liverpool v Manchester United had actually been at Anfield. And only a small fraction of the worldwide TV audience had been in the UK. Many of those who had watched the match had done so via internet streams. And millions of those watching the match – plus millions more not watching it – had followed it on social media.

When the *Guardian* asked football fans about their changing viewing habits, shortly after Red Monday, the newspaper received more than 500 replies. "Even my 78-year old father streams his games now," said one fan. "The cost is ridiculous." In its summary, the *Guardian* reported that some fans had stopped watching football because they were "fed up with the focus on money, celebrity, hype and melodrama", while others still wanted to watch but couldn't bring themselves to pay for Sky Sports and BT Sport. "Unless the TV companies offer deals that are less expensive and more flexible," said the paper, "a growing number of these fans will eschew the old subscription model and watch football online for free."

The idea of fans watching football for free was a terrifying one for the game's stakeholders. For more than a hundred years it had been possible to monetise fans via the turnstile. But, in the 21st century, the vast majority of fans didn't attend matches. They weren't paying for match tickets, and, to make things worse, an increasing number of them weren't paying for TV subscriptions. Could providing football fans with an accessible and affordable legal streaming service cut illegal streaming? Or was it too late to put that bolted horse back in its stable? Perhaps the solution to monetising this new generation of digital fans could be found not in curbing illegal streaming but in harnessing the power of social media.

Social media allowed clubs and other football brands to engage with a new generation of non-traditional fans who might never attend a match, or pay for a TV subscription, or buy merchandise. Writing in the *Financial Times*, Simon Kuper asked reader to imagine a Manchester United fan named Abdul in Kuala Lumpur. Abdul had never been to Old Trafford, or even Europe, but he watched the club's games on TV in his local restaurant, while wearing a bootlegged replica shirt. "The club's total income from Abdul is zero," wrote Kuper. "In fact, for decades United didn't know he existed. Social media changes that."

Manchester United joined Facebook in 2010 and Twitter in 2013. By 2017, the club had more than 70 million fans on Facebook, 10 million on Twitter and 16 million on Instagram. (Real Madrid, the world's most-followed club, had more than 100 million fans on Facebook, 22 million on Twitter and 44 million on Instagram.) These were huge audiences that were incredibly valuable to sponsors. In 2014, the club signed a shirt sponsorship deal with Chevrolet worth £47m per year, more than double the "pre-social media" deal they had with Aon worth £20m per year, which indicated the added value that increased social media visibility had created. And Manchester United had more than 60 club sponsors. So there was ample scope for further monetisation.

Manchester United's huge social media following allowed them to engage with a global community that was thousands of times bigger than their traditional fanbase. "The level we are engaging at, to put it in context, is akin to religion," said the club's managing director Richard Arnold. "John Lennon was famously quoted as saying the Beatles were 'bigger than Jesus'. Whilst we wouldn't want to be disrespectful in that way... the level of engagement and fervour we get is on par with the world's major religions and those are the only things at the same level as Manchester United in terms of that interaction and engagement."

Fans could engage with clubs, players and journalists, and access a continuous flood of football content. With score updates, text commentaries, and highlight videos it was entirely possible to follow a match exclusively on Twitter or Facebook. It was even possible to watch a match via Twitter's Periscope app, which allowed users to film and (illegally) broadcast matches via their smartphones. When Manchester City fan Josh Chambers "Periscoped" an entire away match at Crystal Palace in February 2017, notionally for the benefit of his stay-at-home dad, the stream was watched by more than 139,000 stay-at-home fans. The Periscope audience was ten times bigger than the FA Cup tie's attendance of just 13,979.

Meanwhile, another type of fan broadcast was becoming hugely popular. Fan TV channels, broadcast via YouTube and promoted on social media, were acting as digital soap boxes on which to air views, rants and "bants". The typical format involved post-match interviews with fans as they left the ground, generally captured guerrilla-style with a digital camera, then quickly posted online. These unfiltered hot-takes, delivered in the warmth of victory or chill of defeat, could sometimes be measured, but were often deliriously happy or furiously angry. These colourful extremes of opinion only added to the popularity of fan TV channels.

The most high-profile channel was ArsenalFanTV, which had more than 400,000 subscribers in 2017. Manchester United's Full Time Devils had more than 300,000 subscribers, and Liverpool's The Redmen TV had more than 150,000. Individual video clips were shared on social media, and were watched by audiences far bigger than the channels' subscriber bases, and by audiences that included fans of other clubs. When ArsenalFanTV interviewed player-turned-pundit Gary Neville, who had previously been critical of the channel, the resulting video was viewed 1.2m times, reaching a bigger audience than most of Neville's Sky Sports broadcasts.

The contrast between ArsenalFanTV's regulars and Sky's and other mainstream channels' pundits was clear. The vast majority of professional pundits were former players, and many seemed to share the belief that it was impossible to hold a valid opinion on football "unless you have played the game". This was pure nonsense, as fanzines and other fan-orientated mediums had already proven. Fans had always been deeply knowledgeable about the game they watched week in, week out, and the increased availability of matches from around the world and an abundance of statistics and other information only made it easier for them to dissect and discuss tactics, team selections and endless minutiae. The advent of social media had blown the doors off football punditry's closed shop, and had allowed millions of fans to rush in with almost as many opinions. But TV had been slow to give fans a voice, only displaying occasional onscreen tweets in an effort to demonstrate fan engagement. "After a game you used to hear from everybody else apart from the fans," said ArsenalFanTV founder Robbie Lyle. "Showing the importance of fans, who are the most neglected part of the game, is what we're about."

The prospect of fans creating their own media platforms, from fan TV channels and podcasts to websites and social media accounts, would clearly have an effect on "old media".

But it would also have an effect on the game in general, providing fans with a more powerful voice, and with increased influence. Fans had been neglected for much of football's history, but were becoming much more difficult to ignore, and seemed increasingly keen to take back their game.

Despite everything they've endured, fans have not been driven away from football, and have remained loyal to the game they love. They've been oppressed, vilified, ripped-off, and treated with contempt and disdain. Attempts have been made to marginalise them, and to exclude them from a sanitised reboot of the game. But, while football no longer relies on the clicking of the turnstile, it still relies on fans, whether they attend matches to sing and cheer or stay at home with TV and the internet. Football has big new revenue streams, generating previously unimaginable riches, but all of that only exists because of the remarkably enduring and seemingly unbreakable bond between the fans and the game. Rather than walking away, fans are embracing football in bigger numbers and from further afield than ever before.

"Nearly everything possible has been done to spoil the game," wrote JB Priestley, "but the fact remains that it is not yet spoilt, and it has gone out and conquered the world." Priestley was writing not during the modern era but in 1934, almost 60 years before the Premier League was even imagined. Priestley referred to football as "this uproarious Saturday plaything", and said it was easy to understand why fans would pay to watch 22 men kicking a ball about. "They are not mere spectators in the sense of being idle or indiffer-ent lookers-on," he wrote, noting the vicarious nature of their support. Priestley referred to the "wave of happiness" and "quick comradeship" that football engendered, and described how fans "are driven to despair, are risen to triumph". "It has yet to be proved to me that these men," he wrote, "ever did anything better with their free time and their shillings."

The experience of being a football fan has changed, but the essence remains the same. We modern fans can put down our smartphones, turn off our TVs, and wrap our woollen scarves around our necks. We can head out to the football ground, drawn towards the floodlights, mingling with an ever-thickening throng. There is the buzz of anticipation, a quickening of the heart, an alerting of the senses. Then a push through the turnstile into an intoxicating world of noise and passion. For the next hour and a half, little outside of the white-chalked green field in front of us matters. Football is a release, an escape and a comfort. It's an emotional, communal experience. It's important. It's special.

Football and how we consume it will continue to evolve. The experience of being a fan will be shaped by changes in society, technology and the media. We may gripe at football's failings, and push for necessary improvements or the return of favourite traditions. But we will remain just as captivated by the game as our ancestors from past generations. The emotional connection we have with the game will never be broken. The future of football belongs to its fans.

Bibliography

Books

Athenaeus, *Deipnosophists*, 1.14-15, tr. Yonge & Bohn, 1853

Buchan, Charles, *A Lifetime in Football*, Phoenix House, 1955

Buford, Bill, *Among the Thugs*, Secker & Warburg, 1990

Catton, JAH, *Wickets and Goals*, Chapman & Hall, 1926

Davies, Pete, *All Played Out*, William Heinemann, 1990

Finney, Tom, *My Autobiography*, Headline, 2003

Gibson, Alfred and Pickford, William, *Association Football and the Men Who Made It*, Caxton, 1906

Goldblatt, David, *The Ball is Round: A Global History of Football*, Penguin, 2007

FitzStephen, William, *Descriptio Nobilissimi Civitatis Londoniae*, c.1174–83, translated in Stow, John, *A Survey of London*, 1598

Fletcher, Martin, *56: The Story of the Bradford Fire*, Bloomsbury, 2015

Hines, Barry, *This Artistic Life*, Pomona, 2009

Hopcraft, Arthur, *The Football Man*, Collins, 1968

Hornby, Nick, *Fever Pitch*, Gollancz, 1992

Inglis, Simon, *Football Grounds of Britain*, CollinsWillow, 1996

Le Bon, Gustave, *The Crowd: A Study of the Popular Mind*, Macmillan, 1896

MacKay, Charles, *Extraordinary Popular Delusions and the Madness of Crowds*, Richard Bentley, 1841

Mason, Tony, *Association Football and English Society 1863-1915*, Harvester, 1980

Matthews, Stanley, *The Way It Was*, Headline, 2001

Morris, Desmond, *The Soccer Tribe*, Jonathan Cape, 1981

Nennius, *Historia Brittonum*, c.828

Priestley, JB, *The Good Companions*, William Heinemann, 1929

Priestley, JB, *English Journey*, William Heinemann, 1934

Reynolds, Simon, *Generation Ecstasy*, Routledge, 1999

Rook, Clarence, *The Hooligan Nights*, 1899

Scraton, Phil, *Hillsborough: The Truth*, Mainstream, 2009

Shearman, Montague, *Athletics and Football*, Longmans, Green and Co, 1887

Stubbes, Philip, *Anatomy of Abuses*, 1583

Tabner, Brian, *Through the Turnstiles... Again*, Yore, 2002

Taylor, Matthew, *The Association Game*, Routledge, 2013

Taylor, Rogan, *Football and Its Fans*, Leicester University Press, 1992
Tempany, Adrian, *And the Sun Shines Now*, Faber & Faber, 2016
Thornton, Phil, *Casuals: The Story of a Terrace Cult*, Milo, 2003
Winner, David, *Those Feet*, Bloomsbury, 2005
Laus Pisonis (Praise of Piso), tr. Duff, JW & AM, Harvard University Press, 1935

Newspapers and magazines

Aberdeen Journal, All the Year Round, Athletic News, Bath Chronicle, Bell's Life in London and Sporting Chronicle, Berwickshire News, Biggleswade Chronicle, Birmingham Daily Gazette, Birmingham Daily Post, Blackburn Standard, Bolton Evening News, Buenos Aires Standard, Burnley Express, Burnley News, Celtic View, Charles Buchan's Football Monthly, Chums, Contemporary Review, Coventry Herald, Coventry Telegraph, Daily Chronicle, Daily Express, Daily Mail, Daily Mirror, Daily News, Daily Record, Daily Sketch, Derby Daily Telegraph, Derby Mercury, Dundee Courier, Dundee Evening Post, Dundee Evening Telegraph, Edinburgh Evening News, L'Equipe, Essex Newsman, Falkirk Herald, Financial Times, FourFourTwo, Glasgow Herald, Gloucester Citizen, Graphic, Hartlepool Northern Daily Mail, Huddersfield Chronicle, Hull Daily Mail, Illustrated Police News, Independent, Izvestia, Lancashire Evening Post, Lancaster Gazette, Leeds Mercury, Leighton Buzzard Observer, Life, Lincolnshire Echo, Lincolnshire Standard, Liverpool Daily Post, Liverpool Echo, London Standard, Manchester Courier, Manchester Times, Middlesbrough Daily Gazette, MK Citizen, Monthly Chronicle of North Country Lore and Legend, Morning News, Motherwell Times, Nature, New Scientist, New York Times, News of the World, Newcastle Courant, Nineteenth Century, Northern Echo, Nottingham Evening News, Nottinghamshire Guardian, Observer, Pall Mall Gazette, Penny Illustrated, Portsmouth Evening News, Radio Times, La Repubblica, Scotsman, Sheffield Daily Telegraph, Sheffield Independent, Sketch, Soviet Sport, Sporting Chronicle, Sporting Gazette, Sports Argus, Sportsman, St James's Gazette, STAND, Sun, Sunday Express, Sunday Post, Sunderland Echo, Tamworth Herald, Telegraph, Time, Times, Western Daily Press, Westmorland Gazette, When Saturday Comes, Whitby Gazette, Wired, World Soccer, Yorkshire Evening Post, Yorkshire Post

Reports and articles

Baker, William J, *The Making of a Working-Class Football Culture in Victorian England, Journal of Social History*, Vol 13, No 2, Winter 1979
Cialdini, Robert B, *Basking in Reflected Glory: Three Football Field Studies, Journal of Personality and Social Psychology*, Vol 34, No 3, 1976
Gantz, Walter and Wenner, Lawrence A, *Fanship and the Television Sports Viewing Experience, Sociology of Sport Journal*, Vol 12, 1995
Garnham, Neal and Jackson, Andrew, *Who invested in Victorian football clubs?, Soccer & Society*, Vol 4, Iss 1, 2003

Raney, Arthur A, *Why We Watch and Enjoy Mediated Sports*, *Handbook of Sports and Media*, Taylor & Francis, 2006

Redhead, Steve, *Hit and Tell*, *Soccer & Society*, Vol 5, Iss 3, 2004

Annual Report of the Press Council 1989, Press Complaints Commission, 1989

Changing face of the Premier League, European Professional Football Leagues (EPFL), 2012

Dialect Notes Vol 2, American Dialect Society, 1900

Hillsborough Stadium Disaster: Final Report of Inquiry by Lord Justice Taylor, HMSO, January 1990

Hillsborough: The Report of the Hillsborough Independent Panel, September 2012

Lang Report, HMSO, 1969

Premier League Football Research, European Commission, 2005

Statistics on Football-Related Arrests Season 2008-09, Home Office, 2009

Websites

AFC Wimbledon, www.wimbledonheritage.co.uk

Arsenal History, www.thearsenalhistory.com

BBC Genome Project, http://genome.ch.bbc.co.uk

European Football Statistics, www.european-football-statistics.co.uk

FC United of Manchester, www.fc-utd.co.uk

Football Supporters' Federation (FSF), www.fsf.org.uk

Hillsborough Independent Panel, http://hillsborough.independent.gov.uk

ITV Football 1983-1998, bit.ly/itvfoot

Manchester United, www.manutd.com

Non-League Day, www.nonleagueday.co.uk

Premier League Fan Research, fanresearch.premierleague.com

Spirit of Shankly, www.spiritofshankly.com

Supporters Direct, www.supporters-direct.org

Worldfootball.net, www.worldfootball.net

Film and TV

1950 FA Cup Final, Movietone News, 1950, bit.ly/1950facup

Blackburn Rovers v West Bromwich Albion, Arthur Cheetham, North West Film Archive, 1898, bit.ly/1898film

FA Cup Final 1965, BBC TV, 1 May 1965, bit.ly/1965facup

Football Final, Robert W Paul, Animatograph Films, 1903, bit.ly/1903film

Match of the Day, BBC TV, 22 August 1964, bit.ly/1964motd

Newcastle United v Liverpool, Mitchell and Kenyon, BFI, 1901, bit.ly/1901film

Panorama (from Liverpool), BBC TV, 20 April 1964, bit.ly/1964pano

Panorama (Treatment and the Half-Way Line), BBC TV, 14 November 1977, bit.ly/1977pano

Stairway 13, Rangers TV, bit.ly/stair13
Super Sunday, Sky Sports, 16 August 1992 via Sky Sports Vault, 27 July 2014, bit.ly/1992sky
Wembley FA Cup 1923, British Pathé, 7 May 1923, bit.ly/1923facup
When Football Changed Forever, ITV, 6 October 2016

Epigraph

Page 5 "People come home from..." *Seinfeld*, S06E01, NBC, 22 September 1994

Introduction

10 "Fan, n..." *Dialect Notes Vol 2*, American Dialect Society, 1900
10 "who are called 'fans'..." *Sketch*, 30 April 1913
10 "First League football 'fans'..." *Daily Express*, 3 October 1914
12 Manchester United's claim... club website, 29 May 2012, bit.ly/manuglob
12 average attendance... Worldfootball.net, bit.ly/attenda
12 average UK TV audience... *Bloomberg*, 16 January 2017, bit.ly/uktvaud
12 worldwide in-home TV... Premier League Fan Research, bit.ly/globmed
13 a third of football fans... Kantar Media, 10 June 2016, bit.ly/euro16data

1. Alive with expectation

14 "men ate and drank..." *Westmorland Gazette*, 20 February 1836
14 "No public amusement..." *Derby Mercury*, 28 February 1827
15 "At two o'clock..." *Sportsman*, 17 December 1868
19 "Almost the whole..." Morris, Desmond, *The Soccer Tribe*, 1981
20 "He seized the ball..." Athenaeus, *Deipnosophists*, translation 1853
20 "It is your pleasure..." *Laus Pisonis (Praise of Piso)*, translation 1935
21 "They respond when..." *New York Times*, 10 January 2006, bit.ly/cellsthat
24 "a party of boys..." Nennius, *Historia Brittonum*, c.828
24 "After dinner..." FitzStephen, William, in Stow, *Survey of London*, 1598
24 "a football was thrown..." *Newcastle Courant*, 27 February 1857
25 "At some places..." *Monthly Chronicle Vol 3*, 1889
25 "It may rather..." Philip Stubbes, *Anatomy of Abuses*, 1583

2. Surrounded by partisans

28 "The uniforms..." *Sheffield Daily Telegraph*, 27 December 1860
31 "The spectators numbered..." *Nottinghamshire Guardian*, 3 January 1862
31 "a very fair number..." *Sheffield Independent*, 30 December 1862
32 "attended by a considerable..." *Bell's Life*, 31 October 1852
32 "a match for cock..." *Bell's Life*, 11 December 1853
33 "a most exciting match..." *Bell's Life*, 19 November 1854
33 "the excitement of the spectators..." *Bell's Life*, 5 December 1858

33 "the favourable state..." *Bell's Life*, 17 November 1861
33 "want of room..." *Bell's Life*, 7 October 1849
33 "I well remember..." *Lancaster Gazette*, 31 October 1818
35 "not connected with the game..." *Bell's Life*, 2 January 1842
35 "a pretty and suitable spot..." *Bell's Life*, 7 December 1862
35 "elicited great applause..." *Bell's Life*, 22 March 1863
36 "showed by their applause..." *Bell's Life*, 5 December 1863
36 "the spectators, of whom..." *Bell's Life*, 26 December 1863
37 Cialdini noted that... *Journal of Personality and Social Psychology*, 1976

3. Popular favour

40 "No better proof..." *Glasgow Herald*, 7 March 1870
41 "computed to number..." *Leeds Mercury*, 8 March 1870
42 "a gallery rarely seen..." *Glasgow Herald*, 21 November 1870
43 "in the light of a mere farce..." *Daily News*, 23 March 1871
43 "many ladies..." *Morning News*, 18 March, 1872
44 relatively high admission, *Bell's Life*, 23 March 1872
44 "This was the first..." *Sporting Gazette*, 7 December 1872
44 only 2,500 spectators... *Graphic*, 14 December 1872
45 "A good and fair game..." *Glasgow Herald*, 29 November 1872
45 "it would be too bad..." *Glasgow Herald*, 30 November 1872
46 "On arrival at the ground..." *Sheffield Independent*, 17 March 1873
46 "The enthusiasm was unbounded..." *Glasgow Herald*, 11 October 1875
47 "safely and securely railed off..." *Athletic News*, 3 March 1877
47 "There was a pretty good..." *Bell's Life*, 16 November 1874
48 "The match was announced..." *Sheffield Independent*, 15 October 1878
49 "Football has enjoyed..." *Penny Illustrated*, 8 March 1873
49 "some combination of grace..." *Nature*, Vol 383, October 1996

4. Extraordinary interest

52 "The West End streets..." *Pall Mall Gazette*, 26 March 1888
52 "some hundreds of their local..." *Blackburn Standard*, 25 March 1882
53 "such a reception..." *Manchester Courier*, 3 April 1883
53 "gradually fallen off ..." *Whitby Gazette*, 31 March 1888
53 "The enclosure railed off..." *All The Year Round*, 26 April 1890
55 "The first intelligence..." *Sheffield Daily Telegraph*, 26 March 1888
56 "a degree of popularity..." *Pall Mall Gazette*, 4 April 1885
58 "the increased interest..." *Northern Echo*, 28 April 1888
59 "how immensely the game..." *Times*, 14 April 1888
59 "A few years since..." *Northern Echo*, 14 December 1886
60 "were received by at least..." *Blackburn Standard*, 31 December 1881

60 "power of the spectators..." *Yorkshire Post*, 5 October 1882
63 BBC and ONS figures... BBC website, 15 October 2014, bit.ly/pricefoot & ONS website, 13 May 2015, bit.ly/uklab
63 "In the East End..." *Northern Echo*, 19 October 1889
63 the club's share returns... *Soccer & Society*, Vol 4, Iss 1, 2003
64 urged all clubs with a turnover... *Athletic News*, 5 June 1888
64 "more intelligent" supporters... *Athletic News*, 12 June 1888
64 "against true sport..." *Athletic News*, 18 March 1889
64 "designed to help the club..." *Blackburn Standard*, 20 March 1886
65 "by far the largest sum..." *Sunderland Echo*, 10 January 1888
65 "No words of ours..." Shearman, Montague, *Athletics and Football*, 1887
66 "When the town to be visited..." *Sheffield Independent*, 22 December 1899

5. Howling roughs

68 "aroused the feelings..." *Manchester Courier*, 24 February 1890
69 "Both sides put in all..." *Lancashire Evening Post*, 22 February 1890
69 "The home team..." *Lancashire Evening Post*, 24 February 1890
71 "2,000 howling roughs..." *Birmingham Daily Post*, 11 May 1885
71 "Unfortunately there is too much..." *Burnley Express*, 27 March 1886
72 "the most blackguardly..." *Northern Echo*, 24 December 1887
72 "disgraceful rowdyism..." *Manchester Courier*, 29 March 1886
72 "Your remarks about..." *Manchester Courier*, 5 April 1886
72 "A Football Referee Mobbed..." *Illustrated Police News*, 24 February 1897
73 "Men, it has been well said..." MacKay, Charles, *Madness of Crowds*, 1841
73 "a sentiment of invincible power...", Le Bon, Gustave, *The Crowd*, 1896
74 "Since football became..." Shearman, Montague, *Athletics & Football*, 1887
74 "Happy is the publican..." *Sheffield Independent*, 22 December 1899
75 "The betting mania..." *Middlesbrough Daily Gazette*, 1 March 1889
75 "practical connection with..." *Huddersfield Chronicle*, 14 March 1887
76 "Betting at football..." *Yorkshire Post*, 20 November 1888
76 "a hurricane of criticism..." *Pall Mall Gazette*, 26 March 1888
76 "The multitude flock..." *Nineteenth Century*, Vol 32, October 1892
77 "There's the spectator..." *Chums*, 23 October 1895
77 "Now that the football..." *Derby Mercury*, 4 October 1899
78 "How keenly the onlookers..." *Chums*, 28 September 1892
78 "There is scarcely room..." *Daily News*, 15 October 1892
79 "astonishing increase..." *Contemporary Review*, November 1898
79 "a great deal of the extravagant..." *London Standard*, 29 October 1898

6. Millions of them

80 "a tax on football spectators", *Daily Mail*, 22 April 1901

81 "I think I may safely say..." *Sheffield Daily Telegraph*, 20 April 1901
82 "The great charm of the Crystal..." Catton, JAH, *Wickets and Goals*, 1926
82 "There is, in the first place..." *Sheffield Independent*, 20 April 1901
82 "It is possible to 'do' the city..." *Sheffield Daily Telegraph*, 17 April 1901
83 "The average Londoner does not..." *Daily Mirror*, 23 April 1906
84 "foaming bitter..." *Daily News*, 22 April 1901
84 "The weather attracted everyone..." *Sheffield Daily Telegraph*, 22 April 1901
86 "It would be better..." *Daily Mail*, quoted in *St James's Gazette*, 22 April 1901
87 "On their return..." Gibson & Pickford, *Association Football*, 1906
87 "the finest football film extant..." *Football Final*, Animatograph Films, 1903
90 "Football is too important..." *Coventry Herald*, 21 March 1902
90 "There was a general feeling..." *Edinburgh Evening News*, 5 April 1902
91 "an ocean of faces..." *Scotsman*, 8 April 1902
93 "beyond the power of man..." *Daily Mail*, *Telegraph* & *Sportsman* quoted in *Dundee Evening Post*, 7 April 1902

7. Lost enthusiasm

96 "Football is an excellent thing..." *Times*, 7 November 1914
96 "whole agitation..." *Athletic News*, 7 December 1914
96 "There is a time for games..." *Yorkshire Post*, 3 September 1914
97 "the patriotism of all..." *Manchester Courier*, 7 September 1914
97 "An appeal to good sportsmen..." *Bath Chronicle*, 21 November 1914
98 "the very opposite..." *Liverpool Echo*, 17 December 1914
98 "novel and really funny..." *Liverpool Daily Post*, 26 December 1914
99 "We do not hear of theatres..." *Liverpool Echo*, 29 December 1914
100 "The dominant note was khaki..." *Sports Argus*, 24 April 1915
100 "vastly different crowd..." *Manchester Courier*, 6 September 1915
102 "loud guffaws..." *Scotsman* quoted in *Tamworth Herald*, 14 May, 1881
102 "roughly jostled..." *Nottingham Evening News*, 17 May 1881
102 "an astonishing sight..." *Daily Sketch*, 27 March 1895
103 "the appearance of the..." *Lancashire Evening Post*, 26 December 1917
104 "it is evident there will not be..." *Nottingham Evening Post*, 21 April 1920
104 "probably the finest..." *Sporting Chronicle* q. in *Burnley News*, 4 June 1921

8. Jumbles of men

106 "scarcely to be distinguished..." *Scotsman*, 1 August 1927
107 "The wish to see the..." *Times*, 28 April 1923
107 "Some of the Bolton..." *Yorkshire Evening Post*, 28 April 1923
109 "We expected nothing like this..." *Sheffield Independent*, 30 April 1923
111 "What steps does the right..." *Times*, 1 May 1923
112 "with, no doubt, salutary..." *Sheffield Independent*, 1 May 1923

112 The earliest football programme... *Radio Times*, 12 October 1923
113 "one of the giants..." *Northern Whig*, 5 January 1952
113 "fiasco..." *Observer* quoted in *Yorkshire Post*, 20 January 1927
114 "it was easier to form..." *Sheffield Independent*, 24 January 1927
115 "Directors believe that..." *Yorkshire Post*, 28 February 1927
115 "My husband, when he was..." *Nottingham Evening Post*, 26 February 1927
115 "did not feel disposed..." *Nottingham Evening Post*, 11 February 1927
115 "Did you hear that..." *Liverpool Post* q. in *Yorkshire Post*, 14 March 1927
116 "a mistake..." *Sheffield Independent*, 8 January 1927
116 "Football at the fireside..." *Falkirk Herald*, 15 January 1927
116 "The most vivid description..." *Essex Newsman*, 5 March 1927
117 "Nothing that the BBC..." *Radio Times*, 18 March 1927
117 "in a few years..." *Daily Chronicle* q. in *Edinburgh News*, 13 February 1924

9. Amazing scenes

118 "the so-called World's..." Press Association in *Scotsman*, 31 July, 1930
119 "The enthusiasm of football..." *Aberdeen Journal*, 30 August 1930
120 "It is unpleasant to record..." *Buenos Aires Standard* q. in *Biggleswade Chronicle*, 19 July 1929
121 "They take great care..." *Aberdeen Journal*, 30 August 1930
122 "It seems that people..." *Derby Daily Telegraph*, 2 September 1930
122 "So great was the excitement..." *Nottingham Evening Post*, 11 June 1934
124 "The Association match..." *Times*, 17 April 1937
125 "We are very sorry..." *Aberdeen Journal*, 10 April 1937
125 "The tonic taken if..." *Dundee Courier*, 17 April 1937
126 "Soccer crowds invade..." *Hull Daily Mail*, 17 April 1937
126 "football's biggest day..." *Scotsman*, 17 April 1937
126 "Now for the loudest..." *Dundee Courier*, 16 April 1937
126 "before even the milkmen..." *Dundee Evening Telegraph*, 17 April 1937
127 "Hampden Park with its throng..." *Motherwell Times*, 23 April 1937
127 "Starting on the embankment..." *Scotsman*, 19 April 1937
128 "the mightiest roar..." *Dundee Courier*, 19 April 1937
128 "If ever a match was won..." Matthews, Stanley, *The Way It Was*, 2001
128 "the missing 593..." *Motherwell Times*, 23 April 1937
129 "to give a comprehensive..." *Hartlepool Daily Mail*, 9 September 1937
129 "Bad light yesterday..." *Hartlepool Daily Mail*, 17 September 1937
130 "Please bear with us..." *Sunderland Echo*, 30 April 1938
130 "No football enthusiast..." *Lancashire Evening Post*, 3 May 1938
131 although an enthusiast... *Derby Daily Telegraph*, 5 May 1939
131 "The sets gave excellent..." *Leighton Buzzard Observer*, 2 May 1939

10. Much-needed escapism
132 "In accordance with..." *Western Daily Press*, 9 September 1939
134 "ersatz..."*Aberdeen Journal*, 5 May 1941
134 "great Hampden Park roar..." *Birmingham Daily Gazette*, 5 May 1941
134 "Wartime football was no..." Tom Finney, *My Autobiography*, 2003
135 "The public stood..." *Yorkshire Evening Post*, 15 January 1946
135 "Football strikes..." *Liverpool Evening Express*, 9 November 1945
137 "there was tremendous..." *Lancashire Evening Post*, 11 March 1946
137 "When the crowd began..." *Sunday Post*, 10 March 1946
138 "Crowd Mishap Delays..." *Lancashire Evening Post*, 9 March 1946
138 "the increasing violence..." *Bolton Evening News*, 11 March 1946
139 "Plenty of Room..." *Bolton Evening News*, 6 March 1946
140 "electronically operated indicator..." *Yorkshire Post*, 11 August 1950
140 "the disaster at Bolton..." *Lancashire Evening Post*, 6 July 1946
141 "If the sun did not..." *Times*, 2 September 1946
141 "Nobody could be expected..." *Times*, 7 September 1946

11. Rosettes and rattles
143 "Rosettes and rattles..." *Nottingham Evening Post*, 29 April 1950
143 "monster rosettes..." *Lincolnshire Echo*, 29 April 1950
144 "colours flying..." *Yorkshire Post*, 30 January 1953
145 banned in the early 1920s... *Dundee Evening Telegraph*, 20 February 1924
146 "hat census..." *Dundee Evening Telegraph*, 28 January 1947
146 "fearful state of frenzy..." *1950 FA Cup Final*, Movietone News, 1950
147 "Within the next few years..." *Hull Daily Mail*, 1 April 1950
148 "soccer-suckers..." *Sunderland Echo*, 19 January 1950
149 "Grateful thanks to Frank..." *Sunderland Echo*, 23 January 1950
149 "facetious poppycock..." *Sunderland Echo*, 30 January 1950
150 "sensation..." Reuters in *Times*, 30 June 1950
150 "to protect players..." *New York Times*, 29 January 1950
151 "had not entertained a thought", *Gloucester Citizen*, 17 July 1950
151 eight fans died... *New York Times*, 18 July 1950
152 "the great spectator sport..." *Life*, 7 May 1951
152 "Even those who do not win..." *Times*, 18 April 1951
153 "You may think your club programme..." *Yorkshire Post*, 1 May 1951
153 "Our object is to..." *Charles Buchan's Football Monthly*, September 1951
154 "Surely the game is..." Buchan, Charles, *A Lifetime in Football*, 1955
154 "all brothers together for..." Priestley, JB, *The Good Companions*, 1929
154 "Supporters receive scant respect..." *Sunderland Echo*, 14 March 1951
154 "The Football League clubs..." *Yorkshire Post*, 16 March 1951
155 "not the way to attract people..." *Portsmouth Evening News*, 4 June 1955

155 "There is a hardening..." *Lincolnshire Standard*, 20 March 1954
155 "It is an amazing game..." *Sunderland Echo*, 29 October 1954
156 "awful bias..." *Berwickshire News*, 28 August 1951
156 "football is the most beautiful game..." *Sunday Times*, 16 November 1952
156 "It is as pleasing to the eye..." Hines, Barry, *This Artistic Life*, 2009
157 "a symbolic hush..." *Times*, 10 February 1958

12. Some people are on the pitch

159 "Welcome to..." *Match of the Day*, BBC TV, 22 August 1964
160 "The Kop's noise..." *Liverpool Daily Post*, 24 August 1964
162 "I've never seen anything..." *Panorama*, BBC TV, 20 April 1964
163 "The Kop set this match..." *Daily Mirror*, 20 April 1964
163 "Liverpool's signature tune..." *FA Cup Final*, BBC TV, 1 May 1965
163 "Merseyside terrors..." *Daily Mirror*, 9 November 1963
164 "It is shocking..." *Charles Buchan's Football Monthly*, January 1964
164 "gave laws and a name..." Clarence Rook, *Hooligan Nights*, 1899
165 "Merseyside maniacs..." *Daily Mirror*, 28 January 1964
165 "on trial..." *Daily Mirror*, 13 August 1964
165 "We cannot have a minority..." *Times*, 14 September 1965
165 "dirty unwashed little thugs..." *Daily Mirror*, 16 November 1964
165 "Hear! Hear!..." *Charles Buchan's Football Monthly*, January 1966
166 "the most shameful day..." *Guardian*, 8 November 1965
167 "Soccer Marches to War..." *Sun*, 8 November 1965
167 "These tactics seemed to..." Times, 26 May 1964
168 "Then the shooting began..." BBC News, 23 May 2014, bit.ly/lima1964
169 "Luzhniki's Dark Secret..." *Soviet Sport*, 8 July 1989, via October 20 website, bit.ly/sovspor
169 However, two weeks... *Izvestia*, 20 July 1989, via October 20, bit.ly/izvesti
169 "Crowds everywhere are..." *Daily Mirror*, 11 September 1965
170 "Brazilians will tell you..." *Times*, 15 July 1966
171 "screams, kicks, fists..." *Times*, 23 July 1966
172 "Bravo fans..." *Daily Express*, 13 July 1966
172 "growing, gladdening support..." *Daily Mirror*, 18 July 1966
172 "Nothing has ever gripped..." *Daily Mirror*, 30 July 1966
173 "the most triumphant..." *Sunday Express*, 31 July 1966
174 "This is the slick..." *Charles Buchan's Football Monthly*, December 1968
175 "We see Pay-TV..." *Daily Express*, 9 January 1967
176 "very much a young man's game..." *Times*, 7 August 1968
176 "Past history has..." *Times*, 2 September 1968
177 "very stupid people..." *Daily Express*, 23 May 1969
177 "Football matters..." Arthur Hopcraft, *Football Man*, 1968

13. Villains of the piece

179 "soccer hooligans boasting..." *Daily Mirror*, 2 August 1971
179 "They are usually very placid..." *Daily Express*, 19 April 1971
180 "a mob of about 600..." *Times*, 21 August 1971
180 "Once again, certain sections..." *Guardian*, 21 August 1971
182 "Now this has been very serious," *Stairway 13*, Rangers TV
183 "The Death Steps..." *Daily Record*, 4 January 1971
183 "It was only from the top..." *Times*. 4 January 1971
183 "This was a black, black day..." *Celtic View*, 7 January 1971
185 "not found a single solution..." *Lang Report*, HMSO 1969
186 "the football fan game..." *Times*, 15 January 1968
187 "Players traded punches..." *Daily Mirror*, 1 September 1975
187 "Whatever pleasure there is..." *Times*, 1 September 1975
187 "the new age of violence..." *Daily Mirror*, 25 November 1971
188 "senseless violence among..." *Daily Mirror*, 19 September 1972
188 the unemployment rate... ONS, bit.ly/2nspzuu
189 "for all the world resembling..." *Times*, 26 August 1974
189 "the day the terrace terrors..." *Sun*, 27 October 1975
190 "held the dubious..." Inglis, Simon, *Football Grounds of Britain*, 1996
190 "If we are closed down..." *Times*, 29 December 1977
191 "Close the Lion's Den..." *Daily Mirror*, 13 March 1978
192 "language you don't usually..." *Panorama*, BBC TV, 14 November 1977
194 "What shocked me..." *Guardian*, 25 July 2014, bit.ly/guar2014
195 "the worst invasion..." *Times*, 6 June 1977
195 "Shame of the Scots..." *Daily Mirror*, 6 June 1977
196 "the worst strip..." *Coventry Telegraph*, 6 June 2013, bit.ly/covstrip
197 "has always been a lifestyle..." Thornton, Phil, *Casuals*, Milo 2003
197 "the missing key..." Redhead, Steve, *Soccer & Society*, Vol 5, Iss 3, 2004

14. Victims of contempt

199 "There was a sudden crash..." *Yorkshire Post*, 5 February 1914
200 no mention in the newspaper... *Times*, 13 April 1981
200 "completely unnecessary..." *Report of the Hillsborough Panel*, 2012
201 "put on a boat..." *Daily Mirror*, 13 June 1980
201 "the scum of society..." *Daily Express*, 9 September 1980
201 "It is no good blaming..." *Times*, 8 September 1980
202 "Soccer's Day of Shame..." *Daily Mirror*, 8 September 1980
203 "a brutal example of..." *Guardian*, 4 September 2006, bit.ly/guar2006
203 Leon Brittan's suggestion... *Glasgow Herald*, 16 March 1985
203 "vary from lack of parental..." *Times*, 15 March 1985
204 "Goalies Against Hoolies..." *Guardian*, 30 December 2014, bit.ly/guargoal

204 "There is a build-up of combustible..." *New Scientist*, 30 May 1985
205 "It was sheer hell..." *Times* 13 May 1985
205 "Could any man really be..." Fletcher, Martin, *56*, 2015
206 "Human Fireball..." *News of the World*, 12 May 1985
206 "nouveau riche..." *Times*, 13 May 1985
207 "The wall collapsed..." *Daily Express*, 30 May 1985
207 "Only the English fans..." *Times*, 30 May 1985
208 "If this is what football..." *L'Equipe* quoted in *Times*, 31 May 1985
210 "one of carnival..." *Hillsborough Stadium Disaster: Final Report*, 1990
210 "I was vaguely aware..." Tempany, Adrian, *And the Sun Shines Now*, 2016
212 "Who if not the tanked-up..." *Independent*, 26 April 2016, bit.ly/indyobs
212 "The Truth..." *Sun*, 19 April 1989
212 "unbalanced and misleading..." *Annual Report of the Press Council*, 1989
212 continued to insist he had... Scraton, Phil, *Hillsborough: The Truth*, 2009
212 "The people who died..." *Times*, 17 April 1989

15. Enhanced patriotism
218 concert-goers followed the... *Times*, 5 July 1990
218 "England's roads and places..." *Times*, 7 May 1990
219 "Almost overnight..." Reynolds, Simon, *Generation Ecstasy*, 1999
219 "enhanced patriotism..." BBC News, 15 January 2010, bit.ly/enhapat
220 "determined hooligans..." BBC News, 12 September 2012, bit.ly/dethool
220 Arrests at football matches... *Times*, 5 July 1990
221 "Turin had hooligan psychosis..." Davies, Pete, *All Played Out*, 1990
222 "equivalent to that used by..." *Times*, 5 July 1990
223 "Lots of different kinds..." BBC News, 4 July 2015, bit.ly/ital90
223 "rather better..." *Guardian*, 6 July 1990
224 "1990 may come to be seen..." *Times*, 7 July 1990
223 independent inspection... Inglis, Simon, *Football Grounds of Britain*, 1996
225 "the great untapped resource..." *Observer*, 22 September 1985
225 "This paper isn't going to be..." *When Saturday Comes*, March 1986
226 *WSC* had a circulation of... *Times*, 10 April 1991
227 "Mellor Made Love in Chelsea Strip..." *Sun*, 7 September 1992
228 "We went to opera and football..." *Times*, 30 December 1992
228 "I have measured out my life..." Hornby, Nick, *Fever Pitch*, 1992
229 "I was surprised by what I found..." Buford, Bill, *Among the Thugs*, 1990
229 "I've read no better account..." *Independent*, 11 September 1992
230 the match was watched by 10.3 million... *Times*, 7 June 1989

16. Armchair supporters
232 "Here we go..." Sky Sports website, 27 July 2014, bit.ly/1992sky

234 "a reasonable advertisement for the game..." *Times*, 3 October 1983
236 ClubCall lines for top clubs received... *Guardian*, 16 April 1988
236 By 1989, it was estimated that... *FourFourTwo*, November 2015
238 the deciding vote... *When Football Changed Forever*, ITV, 6 October 2016
238 a satellite dish and receiver cost... *Times*, 11 December 1992
238 "spurned by some..." *Guardian*, 12 August 1992
239 a million Sky Sports subscribers... *Guardian*, 14 December 1992
239 the cheapest Premier League tickets... *Times*, 10 October 1992
240 the lowest ticket prices... Arsenal History, 2 October 2015, bit.ly/arshis
240 "the same old product..." *Guardian*, 15 December 1992
241 "Football is fast becoming..." *Times*, 10 October 1992
241 "The stadium has the look of an airport hangar..." *Times*, 28 August 1995
241 "There is neither the atmosphere..." *Times*, 23 October 1995
241 "tightly-enclosed, inner-city..." *Observer*, 8 November 1992
242 "the nitro-glycerine in human form..." *Guardian*, 26 January 1995
242 "If professional football is to retain..." *Guardian*, 27 January 1995
243 "Why the moral outrage..." *Telegraph*, 21 February 2014
243 "For all the fuss..." *When Saturday Comes*, March 1995
243 "Football fanatics are going online..." *Times*, 3 April 1995
244 experimental Ipswich fans' website... *Guardian*, 14 December 1995
244 Reading's Hob Nob Anyone... *Guardian*, 26 October 2016, bit.ly/guar2016
244 Only 4% of the UK population... World Bank via Google Public Data, 7 October 2016, http://bit.ly/googpop
245 "There were three countries..." BBC News, 9 March 2006, bit.ly/engviol
245 "The supporters' behaviour..." *Times*, 16 June 1996
247 It was the biggest UK TV... BBC News, 25 June 2004, bit.ly/recoaud
248 "A working class game has become..." *Guardian*, 29 April 1996
249 "I used to watch absolutely everything..." *Guardian*, 29 April 1996
249 "Away from home our..." BBC News, 9 November 2000, bit.ly/prawnsa

17. Against modern football

255 "a lack of significant interest..." *MK Citizen*, 3 July 2003, bit.ly/mkcitiz
255 "For the last two years..." *Times*, 19 August 2002
256 "I thought it was possible..." AFC Wimbledon website, bit.ly/afcwimb
257 The manifesto stated... FC United of Manchester website, bit.ly/fcuman
257 Some Manchester United fans... *Guardian*, 26 May 2015, bit.ly/guarfcum
258 There was also some... *Guardian*, 31 March 2016, bit.ly/guarfcu2
258 football did not appear to be suffering... *Premier League Football Research*, European Commission, 2005
258 "Football fans are idiots..." *Guardian*, 2 September 2005, bit.ly/guaridio
258 An Arsenal season ticket... Arsenal History, 2 October 2015, bit.ly/arshis

259 The Bundesliga was the best-attended... Weltfussball.de, bit.ly/weltfuss
261 "Few can seriously question..." *Telegraph*, 17 Nov 2008, bit.ly/telbund
261 "90% of British fans..." BBC News, 12 September 2008, bit.ly/safestan
263 "The socialism I believe in..." Spirit of Shankly, spiritofshankly.com
263 were 185 supporters' trusts... Supporters Direct website, bit.ly/suppfact
264 fans received compensation... BBC News, 25 June 2010, bit.ly/fanscomp
264 "Fans are discriminated..." *Guardian*, 6 March 2010, bit.ly/guarights
264 "I have come to be horrified..." *Guardian*, 22 October 2010, bit.ly/guapoli
265 "I'm delighted..." *Independent*, 26 August 2009, bit.ly/indhool
266 According to the Home Office... *Statistics on Football-Related Arrests Season 2008-09*, Home Office, December 2009
266 Of the 13.6 million fans who... *Changing face of the Premier League*, European Professional Football Leagues (EPFL), 2012
266 average cost of watching... *Telegraph*, 9 September 2008, bit.ly/telcost
266 average matchday cost... *Guardian*, 6 October 2010, bit.ly/guacost
267 "We do not want the return..." *STAND* fanzine, bit.ly/abostand

18. Akin to religion

269 "It is a blockbuster..." Sky Sports via YouTube, October 2016, bit.ly/redmonda
270 "One of the most eagerly..." *Telegraph*, 17 October 2016, bit.ly/mondfoot
270 An average of 2.8 million... *Telegraph*, 18 October 2016, bit.ly/boredra
270 Outside of the UK... Premier League Global Media, bit.ly/fanglob
270 "Here's how we'll line up..." etc, Twitter, 17 October 2016
273 In 2015, the Premier... BBC News, 10 February 2015, bit.ly/2015tel
273 Global deals, including... Guardian, 18 November 2016, bit.ly/guchin
273 audience figures for... *Guardian*, 24 October 2016, bit.ly/guarskybt
274 the Premier League estimated that... Wired, 15 June 2016, bit.ly/wiredill
274 identifying more than 500... Gigaom, 22 September 2009, bit.ly/gigaomf
274 during the Euro 2016... Kantar Media, 10 June 2016, bit.ly/kanteuro
275 "That was a wretched game..." *Guardian*, 17 October 2017, bit.ly/guarlive
275 "Even my 78-year old..." *Guardian*, 26 October 2016, bit.ly/guarstre
276 "The club's total..." *Financial Times*, 21 November 2014, bit.ly/ftfans
276 By 2017, the club had... Manchester United website, bit.ly/manupa
276 In 2014, the club signed... *Independent*, 29 July 2014, bit.ly/indshirt
277 "The level we are..." *Daily Mirror*, 10 November 2016, bit.ly/mirrman
277 When Manchester City fan Josh... *Times*, 3 February 2017, bit.ly/timperi
278 "After a game you used to..." *Telegraph*, 13 October 2016, bit.ly/teleyou
279 "Nearly everything possible..." Priestley, JB, *English Journey*, 1934

Index

Printed in Poland
by Amazon Fulfillment
Poland Sp. z o.o., Wrocław